THE POLITICS OF AGE
AND
GERONTOCRACY IN AFRICA

❖

THE POLITICS OF AGE AND GERONTOCRACY IN AFRICA:
ETHNOGRAPHIES OF THE PAST & MEMORIES OF THE PRESENT

❖

EDITED BY

MARIO I. AGUILAR

Africa World Press, Inc.

P.O. Box 1892
Trenton, NJ 08607

P.O. Box 48
Asmara, ERITREA

Africa World Press, Inc.

P.O. Box 1892
Trenton, NJ 08607

P.O. Box 48
Asmara, ERITREA

Book Design: Wanjiku Ngugi
Cover Design: Jonathan Gullery

Library of Congress Cataloging-in-Publication Data

The politics of age and gerontocracy in Africa : ethnographies of the
    past & memories of the present / edited by Mario I. Aguilar.
        p.   cm.
    Includes bibliographical references and index.
    ISBN 0-86543-597-9 hb. -- ISBN 0-86543-598-7 pb
        1. Age groups--Africa. 2. Gerontocracy--Africa. 3. Aged--Africa.
    4. Africa--Politics and government.   I. Aguilar, Mario I.
    GN645.P66 1998
    305.2' 096--dc21   98-27563
                                                           CIP

CONTENTS

PART III
AGE IN THE POST-MODERN STATE

To Paul Spencer
Nagaat!

PROLEGOMENA

When in 1990 I arrived at the SOAS building in London, in order to pursue research in Anthropology, I was met by a soon-to-retire man by the name of Paul Spencer, who spoke with authority and enthusiasm about firestick patrons, the old and the young, age and gerontocracy, and who became a mentor and a friend. Paul Spencer, I was told at that time, "is a precise man and a very good ethnographer. If you can work with him, he will be the best person for your own research." And he was.

It was only years later, and in the context of a meeting of Oromo specialists in Sweden, that the idea of assessing Spencer's ideas came to me, in the context of a conversation with Paul Baxter. Thus, this volume tries to converse with historical and anthropological perceptions of age and gerontocracy, in the context of a more fragmentized and globalized Africa, than that portrayed in the work of Paul Spencer. However, his perceptions, theoretical models, and ideas concerning the anthropology of age have influenced the essays of this volume, and the work of those who have contributed to the current discussion. Others, such as Paul Baxter, provided encouragement when needed, however were finally unable to write down their own perceptions and wisdom.

Paul Spencer's influence on the shaping of a so-called "anthropology of age," and on other scholars, has been continuous since 1971, when he was appointed Lecturer at the School of Oriental and African Studies. Having completed his D.Phil. in Oxford (1962), under the guidance of E.E. Evans-Pritchard, he worked as a government researcher before taking his first academic post. His whole career continued at SOAS, where he was promoted to Senior Lecturer (1982), Reader (1988), and Professor of African Anthropology (1993).

One hopes that this volume creates new challenging avenues for the continuation, and critical assessment of anthropologists and historians' work on age in Africa, and in other parts of the world.

Mario I. Aguilar
St. Andrews, Scotland
Summer, 1997

PART I
ARCHIVES OF AGE

Introduction

Gerontocratic, Aesthetic and Political Models of Age

❖

Mario I. Aguilar

The elderly are not merely a phenomenon,
but an outcome.
—Paul Spencer

The idea of reliable elders and unreliable youngsters has been central to cultural understandings and perceptions of age by ourselves. After all, it is "our" experience of age, as we exit a particular school system and proceed to do other things. The fact that, we, older human beings, perceive younger men and women in a particular way, speaks of the importance of age in the biological and cultural perceptions of societies, cultures, and nations. Thus, David Kertzer and Oker Madison have suggested, and rightly so, that "age is rivaled only by sex as a universal principle of social differentiation" (1981:109).

Thus, biological perceptions of age, mainly related to a universal human process of ageing, have stressed ageing, in relation to old age, as a process of being, rather than as the result of a longer process of becoming old. From that perspective, studies of the old, such as those conducted by gerontologists, have somehow assumed different methodologies from those pursued by anthropologists and historians. Gerontology pursues knowledge and research about those who are considered old, or retired, or of the third age.

Nevertheless, there are academic differences as well as common concerns between gerontology and the anthropology of aging, that suggest the importance of particular social groups, such as the old, in every society (e.g., Myerhoff 1994 [1979]). That social group of older people is at the center in contemporary studies of age, rather than at the margins of a possible intellectual encounter between disciplines, a reality suggested by Christine Fry almost thirty years ago (Fry 1981:1).[1]

Therefore, through an academic specialization and intellectual fragmentation over time and in research circles, the biological and the cultural sides of the process of aging have been separated, so that both views have in turn, been taken as absolute representations of the same process. Scientific ideas regarding aging have also been taken as universal, while cultural constructions have been portrayed as localized perceptions, within the domain of anthropologists and those studying the particular.

However, and as recently pointed out by Robertson, a viable model of human development "should view the life cycle not within the encapsulated notion of individuality, but within the social relations of reproduction" (1996:591). It is reproduction as a biological and cultural phenomenon that provides the foundation for a universal phenomenon, and for a multiplicity of social differentiations based on age.

4

In the localized realm of Africa and its peoples, paradigms of age have also permeated the social and political changes undergone by peoples and nations in Africa. Those paradigmatic perceptions of age have also portrayed the actual self-reflexive experience of older or younger scholars. After all, social and cultural phenomena, as studied by historians or anthropologists, do help to shape their own writings and (therefore) their own perceptions of Africa—and of themselves—in a shift between "scholarship" and "sentiment", and vice versa (Owusu 1976).

Thus, the systematization of knowledge in a particular manner, as in the case of the study of age, tends to shape not only the (construction of) knowledge about the subject, but also the perceived concerns of the researcher involved. From the perspective of others scholars who are not involved in such particular research, but who profit from the findings and theorizing of such research, a particular topic becomes associated with a particular group of scholars, and not with others.

It is that fact of current scholarship that allows me to suggest that for several decades the study of the anthropology of age has been directly associated with a small group of scholars interested in systems of age in Africa, the so-called age-systems. I would argue, however, that the anthropology of age in the African context (and, indeed, in any context) is certainly larger than the study of those age-systems, due to the fact that perceptions of age are a daily and habitual concern of every person in any given society or nation.

Thus, the bounded and self-contained field of age-systems has been portrayed as related to scholars who tend to avoid talking about social and political change. Those criticisms point to the academic suspicion that all systems of age are being challenged by the invention and political implication of nations and states in Africa. It is true that when significant numbers of African scholars began to appear in the scholarly fortresses of Western Europe and North America, ideas regarding social change dominated the parameters of empirical investigation about Africa. However,

5

already in such a climate, William Arens argued that "social change by its nature is a broad and ill-defined concept that cannot claim a distinct area of inquiry but rather allows for the choice of an infinite variety of areas for discussion" (Arens 1976:1-2; also Karp 1978:1-3). In short, the accusations against those scholars interested in age-systems were precisely related to processes of social change. They did not, in the words of their critics, account for social change.

Looking back at those discussions, one could argue that those critics and their criticisms did not account for the fact that societies that kept their age-systems in progression were less likely to accept the ethnic dissolution brought about by processes of national independence and unification. Many of them, such as groups of pastoralists in East Africa, lived in geographical isolation and experienced an administrative vacuum after the departure of the European colonial officers. Those institutions, even when undergoing rapid change, constituted a growing area of methodological study in the developments of anthropology.

In the same manner that historians reconstruct past events from written archives and manuscripts, anthropologists interested in age used the reconstruction of the age-systems to account for historical processes, especially when oral traditions referred to particular age-sets, their formation and particular activities in a given time in history. Anthropologists suggested that through those processes of writing oral traditions down, social histories could be reconstructed, and even that systems no longer in place could be described, e.g., the case of the Iteso in Kenya (Karp 1978:18-32).

This volume examines those important developments on the anthropology of age and argues for the importance of such research in the context of contemporary Africa. It suggests that cultural perceptions of age and their understanding are fundamental for societal relations of power, and therefore their understanding are fundamental in order to further understand relations of gender, politics and religion. In other words, an understanding of cultural and localized perceptions of age is the key to any understanding of cultural relations of power, and consequently, of knowledge. In such wider perception of age in society, age-systems constituted important models of cultural inclusion—and therefore of cultural exclusion—a predominant phenomenon in any ethnic or national conflict in Africa today.

Historical Developments

It was during the period after World War II that the study of age-class systems of Africa, especially in East Africa, was intensified. It coincided with a quick expansion of anthropological research, and a period in which social anthropology became an established academic profession in Britain (Kuper 1983:121-4).[2] It also followed a colonial realization regarding the actual connections between age-systems, local political leadership, and social organization, recommended as crucial topics for research by anthropologists such as Schapera (Schapera 1949 [in Bernardi 1985: 19]).

It made sense that the colonial administration encouraged such studies, which were not part of contemporary research conducted by non-professional anthropologists. For example, colonial officers and military commanders faced particular problems at times when various age-sets were being constituted. In particular areas, such as Northern Kenya, violence against enemies was required as an element of the passing of age, and the cultural perception of adulthood and warriorhood required periodical raiding of enemies (Fukui and Turton 1979). Thus, the need to understand cultural premises by colonial officers (who in some cases were fascinated by other cultures) was needed in order to establish peace and stability in colonial domains.

At the same time, and on the home front, the continent of Africa dominated the developments associated with the funding provided by the Colonial Social Science Research Council, as well as the usual African interests by social anthropologists in Britain (Goody 1995:81). Thus, anthropological studies of age, particularly in East Africa, reflected the post-war ethnographic explorations of scholars who recognized that age-systems and age-grades were constitutive elements of constructing and perceiving the world. Those scholars were certainly heavily influenced by the studies of Evans-Pritchard on the Nuer of the Sudan (Evans-Pritchard 1940) and his influence on social anthropology from Oxford (Beattie and Lienhardt 1975).

The whole area of anthropological studies of pastoralism also expanded, and those studies dwelt on the obvious, the age organizations predominant in those societies.[3] Ideological constructs, such as the pastoral ideals of Maasai (Spear 1993, Spear and Waller 1993:12-13; Spencer 1993), Boorana (Baxter 1954), or Somali (Lewis 1961), also constituted significant areas for anthropologists to study (full bibliography in Fratkin, Roth and Galvin 1994).

Later on, with the rising of critiques against functionalism, and a growing distrust of classical anthropological monographs, studies of age became less fashionable. After all, in many societies age-systems, as known before the setting of colonial boundaries, had changed or had been temporarily suppressed. In other societies (namely, in segments of large societies based on age, such as the Boorana of Eastern Kenya), rituals that marked the formation of age-sets disappeared (Aguilar 1997a).

Other rituals related to the social perception and creation of age-differences were revived and re-invented in order to stress national identities rather than societal and cultural cohesion (e.g., Kassam 1995). For example, the *gada* system of the Oromo continued to mark cultural constructions of identity and ethnicity, yet during the twentieth century was never celebrated as described by Bahrey in the sixteenth century (Bahrey 1954). Reasons for such dramatic change can be found in the constant diversification and expansion of the Oromo, the cultural pressures exercised by the Amharic conquest in Central and Southern Ethiopia, and the British pacification in Northern Kenya.

Regardless of all those cultural and political changes, aging as a human phenomenon remains universal, and different peoples continue perceiving age in many different manners (Riley 1984).

It is a fact that, in the process of anthropological expansion described above, practitioners and researchers have also expanded the intellectual boundaries of a predominantly Western discipline, so as to include Europe and North America as objects of research and Africans scholars as important agents in the creation and dissemination of anthropological knowledge. With such parameters of change, problems related to age and the creation of "the old" are also being diversified, are being invented and different paradigms for understanding the passing of age developed.

In the first part of this introduction I focus on different ways to understand the passing of age, the cultural creation of the old, and the possible power exercised by the old in Africa (gerontocracy). Models, after all, are not more than an invention in order to describe and interpret the passing of age. Models are therefore complementary rather than contradictory. Fragmentized, they seem to lead to contradiction; however, they represent the intellectual approximation of one and the same social reality.

In the second part of this introduction, I relate the particular contributions made in this volume to such studies, while hinting towards possible future developments in this field, a concern that will be expanded in future collections of essays on age, already in preparation.

Models of Age

As already suggested, the passing of age as a universal, human, and biological process can only be fully understood by looking at its cultural—and therefore localized—processes of construction, perception, change, and adaptation. Perceptions of age do not arise from a given definition but from sociality, from daily and habitual human activities, part and parcel of a larger social continuum. Thus, perceptions of age can change, evolve, and even be challenged by different sectors of a community.

With Africa at large in mind, it is possible to argue that older people are given some kind of social recognition, and that old age seems to be regarded as an attribute rather than a hindrance. If

9

that is not always the case, that was the mythological creation of colonial officers and colonial powers. According to such myth, the elders knew, and they were respected. In the case of the British, for example, indirect ruling to the appointment of local chiefs, who, in the name of the empire, were entrusted with a mediatory role between Europeans and locals. When in doubt, colonial officers consulted elders.

Anthropological studies, in many cases, corroborated such "power of the elders", so that Paul Spencer suggested that in the case of the Samburu, "real power ... is vested in the elders and their control over the *moran* in particular rests entirely on the general belief in their curse" (Spencer 1965:209, cf. 173-210; see also Baxter's contribution to the present volume). In the case of Boorana and their *gada* system, based on age and associated with a complex and democratic way of governance and social organization, assemblies have been recently suggested as "the dominant element of Boorana polity" (Bassi 1996b:153, cf. Baxter and Almagor 1978:19). However, in those assemblies men (and therefore their wives) who have lived longer have a larger say, regardless of structural constructions of systems based on democratic and egalitarian modes of consensus production.

In a vast continent such as Africa, perceptions and constructions of age are certainly created, implemented, and re-created through different societal activities. The idea of models, then, helps the researcher and the reader to systematize many different social and historical processes within the enormous variety and diversity of localized cultural, social, and political systems.

Thus, I suggest that, from the point of view of the researcher, as well as from the people who are becoming older, there are many different ways of becoming old. The reality of being perceived as older than others, or as younger than others, has significant implications not only for groups within a society and for individuals within a group, but also for their society as a whole. Rights and obligations, prohibitions and duties are therefore connected to perceptions by particular individuals, who can be older in biological age, but junior in the ladder of social relations and cultural perceptions, or vice versa.

The tentative models that follow are not the only possible ones, however they seem to illustrate some of the possible ways of constructing—and understanding—cultural parameters of age throughout Africa. As models, they reflect an epistemological tool useful to the researcher, in order to look at social reality from a particular angle. At the same time, each model reflects societal paradigms of construction, perception, and cultural validation of the passing of age. Some of the models are more appropriate to localized societies, and depend on tradition. Other models are significantly more complex, such as gender, and they vary in the way that they challenge or reinvent traditional models in new African contexts.

In those contemporary globalized contexts, such as urban centers, political realms, or public spaces, the young and the old find themselves influenced by pop-culture, or cultural globalization, and at the same time culturally tied to homelands, and to cultural perceptions of themselves by others. Traditional roles and understandings of change, sometimes temporarily, are changed and fixed into a new invented tradition. A striking reminder of such contested arenas between cultural traditions and the difficulties of inter-marriage in a modern African state was the litigation over the body of the Kenyan lawyer Silvanus Melea Otieno, where the old and the young, women and men, traditionalists and modernists, contested each other in the public arena of an African nation, Kenya, always on the making.

On 20 December 1986, SM (as he was known), died at Nairobi Hospital. However, he was only buried in Siaya (Western Kenya) on 23 May 1987, after a long legal contestation that involved his Kikuyu wife, and his brothers and Luo clan-men (Cohen and Odhiambo 1992, Cohen 1994: 94-119). While the problem arose as a consequence of two cultural worlds contesting each other, it is significant that the final ruling allowed the Umira Kager clan to bury SM in Western Kenya. However, the legal dispute explored in court Luo beliefs and burial practices, allowing the "au-

11

thority" of a 66 year old Luo, Johannes Mayamba, to be heard, as he was a respected local politician, Christian, and also "a potent *jabilo*", that is, a manipulator of powerful medicines and magic in Luo culture (Cohen and Odhiambo 1992:59).

Narratives and perceptions of age became crucial in the actual legal dispute, and in the national perception of such dispute, as a 16 year old son of SM gave testimony to the court. For the Luo clan he represented a youngster out of line, who in an unheard manner, expressed his opinion in a public forum. However, for many Kenyans, especially those attending privileged schools throughout the country, he represented a new generation of young and enterprising Kenyans, who were made to belong to a particular ethnic group, however whose aspirations were related to their belonging to a new tribe, "the Kenyans".

Such dispute not only spoke of the diversity in perceptions regarding age, status, prestige, and authority, but at the same time opened other avenues of discourse related to gender. Educated elites of boys and girls, do not tend to follow the ethnically, and therefore localized, constructed parameters of gender production, however they have opinions related to the cultural globalization of age. Such gender issues also became apparent in the SM case, as the litigants on behalf of the Luo clan were males, contesting the legal right of an educated widow to bury her husband at their property near Nairobi, rather than at his father's grave in Western Kenya. Parameters of gendered age in such case became of national interest, and provided public spheres of discourse for the youth and their different perceptions of such complex matters. Thus,

> The youth knew the Otieno story as it came to them through television, radio, newspapers, teachers, parents, bus and *matatu* conversations, market talk, and gossip among house servants, but they also produced their own knowledge of the case. They surveilled adult (read "male") talk at their homes as they brought beer or tea to their fathers' guests; they eavesdropped on women's talk

about the Otienos in the kitchens and backyards, and constructed, daily, meanings into this affair, about which, ostensibly, they had nothing to offer, being merely "children" in the eyes of the grownups, yet fully aware of the way in which this very issue of their own social worth had become, with Patrick's (SM's son) testimony, an issue before the court. (Cohen and Odhiambo 1992: 72)

Thus, age as constructed by localized groups can be interpreted in different ways by other groups, and at the same time by different generations. It is a fact that, in those urban centers such as Nairobi, the passing of age is not dictated by a centralized and unifying ritual or political system, while in the past those localized systems, such as the age-systems, were essential to any cultural construction of ethnicity and identity.

Systems of Age or Age-Class Systems

Age-systems as cultural constructs, and therefore as ways of organizing society as a whole, are only present in non-Western societies. Exhaustive ethnographic surveys related to societies based on age-class systems have not yet been produced (Bernardi 1985: 11), however, they have existed in many African societies. Their distribution in East Africa includes peoples of the Sudan (Nuer, Dinka, Bari, Latuka), Ethiopia (Oromo, Konso, Dassenetch, Mursi), Uganda (Dodoth, Jie, Karimojong, Topotha), Kenya (Boorana, Gabbra, Maasai, Rendille, Samburu, Turkana), and Tanzania (Arusha, Maasai).[4] Thus, age systems are heavily distributed in East Africa, including the age-villages of Nyakyusa, where residence as well as age created a sense of the passing of age, similar to the *muran* villages in Maasai.

Aspects of age-class systems were also present among the Ndembu of Zambia and the Lele of Kasai in Zaire. In southern Africa, the Nguni and their descendants, such as the Xhosa and Zulu (South Africa), the Swasi (Swaziland), Ndebele (Zimbabwe), and the Ngoni (Malawi), developed age class systems that

13

allowed them to carry out military campaigns throughout the region. As in the case of the Roman legions, age-sets allowed for an immediate access to numbers of men who could be easily organized for warfare. That was the case in Maasai and Oromo, and it constituted one major reason for their successful expansion in the past, expansion that secured economic and ecological resources much needed by pastoralists.

Moreover, and due to the fact that we do not have such systems in Western society, important distinctions such as age class systems, age-grades, and age-sets are not part of our everyday language and speech. However, differences between those concepts allow us to appreciate the complexity of those societies based on age-systems, societies which ultimately are organized through the accession to a cultural system based on age. A cultural system, then, allows for the formation of particular groups who are initiated at the same time or who become leaders at the same time or who exit the system at the same time.

In fact, age-sets are made of a group of cohorts who have been culturally perceived as joining the same group, and who exercise obligations towards each other, under a particular age-set name, usually associated with a particular leader. Age-grades, however, refer to a larger category of people, who, within a particular system, have the same culturally perceived status, while they belong to different age-sets. To that effect, an age system contains age-groups, and age-classes, that can also be differentiated from age-sets and their individual members.

The whole discussion of terminology and particular systems of age is rather complex, and it is not the purpose of this section. Rather, the purpose of this short discussion on age systems is to outline such complex systems and their predominant role in the anthropological perceptions of age in Africa to the detriment of any other perceptions. Ultimately, age systems depend on communal rituals, with all their symbolism and cultural understandings.

It could be argued to that effect that the outstanding work of Victor Turner highlighted the fact that rituals as constitutive part of society mark the passing and the construction of age. The idea of rites of passage, a concept borrowed from Van Gennep, suggested that, for example, at the period of circumcision, boys became men, not because they had radically changed their human potential to procreate, but (as suggested by White in the case of the Balovale) because "the novices are reborn as men after a symbolic death" (White in Turner 1967: 152). Thus, stages of a life cycle are marked by communal celebrations, individual changes in social roles, cultural perceptions and expectations, and a re-actualization of personal rights and obligations. In other words, age-systems provide an orderly way of becoming older, a cultural predicament present in most societies and groups that gather together for some kind of public ritual or rite of passage.

Life Cycles and Maturation

Ideas of a life-cycle to be completed between biological birth and death have been common in cross-cultural perspectives of Western and non-Western societies. Thus, particular stages of maturation and growth are implied in the biological cycle of aging (Beall 1984; cf. Fortes 1984:100). Therefore, from birth to death, men and women mature, they grow older, and they assume different roles in society. In Western society, those periods in the life-cycle can be perceived as well defined in the case of old age, and certainly heavily constructed through the influence of law and the development of policies in a particular country. For example, a period of retirement from work at 65 marks a new phase in the life cycle, ritually marked by the end of a public life in the world of work, and at the same time is communally assumed by the production of cards, parties, and good wishes.

Those roles, and especially in the case of the non-Western world, have been embedded with cultural constructions of validation, whereby people are socially recognized, but also they receive "authorization", as to join cattle herds, or to marry, or to sit with elders (Fortes 1984:101).[5] Such a process of maturation is marked by the communal celebration of elaborate rituals that mark

15

the passing of biological age; however, they also define stages of life. Processes of initiation mark, for example, the passing of age of a child into adulthood, and circumcision provides the symbol of adulthood. The rules of such initiation can certainly change, as the ages of those who take part can also be altered. However, the ritual itself, and the elaborate activities before and after such ritual, provide a cultural perception of who is to be circumcised and the time when such passing of age is preferred.

Communal rituals are so effective as markers of such life cycles, that for instance, biological birth does not secure cultural recognition of existence. In the case of the Waso Boorana of Kenya, for example, the naming ceremony marks the start of the life cycle in the case of boys, an occasion on which the father of the newborn gives a name to the baby and therefore allows him to be in relation to other Boorana for the first time. However, cultural perceptions of such a new born baby point to a moment after his biological "birth", when the "foetus" becomes a "person." In the case of Maasai, such social recognition takes place when milk from the herd is introduced into the child's diet. From that moment onwards, the "foetus" becomes a "person" (*oltungani*), "with an independent personality, and he is directly involved in the symbiotic relationship between family and herd" (Spencer 1988:41).

On the other end of the life cycle, members of a society can be perceived as having already exited a cultural system—and the life cycle—even before their biological death. In the case of the Boorana, once again, the *gadamoji* ritual celebrates the passage from an active male adulthood into a period of transition, of elderhood, without any particular active involvement in the community. The passing of age, then, is marked by ritual celebrations that span over a period of three months, after which, and as in the case of the 1995 rituals in Sololo (northern Kenya), as described by A. Kassam,

> the *gadamojjii* elders who were of the right biological age would be treated as women: they would no longer be

16

allowed to carry a spear or engage in any offensive or defensive action; they would be addressed using a female pronoun. They would not participate in the decision-making processes except as arbitrators and would withdraw from active participation in the management of their herds, leaving this to their sons, in the new *Gadaa*. They had now entered the spiritual realm of things and for the rest of their lives they would serenely follow the path of prayer. Their sole responsibility would now be to maintain *nagaya*, the peace of the Boorana, in society. (Kassam 1995: 34)

Those communal rituals are common to every African society, and they are certainly continued at the urban centers, even in the climate of a generalized conversion to Islam and Christianity. While in the African villages people of the same ethnic group pass through rituals and become older at each one of them, members of nations and states also become older by receiving education, assuming social roles associated with marriage and procreation, and by going through a variety of national or localized rituals. Those rituals are authorized and empowered by the state, and allow people to move in the age ladder of a globalized and multi-ethnic cultural perception of age.

In a state such as Kenya, for example, education has become an important marker of the passing of age. Most children go to primary school, and while less children can afford to attend secondary school, there is everywhere a parent's absolute concern for education. That concern is reflected in the collection of school fees amongst relatives and friends. Education is not that cheap, especially as boys and girls attending secondary school must attend school in areas other than their own native ones. Thus, the actual effort to pay for schooling is not alleviated by the fact that schools are at some distance, and transport fees come into the whole effort for education.

In such an African nation though, it is through education that children become adults, boys are transformed into Kenyans, and girls into women, and Kenyans as well. If the age grades present in an age system could be compared to grades in a school, one could argue that a new age-class system has been implemented in the African continent, and especially in the former British colonies. Boys and girls progress together and pass from one grade to the next, in schools that take over their whole lives. It is not uncommon for secondary schools to be boarding schools where activities start by seven in the morning, and where study periods continue till bed time. Through that kind of socialization, strong links between classmates and friends develop, whereby processes such as those described by Monica Wilson in the case of the Nyakyusa villages, also take place. She suggested that while other African groups have villages where boys live together before marriage, "the Nyakyusa themselves associate living in age-villages with decency in sex life—the separation of the sex activities of successive generations, and the avoidance of incest" (Wilson 1951: 159). Their main value was, as suggested by M. Wilson, good company among those who live together, and who, without the pressures of older generations enjoy their sociability.

Nevertheless, educational rituals, such as passing from one grade to the next, or graduations, or the cohesiveness between cohorts (class-mates) for the rest of their lives, create other kind of problems. Those problems arise from the fact that individuals pass through different systems of initiation, or assume different steps in the process of life maturation. It is difficult not to assume that the rural ways of life have continued to implement steps such as communal rituals in the rural setting, and that urban centers, and urbanites within them—have created other ways for the communal perception of the passing of age, such as schools, universities and teacher training colleges. Those new reinventions of cultural settings have then provided an ever-increasing diversification in the ways by which individuals are perceived by others, in terms of age as a cultural marker in society.

This complexity of maturation in urban centers where groups of different ethnic affiliation and self-perception do co-exist has been a particular area absent from the literature. The processes of urbanization have been described, including the relations between "tribes" and "the nation", however the actual relation between age groups in towns and cities, and with their rural counterparts, has only been part of larger studies of ethnicity, that coincided with the urban studies of African cities after independence (e.g., Grillo 1974; Lloyd 1974; Schildkrout 1974). However, processes of age perception, and maturation, also fall into the general processes of variable relationships, suggested by David Parkin as (a) townsmen forging ties on the basis of status grouping, (b) remaining cultural links as members of a particular ethnic group, and (c) national affiliation as a readjusting factor in all relationships (Parkin 1969:180). Thus, a more complex model of age among urbanites needs yet to be untangled, not only in peripheral suburbs and shanty towns, but also among the political and economic elites.

Younger Elites and Older Traditions

Through those economic, political, and cultural variables, present mostly in the larger African cities, African elites have provided in many cases inversions to the age systems, and age models of the rural landscapes. On the one hand the fluidity between town and country has remained a cultural constant; on the other hand, decades of independent life have brought significant changes to the cultural appreciation of age in particular African countries.

As already suggested, the testimony of a youngster in a national case of litigation between ethnic groups, such as the burial of SM, was perceived as incorrect by those affiliated to the rural way of perceiving the world, and quite correct by those brought up in the ideology of the nation. Those youngsters who followed the Otieno saga "hung onto the claim of their age-mate Patrick that he was "of the Kenya tribe" and did not come from "home-squared" or *gicagi*-squared, meaning "real, real home" in the countryside (Cohen and Odhiambo 1992:72). The striking bit of such creation of meaning by youngsters is the actual perception of themselves as older because of their knowledge, acquired through Western schooling, rather than by the knowledge of tradition.

I witnessed the same contestation of age and knowledge during my fieldwork. Boorana men who had pursued university careers were being pushed by their age-mates as those who knew, and therefore should instruct others, playing a significant role in the communal social process of making decisions. While different models of age were being used, perceived, and reinvented in such a society, it was striking to see that education had provided a change in perceptions of age and the passing of time.

The same kind of struggle and dichotomy between the younger elites and the old bearers of tradition can be perceived in the appropriation of cultural symbols that express unity and identity and at the same time relate tradition and modernity in the spheres of the contemporary nation states. For example, political figures who became symbols of unification in the struggles for independence of many African countries assumed that nations would forget their own ethnic quarrels, and that a new generation would be able to work out together, as to create structures for progress and development in those young nations. However, most of them remained as leaders for a considerable number of years, allowing traditional images of gerontocratic elders to be used, images of those who after all had everything, from economic resources to absolute power of decision.

Thus, in the case of those leaders, their education abroad, especially in Europe and the United States, allowed them to gain the authority to become charismatic and patriarchal leaders. As they became older, their charismatic and youthful image of freedom fighters changed into the public perceptions of wise and old men, without whom the young nations could not survive. Some exited due to military coups, or death, or grave illness. Others reluctantly allowed for democracy to be part of their gerontocratic structures.

The case of Hastings Banda in Malawi is an example of such a process of change in the life cycle, combined, however, with

20

the actual connotation of an absence of chronological age, as nobody knew exactly how old he was, and a communal disputation about his origins. It was only through sickness that the life-president of Malawi was replaced, and his trip to South Africa in 1993 triggered conversation by all Malawians about his origins, and even about his future burial place (Englund 1996). Another case is that of President Moi of Kenya, who succeeded Kenyatta after his death in 1978, as a youthful leader, who would prepare a peaceful transition at a time of national crisis. He has managed to be re-elected, and assumed as an *mzee*, a title given to Kenyatta, and to all respected older men. Moi has therefore replaced Kenyatta, in that gerontocratic ladder, so common in contemporary African political systems.

Elderhood and Gerontocracy

The word *mzee* (old man), was already used by European colonial officers as to denote an elder. Elderhood as a social and cultural category expresses in the perception of the outsider, a respected category, of an older and wiser man. Such older man is considered wiser because he has lived longer and therefore "knows". Such colonial perception was appropriated by a centralized colonial administration that needed to organize peoples and territories. The council of elders provided a visible body of people to whom the colonial administration could address concerns related to a colonial policy of indirect rule in the case of the British.

In the 1990s, though, *mzee* is used in East Africa to show respect for older men. Elderhood, however, is not always associated with an active political role, but sometimes with a non-threatening role of advisor and councilor. The old are heard by people in their communities, and the young are accused of not showing any respect for older people. As Spencer has suggested in the case of the Samburu, the *moran* attitude towards the elders is an ambivalent one. They comply with an attitude of compliance towards the elders, so that "observing the correct modes of behav-

21

ior is also understood to be a token of the respect that they should have for one another and for the society as a whole" (Spencer 1965: 145). On the other hand, it is not uncommon for the younger men to dislike the authority and control exercised on them by the elders, that is expressed through songs and conversation (Spencer 1965: 144-9). Those realities that Spencer witnessed forty years ago have indeed permeated into contemporary Africa.

Thus, those social realities of public and private contestation between older men and younger men, and also quarrels between older wives and younger wives have been central to the actual running of African societies. The difficulties of being younger than other men is somehow similar to those faced by women who have to deal with older or younger women, and their proper position in society. For example, Telelia Chieni, a Maasai woman, is proud of understanding her world, where the senior wife is important, and where she shares the seniority of her husband (Chieni and Spencer 1993).

The Problem of Generations and Gender

From her point of view, women have a somehow particular way of looking at the world perceived by others as the world of their husbands. It is clear that historical and economic circumstances have created further change even in societies that are dominated by formalized models of age (Aguilar 1994b;Talle 1987). Therefore, another model of age is constituted by gender factors. Age is certainly perceived and constructed in different manners by men and women.

To that effect, ground-breaking work on women's perception of society has been carried out, even in societies that are perceived as male-dominated and patriarchal, such as Maasai (Talle 1988). Models of age related to gender then, arise from the fact that women perceive society in a somehow different manner than men, and that a different cultural perception comes out of women and men conducting research, as well as from those being researched. In the words of Diane Bell,

> The issue of gender arises because we (ethnographers) do fieldwork by establishing relationships, and by learning to see, think and be in another culture, and we do this as persons of a particular age, sexual orientation, belief, educational background, ethnic identity and class. In particular ... we also do it as women and as men. (Bell 1993:1-2)

Older women perceive the world in a different way than younger women, and vice versa. Generations, as well as groups, tend to challenge each other's views and practices, to the effect that as suggested by Mannheim, they develop an ethos, that sometimes does not reflect their affiliation by age (Mannheim 1952, cf. Aguilar 1998).

Changes in cultural patterns, therefore, will affect future ways of researching and perceiving age in Africa. Not only a focus on women suggests that there are diversified ways of cultural perceptions in a given society or group of people, but famine, war, and the AIDS pandemic have already had a considerable effect on cultural patterns. Recent literature on AIDS in East Africa, for example, suggests that both the nuclear and the "extended" family have been severely disrupted in countries such as Tanzania or Uganda (Wallman 1996).

Age as a Cross-Cultural Paradigm

It is also my suggestion, on introducing models of age, that perceptions of old age are different in industrial and non-industrial societies, whereby the latter can be considered as "distinctly old-age oriented" (Holy 1990:167). With that reality in mind, it is possible to argue that age as a theoretical way of thinking about society provides a way by which all anthropologists and historians could advance research, rather than solely consider it as a subject of research for those who problematize age in a particular social context (Kertzer and Keith 1984:14). After all, any perception of old age reflects a related societal understanding of the passing of age, or the so called "life course". Thus, "the very concept of old age is only intelligible in relation to youth and the lifelong experience of aging" (Spencer 1990a:1). With such understanding, the so called old have passed through many faces of life, they have survived the difficulties of life, and they stand as bearers of cultural traditions. In the case of those who are part of an age-system, the old represent those who have experienced and endured more steps of the system than others.

With those parameters in mind, the contributors to this volume explore different perceptions of the politics of age in an African context. In such a context, the old are those who provide a mediation between the past and the present, because the past is still considered as mandatory in the cultural creation of any present (Tonkin 1992:68-70). The old control society, not only because they are able to utilize economic resources accumulated throughout a longer span of time, but because they are perceived as those who know cultural and religious traditions. That knowledge creates a gerontocratic ladder (Spencer 1965), where the old manipulate knowledge and re-invent tradition so as to create a gerontocracy, a rule of the elders (cf. Roth 1994: 135-8).

Age and gerontocracy, then, are inter-related, so that those who have lived longer try to control the affairs of the present by invoking the past and their own actions in such past. As a reaction, younger men and women contest those manipulative perceptions of the past, however aspiring one day to become old, and therefore respected and listened to by younger men and women.

The Dislocation of Age

That passage of age—the youthful rebellions of every society and of every family—are at the forefront of the ethnographic and historical explorations of age that constitute the following essays. The ethnographies of the past, as represented by Carton and Simpson, explore the colonial periods of Kenya and South Africa. If one has ever believed that systems of age and perceptions of the social and cultural passing of age functioned as colonial

clocks (if those clocks ever existed), Part I of this volume challenges such perceptions.

In the case of the revolt in the Thukela basin, near Natal in 1906 (chapter 1), a colonial Poll Tax imposed on peoples of the regions, brought the defiance of young people against their elders. Instead of obeying, they demonstrated, and created a regional sense of defiance, so that at the end the Natal military crushed the insurrection, killing the chief (Bambatha) and an estimated 3,000 to 4,000 rebels.

The same traces of a political alliance between gerontocrats and the colonial rulers is portrayed in chapter 2. Samburu elders ally themselves with the administration in order to keep cattle, needed by *murran* in order to marry. Thus, the institution of *lmurrano* was reduced to three years, in a systematic colonial manipulation of social change. Changes in Samburu cattle economy were also implemented. It is a fact that all those changes would have been very difficult if the gerontocratic system of elders controlling cattle would not have been a Samburu cultural trait.

From that point of view, explorations of past changes in perceptions of age constitute a significant area that has been under-researched. If the anthropologists with their ethnographic present have been influential in constructing synchronic explorations of age in particular African societies, historians have provided the diachronic complement to such descriptions. If the ethnographic present, so much contested by some contemporary anthropology, seems artificial, complex ethnographic pieces in this volume challenge those current misgivings of dislocated temporalities.

The chapters by Caplan, Talle, and Birch de Aguilar represent complementary visions and local perceptions of age in Mafia Island (Tanzania), Maasai (Kenya), and Chewa (Malawi). If representations of male systems of age and under-represented women provided the bulk of ethnographic representations thirty

years ago, issues of gender complementarity and societal constraints based on age are thus portrayed through local voices and
emic perceptions. Age as a social and cultural category is experienced, rather than invented (Caplan), providing a new interpretation of men and women in a pastoral society (Talle). Those experiences and interpretations are part of cycles of rituals, social celebrations, and aesthetic representations of song and dance, as in
the case of the Chewa of Central Malawi (Birch de Aguilar).

Chapters by Tetelman and Galaty suggest that perceptions of
age, locally constructed, are carried out into the arenas of African
nations, political processes, globalized aspirations, and realms of
mixed temporalities. Politicians, "big men", rulers and ruled take
part in common arenas of generational contestation, where politicians create their own world of gerontocrats who seem to know
and who try to instruct and guide members of their constituen-
cies as children. Violence arises out of injustice, and in the climate of the contemporary nation/state it also reflects old challenges arising from the youthfulness of the younger and their concerns. To that effect, university students' riots in African universities speak of social and political discontent as well as generational clashes, and the rightful rebellion of the young, who see
older men possessing resources and opportunities that they themselves still do not have.

To that effect, perceptions of age in formerly localized societies became diverse, as people from different areas were politically integrated into the continuation of the colonial enterprise,
the independent nations of Africa. It is clear that, while the discourse needed to create those new nations spoke of unity, the
climate of the 1990s speaks of diversity and constant change.
The recent events in the Congo portray a common phenomenon
in Africa. The Belgian Congo became Zaire, however, after the
central symbol of national unity, ex-President Mobutu, exited the
nation, as provinces acquired more power and their respective
senses of self-identity in relation to other peoples and ethnic groups
in the former Belgian Congo. To that effect, boundaries remained,
but became less fluid culturally speaking.

The chapter by Schlee complements the others, bringing to the discussion a somehow contradictory reality. On the one hand, nations have the same laws and the same constitution; on the other hand the practicalities of particular areas within those nations are different. Schlee provides a complementary background to the area where significant numbers of those peoples with age-systems live. According to his analysis, the over-imposed colonial boundaries have been kept during a post-colonial Kenya, challenging peoples within those boundaries to look for different avenues by which to continue their social life and movements. Thus, restrictions and the creation of boundaries provide further changes and movement, rather than constraining peoples within those boundaries. Strategies are developed and practices are changed, in a description of human creativity and the adaptability of human and social perceptions.

It is that sense of social and cultural adaptability that constitutes the thread of all the chapters of this volume. The final chapter particularly challenges any conceptions of age-models as static. *Gada*, the Boorana (Oromo) age-model and one of the most well known in Africa is reinterpreted by the Boorana of Eastern Kenya so as to provide a continuation with their own sense of tradition and genesis, but with the aim of self-generating identity and ethnicity for the following generations to come.

It is clear that more ethnographic and historical research is needed, and it is not plausible in a diversified and fragmentized scholarly community to unify systems simply by a systematic description. It is clear to me that ethnographic presents need to be challenged not by the absence of those timely descriptions, but by a serious and thorough look at the past. That past that comes into the present also proves to be fragmentized, invented, and manipulated. Perceptions of age will be even more diverse in the future, and the comparative analysis of the three—past, present, and future—will certainly open fruitful avenues of theoretical explorations.

As already hinted above, the era of AIDS in the African continent, hopefully decreasing in the near future in its mortality rate, provides a new concept of age for the modern nations of Africa. At the localized level, in countries such as Uganda or Tanzania, significant numbers of people in extended families have died or are infected with the virus. Social and cultural roles have therefore been altered and transformed, reflecting that human gift of adaptation and change. In some countries, famine and war have also changed the perceptions of the old as the most vulnerable. It is a fact that the oldest and the youngest tend to suffer, and even the younger members of society are forced to take arms in the midst of conflict, emulating their older and more mature genitors.

Thus, further essays are needed, and will follow this volume. Those papers will continue arguing against a universal concept of age and gerontocracy, however suggesting that a larger survey of such culturally constructed concepts will lead us to a better understanding of the globalizing process experienced by a significant number of fellow men, women, and children, currently living in their own worlds of mixed temporalities.

NOTES

1. The origins of an anthropology of aging can be traced to monographs by Leo Simmons (1945), Paul Spencer (1965), Margaret Clark and Barbara Anderson (1967), to cite a few. Good critical summaries of the development of the anthropology of aging can be found in Margaret Clark (1973), Christine Fry (1980), Lowell Holmes (1976), Jennie Keith (1980), and Paul Spencer (1990a).
2. Here I must claim an ethnocentric perspective. I am an Africanist, however a social anthropologist, and therefore I give a considerable importance to the influence of social anthropology, as a colonial invention, in the development of academia, particularly scholarship related to the former British colonies and protectorates in Africa.

3. Historical studies on pastoralism were more rare, and the whole area of northern Kenya was unaccounted for (Ogot 1976:xviii), due to the fact that those were considered peripheral areas in the actual formation of the independent African nations.
4. In other societies such as Kalenjin, Pokot, Kipsigis, Nandi, age classes were fully followed before and during the colonial period. Some sorts of age classes also existed among the Embu, Kamba, Kikuyu, Mbeere, and Meru.
5. Processes of Westernization or globalization have made in some urban centers of Africa, such as Nairobi or Johannesburg, difficult to isolate Western and non-Western processes of aging or the passing of time in the life-cycle. In such centers there are different "worlds" that are present, and some people at retirement are faced with their legal retirement as well as their cultural retirement.

Chapter 1

"The New Generation ... Jeer at Me, Saying We
Are All Equal Now":
Impotent African Patriarchs,
Unruly African Sons in
Colonial South Africa

❖

Benedict Carton

"Turning Out ... the Father"

In 1897, Deyi petitioned a white magistrate in the Natal colony of
South Africa "to be relieved from the bondage of his Father's
control."[1] Deyi invoked an "emancipation" clause in the Code of

Native Law, a mix of colonial statutes comprising African customs and British legal strictures.

Earlier, his chief had "take[n] a similar view as the Father," Mbuzikazi, and denied Deyi's plea to be released from filial obligations. Honoring the prerogatives of a generational hierarchy, the chief first asked Mbuzikazi "if he had any objection" to Deyi's request. He said, "'Yes, I object, he is my Son and Heir."[2] The white magistrate subsequently agreed to hear an appeal of the chief's decision, but after ascertaining that "Emancipation as outlined ... is unknown in the Code of Native Law" he too ruled against Deyi. The Native Code, the magistrate decided, only supported the "father's [right] to send a son away ... for misconduct." In such cases, "turning out a son always proceeded from the father in the interests of order and wellbeing in the family."

Deyi's petition was a momentous step. "He was regarded as the alter ego of the father himself so that if he was [seeking to be] turned out it would amount to the father himself being turned out."[3] But Deyi had his own homestead with a wife and small children on a private colonial farm. He knew how lucky he was to live where he could cultivate his own plot and possibly earn wages by laboring for the farm owner. He had already been evicted by other white landlords, and the land that Africans could use had shrunk precipitously since white settlers had recently appropriated thousands more acres of fertile Natal soil.

Deyi's father, Mbuzikazi, was not as fortunate as his son. Like other neighboring homestead patriarchs, Mbuzikazi was deep in debt, scratching an existence in "the thorns," a barren territory of communal land reserved by the colony for Africans. Since the mid-1890s, drought and pestilence had ravaged African agriculture, driving fathers like Mbuzikazi into further poverty. Mbuzikazi borrowed money to survive, as the Natal government authorities sold emergency supplies of grain to stave off famine. His financial burdens worsened, and he could not meet the loan payments. Mbuzikazi then cast his eyes on the property of his son. Deyi gave his own cattle and earnings to his destitute father, but that was not enough for the creditors, who sent "a messenger of the Court" to seize more cattle. Deyi could do little while his "Father took everything," and that was why he "wish[ed] to work [for his] own inheritance for the benefit of [his] children."[4]

African Generational Conflict and Resistance Historiography

Deyi's case epitomizes an unravelling of bonds between fathers and sons, as patriarchs had seen their powers whittled away by the encroachments of white government. Beginning in the 1880s, this chapter explores how tightening colonial rule, expanding opportunities for wage labor, and a series of environmental disasters had, by the turn of the century, transformed generational hierarchies in the Thukela basin of South Africa.[5]

For most of the nineteenth century, the Zulu-speaking people of the Thukela basin lived in the southern periphery of the autonomous Zulu Kingdom (formed in the first decade of 1800) and the northern portion of the British Natal Colony (established in 1845). By 1880, through British military conquest, the Natal Colony imposed its rule over the Zulu Kingdom and drew boundaries for magisterial districts in the Thukela basin. The white government scaled back basin chiefs' authority and compelled homestead patriarchs to surrender more and more taxes, land, and labor to colonists. A series of widespread droughts, locust plagues, and livestock diseases in the 1890s decimated African farming and livestock production, resulting in greater labor migrancy from homesteads.

Dependent on their older guardians for bridewealth cattle (or lobola[6]) and land, growing numbers of young men blamed the loss of their political autonomy and material birthright on African elders whose authority had been manipulated and eroded by the white government. From the middle 1890s onwards, young men increasingly defied their own patriarchs and colonial laws, breaking filial obligations and customary prohibitions against unbridled drinking, fighting, and courting.

33

Historians since the 1970s have interpreted this rebellious-ness as a form of indigenous "resistance" to colonialism. In the 1980s, resistance literature shifted focus from visible protests to a range of ambivalent African responses to white rule, such as begrudging accommodation. Recent gender analyses have elabo-rated strategies adopted by African women to safeguard their families from resource scarcity, a shortage rendered the more acute by settler intrusions. Other scholars have shown how colo-nial "native customary law" and magisterial courts gave African women and youths a forum in which to challenge their patriarchs. These studies of domestic life have laid the foundation for a gen-erational perspective in African historiography.

Generational Hierarchies in the Thukela Basin

In the mid and late nineteenth century, Thukela basin groups were structured according to generational ranking, gender division, and the practice of polygamy. The homestead head, also known as the *umnumzana* and in colonial records as the "*kraal* head", was the patriarch of his residential compound, a cluster of huts arched around a cattle enclosure, the locus of livestock husbandry. He usually had his own hut, as did adolescent boys, while other huts housed his wife and their younger children. Wealthy men with more wives and more children tended to maintain the biggest homesteads. So important were children to a married person's perceived high status that a husband's or wife's infertility would be instant grounds to dissolve a marriage.[7]

Homesteads consumed their own crops and livestock, and bartered for tools, cattle, goats, and building materials. Families engaged in "self-sustaining" activities, favoring subsistence over selling their surplus and wares for cash.[8] As drought, pestilence, and land shortages plagued the Thukela basin in the 1880s, home-steads still showed great resilience, relying mostly on the labor of women who cultivated corn, potatoes, and sorghum, staples of the domestic economy.[9]

Aside from agricultural tasks, wives and their daughters cared for children, cooked, thatched their huts, and made clothes, sleeping mats, and ornaments. Within a hierarchical polygynous homestead, married women delegated the more onerous household duties to unmarried women, including carrying heavy calabashes of water and bundles of wood for fires.[10] The senior wife also had rights to the labor of junior wives; while daughters worked for their mothers and younger girls for their adolescent sisters.[11]

Men rarely farmed except to clear ground or direct a plough hitched to livestock. They dug grain storage pits, built hut infrastructure, and made tools. As males, their province was the rearing of livestock. Ranking married men *(amadoda)* slaughtered the cattle and goats, while boys tended the herds. If an African patriarch was wealthy in cattle, he could attract laborers with no familial ties to himself, rewarding these clients with meat, animal skins, and beer.[12] A father had rights to the labor of his wives and children. Unmarried adult men had rights to the labor of their younger brothers.

Siblings within a homestead also conformed to their own hierarchy based on age-cohort groups. A fledgling patriarch explained how he and his brothers observed their pecking order at meals. "Whenever a beast was killed the principal portions, viz: the brisket [the thick sections of the chest and front legs] ... which are always assigned to the heir, were given to me as my portion, and *mlenze* [the bony legs] were given to [his subordinate brother] as his portion, proving conclusively that I was the heir."[13] Brothers quite close in age and living with their father could vie for the rank of anointed heir, but if a son claimed this title by "self-nomination" without "knowledge of his father", he "would be turned out of his father's *kraal*."[14]

Most fathers sought to nominate their male successor, usually their first son, before dotage prevented them, hoping to avert factional strife among their children. Sometimes a homestead head anointed a younger son when older sons failed to comport themselves nobly.[15] The heir inherited his homestead head's social privileges, residential compound, and personal property.

35

Elder standing was contingent on more than just advanced age. Senior members of a homestead came to power by meriting respect for their distinct knowledge and dignified bearing. During special ceremonies, the patriarch mediated between the spirits of the living and the spirits of the departed (the male ancestors or *amadlozi*). He propitiated the *amadlozi* by pouring libations on the ground, evoking the protection of the divine realm.[16]

Youths achieved a measurably higher stature only after they met the laboring obligations to their homestead head, and he gave them the permission and resources to attain a more independent life. Young men served their homestead head, expecting, in return, the *lobola* cattle that would eventually allow them to wed.[17] However, as young men and women rose in status, not all enjoyed the position of homestead heads and first wives, and this created discord between generations.

Daily practices helped to contain domestic tensions. Customs of deference such as *ukuhlonipha* compelled young males and females and married women to avoid male elders as a demonstration of homage. One homestead head explained that "a male youth (*insizwa*) must make way for a mature man (*indoda*) [and if] he failed to do so, the latter would go to the men of the place of the *mnumzane* [the youth's homestead head], who would fine the boy, asking how he came to regard himself as the equal of a man".[18] When admonishment was not enough, patriarchs could exact severe punishment. If boys allowed a herd to stray from pasture into gardens, reported one homestead head, they "would be beaten."[19]

The patriarch's duty was to safeguard the productive activities of his homestead. He was the custodian of livestock, farming implements, garden land, and money earned by his dependents. As a patriarch matured, his opportunities to take more wives increased, for he would receive *lobola* cattle at the marriage of his daughters.[20] In the early 1880s, African patriarchs testified to a Natal colonial "native commission" that the custom of *lobola* was "not only ... long-existing ... but also [helped] to "build up a *kraal*" to make a man wealthy and great through the cattle received on the marriage of his daughters."[21]

"Shepstone's Downpour"

Most colonists, for their part, denounced bridewealth and polygyny. A government report on "native affairs" in 1881 declared these marital practices "crimes against humanity which have to be put down", although "with gradual extinction [after] the greater spread of Christianity."[22] In 1869, a colonial marriage law launched the official attack on polygyny by fixing the amount of *lobola* on a sliding scale. African men with no political power (the majority "commoners") were to receive 10 heads of cattle for their married daughters, the chiefs' councilors or "headmen" 15 heads, chiefs appointed by the colony 20 heads, and hereditary chiefs a number that they freely determined.

In effect, this gave earning young men the means to compete in a marriage market formerly dominated by older, wealthier, polygynous men. Unmarried younger suitors could buy the requisite 10 head of cattle, undercutting fathers who tried to set *lobola* beyond what male juniors could pay.

The 1869 law also gave single women a voice in determining their nuptial future. An "official witness", an African man appointed by a district magistrate and paid a government salary, was to protect brides from being coerced into unwanted unions.[23] In 1882, a Thukela basin chief reported that, "since the Law has given the right to girls to choose their husbands, old men find difficulty in obtaining young wives. Generally polygamy is on the decrease; the girls belong to the young men."[24] In the 1870s and 1880s, African patriarchs who objected to the 1869 marriage law called it "Shepstone's Downpour", after the secretary for native affairs, Theophilus Shepstone, who was held accountable for the flood of weddings involving youthful brides and grooms.[25]

The 1869 marriage law was a cornerstone of the Natal Native Code, a melange of "customary laws" which, on the one hand, buttressed African patriarchy and, on the other, offered women and youths legal redress against what colonial authorities saw as the tyranny of polygynous fathers. To uphold the Native Code, the Natal colony turned chiefs into the "eyes and ears of the government", recognizing that their "patriarchal system" made Africans "easy to govern" because it promoted "dependence" and obedience.[26] In practice, chiefs collected taxes and fines for the colony. They also enrolled young men from homesteads into mandatory government public works brigades, or *isibalo*, and recruited local laborers for the commercial mining operations in the coal fields of northern Natal and the burgeoning gold industries of the Transvaal.[27]

Despite colonial interference, the institution of chieftaincy retained some sovereignty, with a small ruling elite (a chief and his political councilors, or *izinduna*) exercising rights to the labor and loyalty of homestead heads. Chiefdoms varied in size and scale, the larger ones usually divided into districts, containing many homesteads, and administered by *izinduna*.[28]

Like homesteads, chiefdoms were prone to splinter as a result of political disputes.[29] With no private land ownership, a chief ensured his followers' obedience through reciprocal obligations. Homestead inhabitants offered to *khonza* the chief (i.e. to pay him homage and tribute in cattle, grain, and beer); while young men periodically defended the chiefdom and husbanded his cattle, the females sowed and reaped his fields. A chief, in turn, provided relief during hardship, resolved quarrels, and allotted land.[30]

Chiefs "Have Neither the Means nor the Power... to Control Tribes"

Throughout the 1890s, a series of Natal government actions compromised the authority of chiefs. The secretary for native affairs would balkanize chiefdoms whenever a chief appeared to rule over more than several thousand followers.[31] The colonial system of land tenure merely compounded the problems of fragmentation. Starting in the first decade of British rule in the 1840s, white officials began to divide the colony of Natal into communal

African reserves, private settler farms, and Crown land (from which the government later carved out mission reserves), establishing magisterial districts in all three territories according to natural geographic location. By the turn of the century, the secretary for native affairs assessed the legacy of the three-tier system of landholding: "chiefs ... have neither the means nor the power to ... control tribes, the members ...[of] which are dispersed over a number of magistracies."[32] To bolster what it perceived as frail African leadership, the Natal governor assumed the mantle of "Supreme Chief." Magistrates prosecuted young African men for gang activity or "faction fights,[33] dictated when adolescent boys could enlist in ceremonial regiments, and approved chiefs' successors and new headmen.[34]

Yet chiefdoms experienced colonial incursions unevenly as a consequence of inconsistent government policies. From the Natal capital of Pietermaritzburg northward the influence of white rule decreased.[35] Some chiefs on the south side of the Thukela basin, with the largest number of their followers in the colony proper, were able to muster their young men into labor and fighting corps, and to punish criminals.[36] In southern Zululand, the powers of some appointed chiefs were curtailed in the 1880s, but many hereditary chiefs still collected their own tribute from homesteads.[37]

Britain declared Zululand an English colony in 1887, fueling the ambitions of Natal whites to settle Zululand. The London Colonial Office, however, insisted on keeping them out to maintain the territorial integrity of most chiefdoms and preserve Zulu patriarchy. But beyond this, colonial rule was less of a blessing for the people of Zululand. After the Zulu defeat by British forces in 1880, the resident commissioner in Eshowe modified aspects of "native customary law," such as fixing bridewealth on a sliding scale. During the 1890s, the guarded approach of the London Colonial Office to Zululand would be reversed.

In 1893, the Natal colony became self-governing with a cabinet "responsible" to a locally-elected parliament. For the first time, white settlers oversaw the native administration and began to pressure Great Britain to relinquish its hold over Zululand. In 1897, Great Britain allowed the Natal government to annex Zululand as a province. The governor now presided over the newly-expanded Natal colony. The secretary for native affairs, with two deputies, the under secretary for native affairs in Pietermaritzburg, Natal, and the resident commissioner in Eshowe, Zululand, were in charge of white district magistrates and their African proxies, hereditary and appointed chiefs, headmen, and "official witnesses."[38]

Magistrates usurped even greater control over local affairs within chiefdoms. They became the final arbiters of feuds over garden and pasture boundaries.[39] One Thukela basin elder complained that in land disputes followers would tell their chief to "go away; this place was given to me [by the colony]."[40] To enforce rulings in succession fights, magistrates sent Natal policemen to banish rebellious factions from chiefdoms.[41] In southern Zululand, magistrates overturned on appeal chiefs' judgments in civil cases.[42] Finally, there was the *isibalo* policy, which magistrates instituted to funnel young men from homesteads into low-paying government projects such as building roads. During *isibalo* recruitment drives, chiefs and homestead heads drummed up the necessary labor, employing coercion when they encountered recalcitrant youths.[43] But compulsion could backfire and strain generational authority. An African patriarch said "road party work is a grievance ...The young people are now deserting their fathers because of the *isibalo*, because they are very much afraid of it. The work is hard. They earn nothing, and are given little food."[44]

"We Have No Place ... To Build or Plough"

While the colonial government stifled the authority of chiefs, Natal settlers strangled the ability of African cultivators to maintain subsistence.[45] Since the 1890s, colonial farmers appropriated ever-larger expanses of homestead land, forcing African cultivators to use up their own fallow fields and stores of grain.[46] The territories that homesteads viewed as safety valves (for instance, the mission reserves) were by the mid-1890s overcrowded and plagued by boundary fights.[47] A chief in Nkandla told a visiting secretary for native affairs in 1898 that his chiefdom was "in trouble about land." The secretary asked, "What trouble? As far as I can see there is plenty of land," to which the chief said "We have no place ... to build [homesteads] or plough." The colonial official responded "There is one thing you must remember and that is ... I am not here for the purpose of unsettling anything that has already been settled. It may be unfortunate that you have only a small piece of land, but where is there other land to be found?"[48]

With African agriculture hobbled, unmarried young men departed from their homesteads in greater numbers. Most left to work in the industrial centers of the Transvaal, but some entered service on commercial farms in Natal.[49] Although customary fealty required wage-earning sons to send money to their homestead head,[50] some squandered their pay in the towns.[51] Other labor migrants deserted their rural families, melting into the slums and workers' hostels around industrial areas.

By the mid-1890s, natural calamaties made homestead heads even more dependent on the wages of their migrant sons. Swarms of locusts descended on the Thukela basin and devoured sprouting crops,[52] forcing homesteads to use their entire savings to buy food transported from neighboring colonial territories to stave off famine.[53] A magistrate who observed food shortages in his own district urged the government to distribute relief supplies to African patriarchs,[54] but officials in the "native administration" insisted that emergency provisions be sold at "cost price."[55] In southern Zululand, a magistrate sent a telegram to colonial officials in Eshowe, saying "I fear that there will be many deaths from starvation unless some means are provided by the Government for ... those who are not in a position to purchase food", to which the resident commissioner replied that the magistrate should assist only "people destitute of food, who have neither cattle or money to buy, and as far as possible, deal with such cases by lending or giving grain in limited quantities for their use. You should satisfy yourself that no men fit to work receive any aid."[56] Driven by the scarcity of food, homestead heads asked the Natal colony to suspend the seasonal "game law" so that they could hunt without restrictions for their survival.[57]

As the locust infestation subsided in the middle of 1896, farmers again ploughed and seeded, but drought and the hot spring sun scorched their fields. Mingling with stories of parched earth and spreading hunger were rumors of an apocalyptic cattle disease called rinderpest.[58] The plague had traveled from east and central Africa southward into the Cape. In late 1896, rinderpest entered Natal,[59] prompting white stock-owners to inoculate their herds with bile from infected cows, the only known cure.[60] The government inaugurated a vaccination campaign in the chiefdoms,[61] but Africans rejected the bile remedy because they feared intestinal fluid from dying or dead cattle would "bring ... the disease nearer to them."[62] By 1898, nearly 93 percent of homestead cattle in southern Zululand had perished,[63] and in northern Natal 90 percent.[64]

In just four years, many Africans had slid into ruin. Thukela valley homesteads had in decades past overcome dire agricultural crises, sometimes with relief from colonists,[65] but now adversity persisted since herds took far longer to recover than did crops. Cattle, unlike grain, symbolized wealth and leverage for homestead heads accustomed to endowing hard-working, obedient young men with gifts of cattle.[66]

To unmarried African youths rinderpest would not only dim their future with the specter of lingering hardship, but would also continue to frustrate their expectations of the material advantages and exalted status accorded to patriarchs. The Umvoti magistrate wrote in 1897 that "in many instances the fathers of the girls refuse to take the *lobola* for fear of losing the cattle almost immediately."[67] A chief in the northern Thukela valley confirmed this official sentiment; that "many natives will, for a long time to come, fail to comply with the custom regarding the giving of *lobola*", undermining the matchmaking of homestead heads.[68] Indeed, elders' reliance on their sons grew exponentially as the material base of homesteads steadily shrank during the Anglo-Boer war from 1899–1902.

At the start of the war between Briton and Boer, mining operations in the Transvaal, Cape, and Natal stopped production and sent their workers home. The subsequent flood of labor migrants returning to the Thukela basin created instant food shortages for homesteads.[69] When the Anglo-Boer war ended in May 1902, the dormant South African economy revived, and Transvaal employers started aggressively to recruit African workers from the Thukela basin.[70] The majority of the labor migrants were adolescent males and young men, followed by boys under the age of 15 years old. Far fewer young women migrated, entering domestic "service" in white Natal households.[71] In the districts of Mapumulo, Kranskop, and Nkandla, magistrates estimated that 50 percent more females than males lived in homesteads.[72]

"[W]e Are Scattered by the White People"

Migrant wages were trickling back to rural fathers, but taxes and rents on farms consumed this supplemental income. In 1903, the Natal colony doubled the hut tax on Crown territory in order to halt an influx of indigent Africans onto that land.[73] One male elder saw the rising taxes as a sign that the "Government did not like to see people eating, because when they saw them chewing anything, they seem to put their fingers into their very mouths and scoop the food out to eat themselves."[74] Homestead heads borrowed from colonial usurers to pay the higher taxes, unaware that these loans accrued heavy interest.[75] In addition, white farmers in northern Natal and elsewhere raised rents and evicted homestead tenants who were in arrears.[76] Chief Bambatha and his council of elders told the Kranskop magistrate of "hardships suffered ... on private lands through heavy rents [and] unreasonable demands for service in lieu of rents."[77]

The lull in natural calamity was short-lived; after the Anglo-Boer war another spate of disasters ensued. In 1903, locusts reappeared to eat homestead gardens, while new outbreaks of deadly livestock diseases struck cattle herds, imperiling entire chiefdoms with starvation.[78] After meeting with homestead elders from southern Zululand, a magistrate summarized their grim predicament: "with locusts, drought, ... extensive removals or payment of rent to Europeans—they [have] almost insurmountable difficulties."[79] *Ilanga Lase Natal*, a Zulu language newspaper published by a mission-educated African editor named John Dube, chronicled an ailing homestead economy that only twitched to life with the injection of wages. "We know that in addition to the poverty which we [experience], more especially on those [African] reserves where the soil is unproductive, and where a livelihood is obtained only by the purchase of food, there is great bitterness amongst our people."[80]

In the Thukela basin, harvest time, normally a celebration of largesse, highlighted African elders' inability to deliver their families from hardship. During a visit to a magistrate near Durban in 1905, homestead patriarchs recounted how they coped with the recent travails: "when famine threatened us, we were saved by our sons. They earned the money [to pay for] Government Taxes ... the landlords' rents [and] rice, beans, [and] imported mealies."[81] By 1902, homestead production of staples in Natal had declined 75 percent in one decade.[82] Although African cultivators still planted half the annual corn harvested in Natal, they had many more mouths to feed, with births having risen by a third since the early 1890s. According to the 1904 Natal census, Africans now comprised nine of ten people in Natal; and one in two homestead inhabitants was 20 years old or younger.[83]

By contrast, a handful of colonists in Natal wielded, as one missionary remarked wryly, "a divine right ... to the land." White settlers owned 8,000,000 acres, or two-thirds of the colony's land south of the Thukela river.[84] They produced half of the corn harvested yearly and virtually all of the lucrative exports such as sugar, tea, tobacco, and wattle trees.[85] In 1904, a joint imperial and colonial Zululand-Lands Delimitation Commission "threw open" to white sugar planters a fertile 70-mile band of ocean coast from the Thukela River northwards.[86] In 1905, the first Natal farmers crossed into Zululand, uprooting homesteads from shore-line districts to make way for private sugar farms.[87]

The majority of African young men, who as they matured would not remain in their homestead, and young women, who would leave their family to join landless husbands, faced formidable obstacles in the search for their new homestead sites.[88] One male elder in southern Zululand asked a magistrate: Since "we are scattered by the white people, who have taken up the farms ... where are we going to put our children?"[89] In *Ilanga Lase Natal*, John Dube wrote that "the land where the white man found us—the land where our fathers have been buried from time immemorial ... has been wrested away from us."[90] To the homestead heads who communicated with the souls of departed forbears, the loss of ancestral land was profoundly disquieting. Without access to burial sites, homestead heads were deprived of the domicile of their patriarchal spirits, whose wrath could be directed against any disobedient family member.[91]

"Fighting Between the Young Men will be Inevitable. The Elder Men are Tired of Restraining Them"

With the material and spiritual base of African patriarchy eroded by colonial intrusions and natural disasters, youths saw their homesteads descend into privation, and their homestead heads unable to halt the slide. With dwindling reminders of their father's power, sons became restless, and some obstreperous. The social mechanisms that normally checked their unruliness depended on their homestead head's forceful authority. Now vulnerable, patriarchs could not readily subdue rowdy young men who, spurred on by beer and their newfound hubris as wage-earners, increasingly engaged in brawling and flagrant pursuits of young women.

At beer gatherings, homestead guests were expected to sip politely from a pot of brew. Drinking order fell along hierarchical lines, with homestead heads and married men usually imbibing first, then passing the beer pot to unmarried men. The latter were to stay sober enough to obey the presiding homestead head's commands, and should any "quarrels, wranglings and fightings" arise, they would be tamped down by the older male host. Rarely did women join in the festivities, although they could drink in the privacy of their own huts.[92]

By the late 1890s, however, decorum at beer parties had been sufficiently corrupted, at least in the eyes of some homestead heads and colonial officials, to require policing by government authorities. In 1898, the Natal Legislature passed a law that proclaimed "Rules for controlling ... the gathering of Natives ... for the purpose of feasting or beer drinking." The "beer regulations" stipulated that the "host ... whether he be Chief, headman, kraal head ... shall be held responsible for the good conduct and order of his guests and visitors, and such others as may partake of the beer." Young men, recognized as being sources of potential trouble, were to be closely watched; if they sat "down to drink beer in the company of the [elder] men (*amadoda*) ... unless specially invited so to do by the principal man" they would "be guilty of an [indictable] offence." The law barred young women altogether from beer gatherings and imposed stringent penalties on revelers who violated customary prohibitions against carousing or "insulting gestures ... intended to provoke a breach of peace."[93]

Despite these attempts at vigilance, American Board missionaries in northern Natal claimed the government was not doing enough "to deal with licentious [drunk] young men in our stations," suggesting that the transgressors be "cooled off" in *isibalo* service.[94] Intoxicated aggressive young men increasingly marred beer celebrations when they squared off against one another with fists, stones, and sticks, ignoring patriarchal cries for peace. One homestead head complained that "Nowadays [he] found mere children attending these gatherings ... [T]he *kraal*-head had no authority to send them about their business because if he told them to go home, they would simply say they would not, and then, if he struck them, they would at once go and report him to the Magistrate."[95] Another elder in 1898 bemoaned the recent appearance of impudent young men. "I know that abusing of parents by their own sons has greatly increased in this country. The behavior of today is beyond me. Your own child can abuse you even as he helps himself to your food."[96]

The Natal government reported strife at homestead gatherings as "faction fighting," and when these clashes exploded into public view, African patriarchs incurred magisterial reprimand and fines for not preserving "good order."[97] Without the wages contributed by migrant sons, homestead heads faced difficulties in paying financial penalties, and, in some cases, their dependency on these earnings made them awkwardly beholden to the very young men accused of creating the upheavals.

Faction fighting, however, had long been part of life in the Thukela basin and elsewhere in Zulu-speaking Natal and Zululand. Combat between groups of young men resulted from a range of antagonisms. With homesteads and herds crowded together in districts like Umsinga, Umvoti, and Kranskop, conflicts arose over land; when these squabbles threatened to become violent, homestead heads in one valley might organize their sons into an armed band or regiment, in anticipation of vying with their enemies in the next valley.[98] Thus did bloody feuds begin between rivalrous homesteads, and between rivalrous chieftaincies. Occasionally mere sniping between cattle herders incited a numbers of melees among boys.[99]

But in the late 1890s and early 1900s, there was turmoil on an unprecedented scale, spawned by drunk and volatile young men. The fiercest tussles among male youths tended to originate at marriage celebrations when competition over the affections of girls kindled jealousies and vendettas. Few large ceremonies attracted so many available young women. Eager to show their mettle at the wedding, bands of young men danced, goading one another before an enthusiastic female audience. Such demonstrations of prowess often erupted into melees, scattering the host and other patriarchal authorities charged with keeping the peace. A magistrate in northern Natal wrote in 1902 that "it often transpires [in] faction fight cases that young men of one tribe simply defy the official witnesses in charge of the wedding."[100] Chief Tulwana in Umsinga similarly reported an incident at a "bridal party" where young men from an adversarial chiefdom raided his territory, prompting his men [to exclaim] "they [the attacking young men] will reach the *kraal* and kill us" [but] the boys [vowed] "we shall not allow them to come to our *kraal*". In the resulting battle between the rival "*impi*" or regiments of young men, the "men (*amadoda*) did not succeed in keeping the boys back."[101] After rinderpest decimated homestead herds, chief Magqanqu in Lower Tugela district lamented that "marriage season [saw more] collisions [between groups of young men], owing to the opposite factions living in close proximity. Fighting between the young men will be inevitable. The elder men are tired of restraining them."[102]

In the absence of bridewealth cattle, a daughter's outright refusal to marry an elder man might no longer jeopardize her future. The under secretary for native affairs said in 1904 "young men do not suffer under anything like the disability their fathers were accustomed to with regard to marriage, as any young fellow who is industrious can easily earn enough to purchase sufficient cattle [from the healthy stock owned by white farmers] to *lobola* a wife with."[103] With myriad younger suitors calling, single women became more discerning about who their husbands would be, knowing that emboldened young men could pledge future *lobola* and challenge the grooms of their fathers' generation.[104]

Girls were now receiving recurrent visits from unmarried men, flush with the means to acquire bridewealth with their own wages, and these frequent courting episodes heightened the likelihood for faction fighting. Chief Mabizela in Weenen district explained "my people became lovers of girls of the Amabaso people [who were his rivals] in the Umsinga Division and one of these days a member of my Tribe will go to see his girl and will, while there be assaulted by the Amabaso's young men, he will then come and tell other members of his (my) Tribe what has occurred and they naturally will take his part and a faction fight will ensue."[105]

In Mapumulo criminal court, the cases of faction fights involving young men soared from 124 in 1896 to 631 in 1897. The Mapumulo magistrate warned "the natives of [his] intention to pass somewhat severe sentences [for] faction fighting ... which is as a general rule confined to young men."[106] By 1903, the rowdiness in the district exasperated him; the magistrate "found ... the youth the most unruly community I have had to deal with during nearly 17 years experience in various parts of Natal and Zululand."[107]

The climbing number of faction fighting cases in other districts also reflected unmarried sons' growing disregard for their elders.[108] From 1900 to 1905, faction fight incidents in Eshowe, Mapumulo, and Kranskop districts appeared to be mounting at a rate never before documented in criminal records. In Kranskop alone, the number of faction fight cases tripled from 1904 to 1905. The Thukela basin had become the center of such conflicts in Natal and Zululand. In 1905, the office of the colonial secretary tabulated all the faction fights heard by magistrates. The six district courts abutting the Thukela River south of Zululand tried nearly 30 percent of all cases of faction fighting in Natal. On the north side of the river, more than half the faction fights cases were heard in just two Thukela basin courts in Eshowe and Nkandla.[109]

"We Are All Dogs on Account of Our Children"

The Natal government tried to curb the upsurge of youth violence, partly by buttressing the faltering African patriarchy. The magistrates' role as final arbiters in faction fight cases underscored just how difficult it was for homestead heads to discipline their fractious sons. When public disorder and family disputes threatened to disrupt domestic life, male elders quickly turned to colonial officials to stanch the trouble. Obedience to, if not reliance on white rulers had become equated with the most privileged generation, yet for most African patriarchs, this relationship of dependency was at best uneasy, or in the words of one homestead head, an "in between" state of defeat.[110]

Colonial officials, some of whom were no older than young heir-apparents in homesteads, alternately reduced and amplified the generational standing of African men. In 1906, the homestead head Socwatsha "found nowadays" that headmen were "mere whippersnappers."[111] The governor could now chose commoners as chiefs, who, asserted one male elder named Mbovu, would be "obliged to pick a man [as his political representative at the district court] who is of no rank, and yet owing simply to his ... being known at the court house he is made not only equal to but above those of rank, who are regarded by the Government as ordinary people."[112] Mbovu measured colonial encroachment in generational terms. "We have mixed up old habits and customs; [once] cases were heard by our chiefs [but] now the Government does so ... The children too are no longer our own for we may not demand what cattle we wish... We of hereditary rank are of no account for we have been set on one side."[113] *Ilanga Lase Natal* leveled an analogous criticism: "Let us not be shoved aside by supercilious young magistrates. Let just men be chosen for us, not boys [and] Let the chiefs and parents of children be supported in the just control of the young."[114]

The stripping away of fathers' powers fostered disrespect within chiefdoms and homesteads. In a northern Natal district where many unmarried men entered colonial society through labor migrancy, a male elder reported in 1900 that "at public meetings of natives some of the young men get up and speak in English. The older men strongly object and (say) ... they (would be) quite ready to leave and hold their meetings apart. This speaking of English, when there is no necessity for so doing, is due to a species of pride and sense of importance."[115] Homestead head Mbovu spoke for his fellow patriarchs when he lamented, "We are all dogs on account of our children in spite of the fact that we *lobola*'d their mothers."[116] He foresaw a widening schism because "the country belong[ed] to the new generation – *abatsha*" who "jeer at me saying we are all equal now."[117]

Mkando, an aged homestead head, mourned the twilight phase of his generation's reign: "Over and over again [the Natal colony] promulgate[s] fresh laws and we abide by them cheerfully, and this sort of thing has continued until we have become old and grey-headed, and not even now, advanced in years as we are, do we know the meaning of [white rule]. We cut away the wild forests for sugar plantations and towns; we dig your roads ... We are made to live on farms and pay rent, and are imprisoned if we cannot pay ... Our children ... We have no control over them. We are in trouble. Our children lose contact with their homes, and we lose that wealth which according to ancient customs is vested in them."[118]

NOTES

1. Annexure C, Deyi of Madulini v. Mbuzikazi, 1 July 1897, 1/1/SNA 1/1/278 1962/1897.
2. Annexure A, Deyi of Madulini v. Mbuzikazi, 1 July 1897, 1/SNA 1/1/278 1962/1897.
3. Magisterial Notes, Deyi of Madulini v. Mbuzikazi, July 1897, 1/SNA 1/1/278 1962/1897.
4. Annexure A, Deyi of Madulini v. Mbuzikazi, 1 July 1897, 1/SNA 1/1/278 1962/1897.
5. This chapter is part of a larger narrative of generational conflict told in Carton (forthcoming).
6. *Lobola* is a verb meaning "to offer bridewealth," usually in the form of cattle. *Lobolo* (*ilobolo*) is the noun for bridewealth. Today, many Thukela basin residents say that *lobola* was, and it still is, the preferred term to describe both bridewealth cattle and the action of giving bridewealth cattle.
7. Unless otherwise noted, the primary evidence for this chapter comes from the Natal Archives, Pietermaritzburg, South Africa. Minute (hereafter Min.) Magistrate (hereafter Mag.) Entonjaneni, 5 Oct. 1903, 1/MEL 3/2/10 PB906/1903.
8. A "self-sustaining" homestead relied on a range of productive practices and flexible responses to external challenges. In con-

trast, a "self-sufficient" homestead was, by definition, a closed economic unit.

9. Blue Books Natal 1884-1889, Crops and Produce by Natives, Native Stock, Average Market Values; 1884 Statistics (hereafter Stat.), pp. X6-11; 1885 Stat., pp. X6-11; 1886 Stat., pp. X6-7, 14-5; 1887 Stat., pp. X6-7; 1888 Stat., pp. X6-7; 1889 Stat., pp. X6-7; 1/NCP 7/2/1/1-6. Less accurate statistics are in the Blue Books Natal 1879-1883, Acreage Cultivated, Crops by Natives, Stock Estimates by Natives, Animal Production, Average Market Value; 1879 Stat., pp. AA8-15, Mag. Reports, pp. JJ6-16; 1880 Stat., p. AA7, Mag. Reports, pp. JJ105, 111; 1881 Stat., pp. X7-13, Mag. Reports, p. GG45; 1883 Stat., pp. X6-11, Mag. Reports, p. GG11; 1/NCP 7/1/27-31. Colonial Veterinary Surgeon, Revenual Auditor, Supp. Blue Book, Natal Departmental (hereafter Dept.) Reports, 1884-1889; 1884 Veterinary Surgeon Rep., pp. H17, 20-1; 1885 Reports Magistrates, pp. B27, 29; 1887 Reports Magistrates, p. 46; 1889 Reports Magistrates, p. B98; Supplemental (hereafter Supp.) Dept. Reports Natal, 1/NCP 7/2/2/1-6.

10. Testimony of Madama, Umvoti, 21 Feb. 1882, *Evidence Natal Native Commission 1881(-2)*, 1/NCP 8/3/20, pp. 248-9. Rep. Mag. Umsinga, Supp. Blue Book Natal 1886, 7/2/2/3, p. B187. Testimony of Mqayikana, 12 Nov. 1897, p. 34; Testimony of Ndukwana, 5, 18 April; 2, 17 May; 3, 11 Sept. 1903; pp. 363-4, 366, 370, 372, 375-6, 378; *James Stuart Archive Vol. IV* (1986). Report (hereafter Rep.). Mag. Lower Tugela 1902, 1/SGR 4/1/7 LTD 132/1903. Testimony of Ndukwana, 11 Sept. 1903, File #61, Notebooks, James Stuart Papers, Killie Campbell Library, Durban, South Africa. Testimony of Mkotana, 1 June 1905, *James Stuart Archive Vol. II* (1982), p. 228. Zulu History, (c. 1930), H.C. Lugg, File #2, H.C. Lugg Papers, Killie Campbell Library.

11. "Rights" in labor based on generational ranking: J. Stuart, "The Zulu Tribal System," 1907, File #26, p. 121, James Stuart Papers, Killie Campbell Library, Durban. Circular (hereafter Circ.). R 471, 1894, 28 Feb. 1894, Resident (hereafter Res.) Commissioner (hereafter Comm.), Eshowe, to Mag. Nkandla, 1/NKA 3/

2/2/1 NK Confidential (hereafter Conf.) 7/1910. Min. Mag. Umvoti, 29 June 1904, 1/SNA 1/1/312 1341/04.

12. Securing the labor of clients: Testimony of Ndukwana, 12 Sept. 1900, *James Stuart Archive Vol. IV* (1986), pp. 269-70. Testimony of J. Kumalo, 31 Dec. 1900, p. 250; Testimony of Mxaba, 2 Jan. 1901, p. 252; *James Stuart Archive Vol. I* (1976). Government Notice of Beer Drinking Act 5 1898, 1/SNA 1/1/296 2557/ 1902.

13. Statement of Lukulwini, 7 Feb. 1905, 1/SNA 1/1/315 2525/1904.

14. Brothers jostling for social position: Testimony of Ndukwana, 9 Nov. 1903, File # 61, p. 31, James Stuart Notebooks, Killie Campbell Library. "Self-nomination": Letter Mag., Inanda, to Civ. Comm., Eshowe, 1/SNA 1/1/315 R212/1905.

15. Annexure A, Statement of Lugubu, 8 Feb. 1905; Telegram Civ. Comm., Eshowe, to Mag. Newcastle, Inanda, and Umlalazi, 1 Feb. 1905; 1/SNA 1/1/315 2525/1905.

16. H.C. Lugg, "Zulu Fibres and Their Uses", p. 2, H.C. Lugg Papers, Killie Campbell Library. Testimony of Mkando, 12 Aug. 1902, pp. 168-9; Testimony of Ndukwana, Mkando, and Dlozi, 13 Aug. 1902, pp. 171-2, 174; *James Stuart Archive Vol. III* (1982). Testimony of Msimanga, 28 Feb. 1922, *James Stuart Archive Vol. IV* (1986), p. 41. A. Bryant, "Notes on Magic, AbaNgoma, Ancestor Worship, Divination and AmaDlozi," (c. 1900), A. Bryant Papers, Killie Campbell Library.

17. Testimony of Kumalo, 16 Dec. 1900, *James Stuart Archive Vol. I* (1976), p. 237.

18. Testimony of Ndukwana, 3 Sept. 1903, *James Stuart Archive Vol. IV* (1986), p. 376.

19. Testimony of Ndukwana, 9 Nov. 1903, File #61, p. 31, James Stuart Notebooks, Killie Campbell Library.

20. Testimony of Induna Class, 30 Jan. 1882, p. 333; Testimony of Umnini, 15 Feb. 1882, p. 193; *Evidence Natal Native Commission 1881(-2)*, 1/NCP 8/3/20. *Report Natal Native Commission 1881-2*, 1/NCP 8/3/19, p. 13. Testimony of Ndukwana, 15 July 1900, *James Stuart Archive Vol. IV* (1986), pp. 267-8. Testi-

mony of Mbovu, 7 Feb. 1904, *James Stuart Archive Vol. I* (1976), p. 28. Testimony of Sibindi, 11 April 1907, *Evidence Natal Native Affairs Commission 1906-7*, 1/NCP 8/3/76, p. 846.

21. *Report Natal Native Commission 1881-82*, 1/NCP 8/3/19, p. 13.
22. Ibid. p. 12.
23. Testimony of Umnini, 15 Feb. 1882, *Evidence Natal Native Commission 1881(2-)*, 1/NCP 8/3/20, p. 193. Testimony of Joko, 1 Feb. 1882, pp. 354-5; Testimony of Homestead Head Madama, 21 Feb. 1882, p. 249. *Evidence Natal Native Commission 1881(-2)* 1/NCP 8/3/20.
24. Testimony of Chief Domba, 31 Jan. 1882, *Evidence Natal Native Commission, 1881* 1/NCP 8/3/20, p. 335.
25. "Shepstone's Downpour": "The Paying of Bride-Price, uBaxoxele," pp. 4-5, File #79, James Stuart Papers, Killie Campbell Library.
26. *Report Native Affairs Commission 1906-7*, 1/NCP 8/3/75, p. 13.
27. *Isibalo*: Testimony of J. Matiwane, 10 Feb. 1881, p. 148; Testimony of Umnini, 15 Feb. 1882, p. 199; Testimony of Teleku, 13 Feb. 1882, p. 176; *Evidence Natal Native Commission 1881(-2)* 1/NCP 8/3/20. *Report Natal Native Commission 1881-2*, 1/NCP 8/3/19, pp. 4-5. Rep. Mag. Umsinga, Supp. Blue Book Natal 1885, 1/NCP 7/2/2/2, pp. B39, B46. Mine labor recruitment: Official Telegrams and Correspondence, Vol. 758, 1894-1896, 1/ZGH.
28. Certain chiefly lines of descent, like those of homestead heads, endured over time. Rep. Mag. Krantzkop, Condition of Natives, 31 Dec. 1898, 1/KRK 3/1/2 KK1A/1899. Testimony of J. Kumalo, 20 Oct. 1900, pp. 43-4, File #59, Notebooks, James Stuart Papers, Killie Campbell Library. Testimony of Ndukwana, 21 Oct. 1900, *James Stuart Archive Vol. IV* (1986), p. 316. Testimony of N. Nembula, 7 May 1905, p. 90; Testimony of Mayinga and Dinya, 11 July 1905, pp. 257-8; *James Stuart Archive Vol. II* (1979).
29. Often political disputes could propel an exodus of followers from a chiefdom. Testimony of Mageza, 20 Feb. 1905, p. 73; Testimony of Maziyana, 30 April 1905, p. 300; *James Stuart Archive Vol. II* (1979). Testimony of Lugubu, 4 Mar. 1909, *James Stuart*

Archive Vol. I (1976), pp. 281-3. Testimony of Mbokobo, 5 Nov. 1913, *James Stuart Archive Vol. III* (1982), pp. 6-15.

30. Letter Mag. Eshowe to Chief Dunn, Eshowe, 6 Sept. 1894, Eshowe Letter Book, 1892-1897, 1/ESH 3/1/3. Min. Civil (Civ.) Comm., Eshowe, to SNA, Pietermaritzburg, 21 Jan. 1898, 1/SNA 1/1/ 279 25/1898. Statement of Chief Kula, Umsinga, 26 Nov. 1902; Statement of Chief Bande, Klip River, 3 Dec. 1902; 1/SNA 1/1/ 298 3531/1902. Statement of Chief Nondubela, Umsinga, 1 May 1903; Min. Mag. Umsinga, 1 May 1903; 1/SNA 1/1/301 1442/ 1903. Statement of Headmen Sandanezwe and Mankamfana, Nkandla, 7 Oct. 1905; Min. Mag. Nkandla, 7 Oct. 1905; 1/SNA 1/1/328 2672/05.

31. *Report Natal Native Commission 1881-2* 1/NCP 8/3/19, pp. 33-4. List of Chiefs and Salaries Paid to Chiefs, Blue Book, Dept. Reports Natal, 1899-1901, 1/NCP 8/2/1. Statement of Chief Kula, Umsinga, 26 Nov. 1902, 1/SNA 1/1/298 3531/1902. Statement of Chief Mtamo, Krantzkop, 28 Nov. 1902; Min. Mag. Krantzkop, 24 Oct. 1902; Statement of Maweni, Krantzkop, 22 April 1903; 1/SNA 1/1/298 3668/1902. Letter SNA to Prime Minister, Pietermaritzburg, 15 Aug. 1904, 1/SNA 1/1/311 1149/1904. See also Prime Minister Papers Nos. 761-1215 (1904), Vol. 49 1/PM 1120/1904.

32. Rep. SNA, Aug. 1900, 1/SNA 1/1/290 1430/1900.

33. Miscellaneous (hereafter Misc.). 1914, Minutes of Interviews with Native Chiefs, 1914-1925, 1/SNA I/9/4, p. 1. This source discusses early 1890s legal jurisdiction accorded to chiefs and district magistrates.

34. *Report Natal Native Commission 1881-2,* 1/NCP 8/3/19, pp. 5-6. Succession: Min. Mag. Stanger, 11 Aug. 1893, 1/SGR 4/1/4. See succession cases in SNA records: 1/SNA 1/1/281 1109/1898; 1/1/290 1430/1900.

35. In the early 1880s, colonial officials urged "greater supervision" of Africans in reserves. "The distance at present existing between seats of Magistracy, and the size of Magisterial Divisions," especially in northern Natal where districts such as Umvoti were the largest in the colony, concerned a Natal government bent on ex-

panding its police and revenue-collecting powers. *Report Natal Native Commission 1881-2,* 1/NCP 8/3/19, p. 4.

36. Min. Mag. Weenen to Under Secretary for Native Affairs (here after USNA), Pietermaritzburg, 29 Dec. 1896, 1/WEN 3/2/2 117/ 1897. Blue Book Natal 1904, 1/NCP 8/2/5, pp. 120-136.

37. Letter Res. Comm., Eshowe, to Governor, Pietermaritzburg, 16 Feb. 1894, 1/ZA Vol. 44. Min. USNA, 22 April 1903, 1/SNA 1/ 1/300 1141/1903. Min. Prime Minister, 2 April 1903; Letter Secretary (hereafter Sec.) Prime Minister to SNA, Pietermaritzburg, 7 May 1903; 1/SNA 1/1/300 1145/1903. Fines were most often in the form of cattle.

38. There were 231 chiefs in Natal and 83 in Zululand, close to one-half of them hereditary. Rep. USNA 1905, Dept. Reports 1905, 1/NCP 8/2/6, p.ii. The 1905 Report describes the colonial administration following the 1897 annexation of Zululand.

39. Supreme Chief vs. Luji Ndabezita, 10 Aug. 1895, Umsinga, 1/ SNA 1/1/207 36/95. Min. SNA, Application of Chief Mqawe for Removal, 1895, 1/SNA 1/1/206 910/95.

40. Testimony of Ndukwana, 28 Dec. 1901, *James Stuart Archive Vol. IV* (1986), p. 351.

41. Min. SNA, Statement of Magqanqu, Acting Chief Inkwenkwenzi, Lower Tugela, 21 April 1900, 1/SNA 1/1/293 566/1900. Min. SNA, 24 Nov. 1900, 1/SNA 1/1/290 2093/1900.

42. Letter Res. Mag. Eshowe, to Chief John Dunn, Eshowe, 11 June 1894, 1/ESH 3/2/2 E313/94. Min. Mag. Nkandla 1895, 1/NKA 3/2/1/1 4098/95. Magistrates in Nquthu, Nkandla, and Eshowe districts also reversed the decisions of chiefs on appeal. Case No. 5, 6 Feb. 1893; Case No. 10, 10 Feb. 1893; Cases Adjudicated Nqutu 1887-1894, 1/NQU 2/2/1/2/1. Case No. 49, 2 Nov. 1894, Native Civil Record Book Nqutu, 1894-1899, 1/NQU 2/2/1/2/2. Nkandla Civil Record Book 1894-1900, 1/NKA 2/2/1/1/3. Eshowe Civil Record Book 1895-1901, 1/ESH 2/2/1/2/4. Min. SNA, 9 Nov. 1898; Minutes Meeting between Nkandla Chiefs, SNA, Civ. Comm. Zululand, and Mag. Nkandla, 29 Aug. 1898, 1/SNA 1/1/282 2419/1898.

43. Testimony of Umnini, 15 Feb. 1882, *Evidence Natal Native Commission 1881* 1/NCP 8/3/20, p. 192. Statement of Chief Nongamulana, 25 Sept. 1905, 1/SNA 1/1/327 2576/1905. Testimony of Bubula, 14 Feb. 1907, *Evidence Native Affairs Commission 1906-7*, 1/NCP 8/3/76, p. 768.

44. Testimony of Beje, 26 Dec. 1906, *The James Stuart Archive Vol. IV* (1986), p. 54.

45. From the late 1870s to the early 1890s, the African population also doubled, heightening the land crisis affecting homesteads. Blue Book Natal 1880, 1/NCP 7/1/28, pp. JJ108, JJ111. Blue Book Natal 1886, 1/NCP 7/2/1/3, pp. X6-7. Blue Books Natal 1892-1893, 1/NCP 7/2/9. Stat. Yearbooks, Natal 1894-1895, 1/NCP 7/3/1-2.

46. In the coastal district of Lower Tugela, land devoted to corn crops rose from 5,500 acres in 1879 to about 13,000 acres in 1893. In the interior districts of Umvoti, the acreage used by homesteads went from 2,600 to 23,000, in Weenen, from 5,500 to 34,000, and Umsinga, from 6,300 to 21,000, during the same time period. Native Land Cultivated and Stock Estimates, Blue Books Natal, 1879, pp. AA8-9, 11; 1880, p. AA7; 1881, pp. X7, 11; 1883, pp. X6-7, 10-11; 1/NCP 7/1/27-29, 31. Native Land Cultivated and Stock Estimates, Blue Books Natal: 1884, pp. X6-7; 1885, pp. X6-7, 11; 1886, pp. X6-7, 11; 1890-1891, pp. X6-7, 11; 1891-1892, pp. X6-7, 12-13; 1892-1893, pp. X6-7, 11; 1/NCP 7/2/1/2-9. Part I. Stat. Summary, Stat. Yearbook Natal 1906, 1/NCP 7/3/13, p. 6.

47. Min. SNA to Rev. Wilcox, Re: ABM Mission Reserves in Mapumulo and Umvoti districts, Oct. 1895, 1/SNA 1/1/208 1352/1895.

48. Testimony of deputation of Nkandla Chiefs, 29 Aug. 1898, 1/SNA 1/1/282 2419/1898.

49. Return Blue Book Natal, July 1892, 1/SNA 1/1/161 1013/1892. Min. Mag. Nqutu, 24 Jan. 1893, 1/NQU 3/3/5 NQ48/1893. Min. SNA, 6 Jan. 1894, 1/SNA 1/1/180 92/1894. Min. SNA, 6 April 1894, 1/SNA 1/1/184 431/1894. Min. SNA, 6 July 1894, 1/SNA 1/1/187 878/94. *The Star*, 25 Oct. 1895, 1/SNA 1/1/210 1320/

95. *Standard and Digger News*, 28 Oct. 1895, 1/SNA 1/1/210 1336/95.

50. See elders' testimony in *Evidence Native Affairs Commission 1906-7*, 1/NCP 8/3/76, pp. 316, 767-8, 855.

51. Annual Rep. Mag. Weenen 1893-94, Dept. Reports Natal 1893-4, 1/NCP 7/4/1, p. B5. Min. Mag. Lower Tugela, 8 Jan. 1895, 1/SGR 4/1/5 LTD 910/94.

52. Min. Col. Sec. to Mag. Kranskop, 21 Sept. 1895, 1/KRK 3/1/1 KK435/95. Stat. Yearbook Natal 1895, 1/NCP 7/3/2. Stat. Yearbook Natal 1896, 1/NCP 7/3/5.

53. Rep. Res. Comm., Eshowe, 21 Mar. 1895, 1/ZGH Vol. 763 Z208/1895.

54. Rep. Mag. Entonjaneni, 31 Aug. 1895, 1/MEL 3/1/1/5, p. 281.

55. SNA Circ. No. 4, to Natal Magistrates, 12 Feb. 1896, 1/SNA 1/1/216 203/96. *The Times of Natal* also cautioned in September 1896 that even starvation in the countryside warranted "the greatest discretion ... in giving relief, so that natives who are able to work ... shall not be encouraged to idle about their kraals." Newspaper article excerpted from 1/SNA 1/1/229 1540/96.

56. Min. Res. Comm., Eshowe, to Mag. Emtonjaneni, 19 Mar. 1896, 1/MEL 3/2/7 PB145/1896.

57. Min. SNA, 30 Oct. 1896, 1/SNA 232 1801/1896.

58. *The Natal Mercury*, 7 Oct. 1896, SNA Min., 18 Sept. 1896, 1/SNA 1/1/230 1676/96.

59. SNA Min., 18 Sept. 1896, 1/SNA 1/1/229 1557/1896.

60. Precautionary measures: SNA Min. 9 Oct. 1896, 1/1/230 1676/1896. SNA Min. 30 Oct. 1896, 1/SNA 1/1/232 1801/96. Bile remedy: SNA Min., 31 Aug. 1897, 1/SNA 1/1/252 1636/97.

61. SNA Min. Papers, 1/SNA 1/1/250 1401-1500 (1897); SNA Min. Papers, 1/SNA 1/1/251 1501-1600 (1897).

62. SNA Min., 11 Sept. 1897, 1/SNA 1/1/255 1972/97.

63. Annual Rep. Mag. Eshowe, Blue Book Returns Natal 1897, 1/ESH 3/1/4, p. 192.

64. For a typical northern Natal district see: Rep. Mag. Kranskop, Condition of Natives 1897, Circ. SNA No. 14, 16 Oct. 1897, 1/KRK 3/1/2 KK 2021/1897.

65. Indeed, colonial statistics, although sketchy at best, showed that African crop acreage and yield had actually increased steadily from 1855 to 1906. Homestead output declined precipitously from 1894 to 1896, but production recovered just three years later to match previous levels, and then in 1900 started to climb again. See, Returns Produce, Stock, &c. Total Number of Acres in Crops, Blue Book Zululand 1889-90, Vols. 848-9, p. 2U; Blue Books Zululand 1891-5, Vols. 850-4, p. 2Y; 1/ZGH. Part I Stat. Summary Land Cultivation, Live Stock and Coal Mining, Stat. Yearbook Natal 1906, 1/NCP 7/3/13, p. 6. From 1897 onwards, agricultural statistics for Zululand were in the Natal Yearbooks.

66. Cattle had a far longer gestation period than crops. In 1896, government officials tallied 738,732 cattle in Natal proper; there was no count of cattle in Zululand that year. A year later, the estimated number of cattle in Natal *and* Zululand was 278,558. The number of cattle in Natal and Zululand did not reach the 700,000 mark until 1905, when the combined amount was still less than the 1896 level. Stat. Summary, Land Cultivation, Live Stock, and Coal Mining, Stat. Yearbook Natal 1906, 1/NCP 7/3/13, p. 6.

67. Min. Mag. Umvoti to SNA 27 Oct. 1897, 1/SNA 1/1/263 GT721/ 1897.

68. Letter Mag. Melmoth to Sec. Res. Comm., Eshowe, 14 Oct. 1897, 1/MEL 3/1/1/1/6.

69. Rep. Pop. Zululand, Dept. Reports Natal 1902, 1/NCP 8/2/2, p. C2. Rep. Mag. Eshowe, p. 70; Rep. Mag. Krantzkop, p. 34; Dept. Reports Natal 1903, 1/NCP 8/2/3. Testimony of Mrs. H. Sibisi, Chesterville, Natal, 13 Mar. 1979, p. 10, Tape #1, "Mapumulo District pre-Bambatha "Disturbances," Bambatha "Disturbances," "Migrant Labor from Zululand," Oral History Project Relating to the Zulu People, Killie Campbell Library.

70. The high rate of labor migrancy was remarkable, given the restrictions the Natal government placed on African mobility. The colony required African men to apply for "Outward Passes" from their magistrates before leaving their homesteads, as well as for "Inward Passes" to cross back into Natal. Rep. Mag. Nkandla, Dept. Reports Natal 1902, 1/NCP 8/2/2, p. C5. *South African*

Native Affairs Commission 1903-5, Vol. 3 (Natal) (Cape Town, 1905), pp. 531-8.

71. Women and domestic service in towns: Rep. SNA, Aug. 1900, 1/ SNA 1/1/290 1430/1900. Statistics on the sex and age of labor migrants, see Rep. USNA, 20 July 1906, Dept. Reports Natal 1905, 1/NCP 8/2/6, p. iii.

72. Rep. Mag. Nkandla, Natal Dept. Reports 1903, 1/NCP 8/2/3, p. 73. Rep. Mag. Mapumulo, p.6; Rep. Mag. Krantzkop, p. 33; Natal Dept. Reports 1904, 1/NCP 8/2/5.

73. Migrant wages and homestead savings: Rep. Mag. Umlalazi, p. C12; Rep. Mag. Mahlabathini, p. C15; Natal Dept. Reports 1902, 1/NCP 8/2/2. Rep. Mag. Mapumulo, Natal Dept. Reports 1904, 1/NCP 8/2/5, pp. 6-7. Doubling hut tax on Crown land, *Ilanga Lase Natal*, 28 July 1905.

74. Testimony of J. Mpetwana, 10 Jan. 1907, *Evidence Native Affairs Commission 1906-7*, 1/NCP 8/3/76, p. 716.

75. Debt and usury: Testimony of Dhlozi, 29 July 1902, *James Stuart Archive Vol.III*, (1982), pp. 155-6. Min. USNA 25 Aug. 1902, 1/ SNA 1/1/296 2277/1902, p. 4. Rep. Mag. Kranskop, Natal Dept. Reports 1903, 1/NCP 8/2/3, p. 34.

76. Tenants burdened by higher rents, Testimony of Headman Banana, Entonjaneni, 16 May 1907, p. 871; Testimony of Headman Nomdwana, Umvoti, 15 April 1907, p. 863; Testimony of Mbanjane, Krantzkop 13 April 1907; *Evidence Native Affairs Commission 1906-7*, 1/NCP 8/3/76. White farmers evict insolvent homestead heads and their families: Min. Assist. Mag. Umvoti to USNA, 20 July 1905; Min. Mag. Umvoti to USNA, 1 Nov. 1905; 1/SNA 1/1/324 1912/1905. *Report Native Affairs Commission 1906-7* 1/NCP 8/3/75, p. 27.

77. Statement of Chief Bambatha and elders, 25 Aug. 1902, 1/SNA 1/1/296 2277/1902.

78. Rep. Natives in Zululand, Natal Dept. Reports 1904, 1/NCP 8/2/5, pp. 89-90.

79. Min. Mag. Umlalazi, 24 Oct. 1905, 1/SNA 1/1/329 2840/1905.

80. *Ilanga Lase Natal*, 28 July 1905, 1/SNA 1/1/324 1945/1905.

81. Statement of Chiefs, District Headmen, Official Witnesses, and *Kraal*-heads, Pinetown, 7 Oct. 1905, pp. 2-3, 1/SNA 1/1/328 2833/1905.
82. Director's Rep. Natal Agric. Dept. Annual Rep. 1902, Natal Dept. Reports 1902, 1/NCP 8/2/2, pp. 15-7.
83. The statistics from this colonial census were probably estimates. Census of Natal, April 1904, p. 28, 1/NCP 8/3/64.
84. ABM Report, "The Attitude of Government and Colonists Toward Missionary Work among the Natives," 17 July 1903, p. 2, 1/ABM A/1/9.
85. Pop. Stat., Natal Blue Book 1901, 1/NCP 7/3/8, p. 13. Rep. Sec. Minister of Agric. June 1906, Natal Dept. Reports 1906, 1/NCP 8/2/7, p. 8. Director's Rep. Natal Agric. Dept. Annual Rep., Natal Dept. Reports 1902, 1/NCP 8/2/2, pp. 3, 41.
86. Third Ad. Interim Rep. Zululand-Lands Delim. Commission 1902-4, 1/NCP 8/3/65, p. 6.
87. Sugar Planters and long-term leases: Min. Comm. Native Affairs, Eshowe, to Mag. Eshowe, 20 Sept. 1905, 1/ESH 3/2/5 E1266/1905. Min. Comm. Native Affairs, Eshowe, 18 Sept. 1905; Letter Comm. Native Affairs, Zululand, to Minister Native Affairs, 13 Oct. 1905; 1/SNA 1/1/329 285/05. Rep. Mag. Umlalazi, Natal Dept. Reports 1905, 1/NCP 8/2/6, p. 95.
88. Pop. Stat., Natal Blue Book 1901, 1/NCP 7/3/8, p. 13. Rep. Sec. Minister of Agric., June 1906, Natal Dept. Reports 1906, 1/NCP 8/2/7, p. 8.
89. Testimony of Ngonsongoso, Eshowe, 16 Mar. 1906, p. 7; Min. Mag. Eshowe, 20 Mar. 1906; 1/ESH 3/2/5 418/1906.
90. Excerpts from *Ilanga Lase Natal* in *Natal Mercury*, Dec. 1906, Natal Society Library, Pietermaritzburg.
91. J. Stuart, "The Zulu tribal System," (c. 1900), p. 121, File #26, James Stuart Papers, Killie Campbell Library. Min. Mag. Lower Tugela, 11 Aug. 1893, 1/SGR 4/1/4 LT 99/93. Testimony of Mcotoyi, 15 April 1905, *James Stuart Archive Vol. III* (1982), pp. 59-61, 69. Min. Mag. Nkandla, 5 Dec. 1904, 1/SNA 1/1/315 2525/1904.

92. Statement of Chief Mabonjana, Lower Umzimkulu, 25 June 1903; Min. Mag. Lower Umzimkulu, 25 June 1903; 1/SNA 1/1/302 2158/1903. Testimony of L. Mxaba, 2 Jan. 1901, *James Stuart Archive Vol. I* (1976), pp. 252-3. Testimony of Bikwayo, 18 Oct. 1903, File #61, Notebooks, James Stuart Papers, Killie Campbell Library.

93. Government Notice Act 5, 1989 issued by Principal Under Sec. Col. Sec., 5 Jan. 1903, 1/SNA 1/1/296 2557/1902.

94. Min. ABM, 30 June 1898, Minutes American Board Mission Vol. VII, p. 378, June 1893 - Feb. 1900, 1/ABM A/1/2.

95. Testimony of Nkantolo, 15 Feb. 1907, *Evidence Native Affairs Commission 1906-7*, 1/NCP 8/3/76, p. 774.

96. Testimony of Gama, 18 Dec. 1898, *James Stuart Archive Vol. I* (1976), p. 137.

97. Memo. Acting Chief Magquanqu, Lower Tugela, 21 April 1900, 1/SNA 1/1/293 566/1900. Min. Mag. Weenen, 1 Sept. 1900, 1/ WEN 3/2/3 W890/1900.

98. Min. SNA to Mag. Krantzkop, 29 Jan. 1902; Statement of Zikizwayo, Umvoti, 24 July 1902, 1/SNA 1/1/295 299/1902. Min. Mag. Umsinga to SNA, 7 feb. 1902, 1/SNA 1/1/295 R193/02. Statement of Chief Bambatha, Umvoti, 22 Aug. 1902; Minutes Meetings between SNA and Krantzkop Chief Bambatha, et al., 25 Aug. 1902, 1/SNA 1/1/296 2278/1902. Min. Mag. Umsinga to USNA, 25 Nov. 1903, 1/SNA 1/1/306 3601/1903. Rep. Mag. Krantzkop to SNA, 16 July 1904, 1/SNA 1/1/305 3077/1903.

99. Papers Faction Fight, Jan. 1898, Stanger Court Depositions 1898-1900, 1/SGR 1/5/1/5 LTD 312/98. Annual Rep. Mag. Conditions of Natives 1898, Krantzkop, 1/KRK 3/1/2 KK1A/1899. Lower Tugela Admin. of Native Law Criminal Record Book, 1892-1899, 1/SGR 1/2/2/1. Min. USNA, 5 Nov. 1900, 1/GTN 3/2/8 G577/1900. Statement of Zikizwayo, Umvoti, 24 July 1902, 1/SNA 1/1/295 299/1902. Min. SNA to Mag. Krantzkop, 29 Jan. 1902, 1/SNA 1/1/295 299/1902. Letter Clerk Umsinga Court to Mag. Umsinga, 13 Feb. 1904, 1/1/308 342/1904. Court Statement of Homestead Head Mutiwentaba, Mapumulo, 18 May 1905; Min. Mag. Mapumulo, 18 May 1905, 1/1/321 1234/05.

100. Min. Mag. Estcourt, 28 Jan. 1902, 1/SNA 1/1/295 W45/1902.
101. Statement of Chief Tulwana, 16 Nov. 1903, 1/SNA 1/1/306 3601/ 1903.
102. Memo of message from chief Magqanqu, 20 April 1900, 1/SNA 1/1/293 566/1900.
103. MIN. USNA, 6 Jan. 1904, 1/SNA 1/1/306 3437/1903.
104. Testimony of S. Mabaso and J. Kumalo, 16 Dec. 1900, *James Stuart Archive Vol. I* (1976), p. 237.
105. Statement of Chief Mabizela, Sept. 28, 1904, 1/SNA 1/1/297 2669/1902, AG 2521/1904.
106. Soaring number of faction fight cases: Rep. Mag. Mapumulo, Dept. Reports Natal 1897, 1/NCP 7/4/4, p. 33. Severe sentences for young men: Rep. Mag. Mapumulo, Dept. Reports Natal 1899, 1/NCP 7/4/6, p. B33.
107. Min. Mag. Lower Umzimkulu (former Mag. of Mapumulo), 23 Jan. 1904, 1/SNA 1/1/307 3867/1903.
108. Min. Mag. Estcourt to SNA, 28 Jan. 1902, 1/SNA 1/1/295 45/ 1902. Min. Mag. Umsinga, 31 July 1902, 1/SNA 1/1/297 2567/ 1902. Statement of Chief Tulwana, Umsinga, 16 Nov. 1903; Min. Mag. Umsinga, 14 Nov. 1903; 1/SNA 1/1/306 3601/03.
109. Return Native Assault and Faction Fighting Cases, 31 Mar. 1905, 1/CSO Vol. 1793. Rep. Mag. Eshowe 1904, p. 92; Rep. Mag. Mapumulo 1904, p. 8; Rep. Mag. Krantzkop 1904; Dept. Reports Natal 1904, 1/NCP 8/2/5. Rep. Mag. Krantzkop, Dept. Reports 1905, 1/NCP 8/2/6, pp. 33, 35.
110. Testimony of Mbovu, 16 Sept. 1904, File #41, pp. 4-7, Note books, James Stuart Papers, Killie Campbell Library.
111. Testimony of Socwatsha, 19 Dec. 1906, *Evidence Natal Native Commission 1906-7*, 1/NCP 8/3/76, p. 710.
112. Testimony of Mbovu, 7 Feb. 1904, *James Stuart Archive Vol. III* (1982), p. 28.
113. Testimony of Mbovu, 13 Sept. 1904, File #61, pp. 1-6, James Stuart Notebooks, Killie Campbell Library.
114. *Ilanga Lase Natal* article excerpted in the *Natal Mercury*, Dec. 1906, Natal Society Library, Pietermaritzburg.

115. Testimony of Kumalo, 9 Dec. 1900, *James Stuart Archive Vol. I* (1976), p. 230.
116. Testimony of Mbovu, 16 Sept. 1904, *James Stuart Archive Vol. III* (1982), p. 34.
117. Testimony of Mbovu, 16 Sept. 1904, File #41, pp. 4-7, Note books, James Stuart Papers, Killie Campbell Library.
118. Testimony of Mkando, 29 July, 1902, *James Stuart Archive Vol. III* (1982), p. 155.

Chapter 2

GERONTOCRATS AND COLONIAL ALLIANCES

❖

George L. Simpson

This chapter is a study of the suppression of the Samburu *murran*, or "warriors," as part of the Samburu age-grade system during the colonial era. Tracing the history of the Samburu back to their first contacts with Europeans, particular attention should be paid to the period of the Mekuri *laji*, or age-set, when the "domestication" of the warriors was essentially completed. Based on a close examination of the archival records, the present work revisits and confirms Paul Spencer's conclusions regarding British-Samburu relations (Spencer 1965, 1973). In addition, it combines Spencer's insights into Samburu society with perspectives based on Robert

Tignor's study of colonial rule and the Kenya Maasai. This chapter will show that an alliance of convenience emerged between Samburu elders, or gerontocrats, and colonial administrators that was largely at the expense of the *murran*. The nature of this relationship was complex and often contradictory, with neither side fully trusting the other and each seeking to enlist support from whatever sources of authority it could enlist. In the end, the broader range for initiative that the Kenya administration gave to the elders further strengthened the power of the gerontocrats within Samburu society, albeit at the cost of creeping colonial encroachment into the affairs of the Samburu (Ranger 1969:300).

To understand British administration over the Samburu, one must first recognize that its nature evolved over four decades of colonial rule. At first, the new European proconsuls were content to establish what John Lonsdale has called an "awkward paramountcy," or a rough kind of peace in Samburu domains. After the First World War, however, the British moved to a second stage of occupation, whereby they sought "the bureaucratization of force," through closer administration and the recruitment of local elites as agents of their rule (Lonsdale 1989:8, 22-3). In the case of the Samburu, this meant the manipulation of traditional sources of authority based on seniority and age-grade organization (Lonsdale 1989: 12-3). This latter phase of colonial advancement was prolonged due to the difficulty of governing the widely dispersed pastoralists who lacked traditions and institutions of centralized rule not to mention the marginality of the Samburu to the Kenya economy and the colony's political affairs.[1] Only when the Samburu came into direct conflict with European settlers in the Rift Valley, did Nairobi consolidate its hold on the Samburu and compelled "law and order" on its unwilling subjects.

As it was the case elsewhere on the African continent, the British found it a procrustean enterprise to graft colonial institutions onto traditional political structures.[2] Spencer's classic study shows why this was the case, too, for the Samburu. Part of the reason for this difficulty was, as Spencer has subtly argued, the vague and sometimes erroneous understanding that the colonial administration had of the Samburu polity and the interrelationships between their political, social, and economic institutions and customs. An example of this was the British understanding of *murran* as simply warriors and their failure to recognize other social and economic aspects to the Samburu age-grade system. A second factor in the British misreading of the Samburu had to do with the fact that it was the elders rather than the *murran* who explained the nature of Samburu institutions to the administration and it was to the advantage of the gerontocrats to interpret "traditions" to their advantage. Moreover, as the administration was primarily concerned with "law and order," field officers were readily inclined to accept explanations that fit in with what they wanted to hear (Spencer 1973: 175-7).

Tignor's study of the Maasai under colonial rule is also instructive for our understanding of alien rule over the Samburu. Tignor, was correct when he declared that his study of the Maasai would likely have implications for other groups who have age-sets. Tignor's argument that "Maasai warriors were a significant element in blocking colonial change," can be applied *mutatis mutandis* to their Samburu counterparts. There is likewise a striking resemblance between the means and, even more so, the ends of British policy in both Maasai and Samburu areas. Tignor's description of District Commissioner (DC) Rupert Hemsted's plan to transform Maasai society by strengthening the authority of Maasai elders and "suppress[ing] those aspects of the warrior organization which they [the administration] felt were inimical to social change and orderly government" reads like a carbon copy of what H.B. Sharpe (see below) was trying to accomplish in Samburu realms (Tignor 1976: 73, 80). Furthermore, Tignor's observation that Maasai elders were often willing to collaborate with the colonial administration on economic grounds appears quite plausible for Samburu elders as well.[3]

The relationship between the British and the Samburu developed over an extended period with the slow advance of colonial administration north of the Ewaso Nyiro River. Although Europeans first encountered Samburu at the time of the Teleki expedition to Lake Turkana in 1888-9, the first official contact with the Samburu did not come until 1902. This was seven years after the British had established the East Africa Protectorate (EAP), when a former North Dakota rancher and now junior administrator named H.R. Tate led a government expedition through Samburu lands.[4] Six years later, the Rift Valley Provincial Commissioner (PC), Stephen Bagge, held a series of *barazas,* or public meetings, with Samburu elders, where he discussed bringing the pastoralists under colonial administration. Interestingly, Bagge told his superiors that the Samburu had expressed an eagerness not only to come under alien rule, but also to pay taxes into the bargain.[5]

More likely, the Samburu were eager to find allies to support their claims to grazing and water rights against those of neighboring groups such as the Turkana and Borana. Certainly, the elders must have had only the vaguest idea concerning the kind of administration that the British official was proposing. In any event, collaboration with the British proved advantageous to the Samburu by 1913, as the latter were rewarded with captured livestock for participating in several so-called punitive expeditions against the Turkana to the northwest. Moreover, the Samburu decision to cooperate with the British must have seemed equally astute since colonial rule had thus far amounted to little more than the occasional payment of stock as "tribute" for the meager forces that Nairobi had dispatched to police its vast northern frontier.[6]

The gains to be had by collaboration, however, were illusory, as the Samburu willingness to work with the British soon proved to have deleterious repercussions. This was dramatically illustrated when the Samburu moved without permission onto the Leroghi plateau, which had been vacated by the Maasai after 1913 to make land available for white settlement.[7] Over the next few years, large numbers of Samburu moved with their cattle from their lowland environs to the richer grazing of the plateau. As the British presence in Samburuland before the First World War amounted to a few irregular patrols launched from Mount

Marsabit, little was done to halt the initial "encroachments" of Samburu onto the former Maasai lands.[8]

Concerned that the Samburu were advancing beyond their traditional "tribal" domains and fearful of the introduction of cattle disease into European herds in the Rift Valley, Governor Sir Henry Belfield ordered local colonial officials in 1914 to remove Samburu beyond the north bank of the Ewaso Nyiro.[9] Belfield's action was significant because it was the first government intervention in what would be a prolonged land dispute. It also indicated something about the direction alien rule would take once the colonial administration established itself in Samburuland. The Samburu supplied the British with thousands of cattle and small stock at below-market prices during the First World War, but were rewarded in turn with regulations that hamstrung local exchange networks when it suited the purpose of the colonial administration. Thus, Nairobi closed the entire Norther Frontier District (NFD)—of which Samburuland was a part—to outside traders and imposed cattle quarantines to prevent the spread of animal disease to the south. Meanwhile, local officials at times interfered to prevent Samburu trade with their Rendille and Meru neighbors.[10]

Yet all the while, the "awkward paramountcy" that the British government had established in Samburuland was unable to meet even its modest, self-imposed mandate of providing protection, or extending the *pax Britannica*, to its African subjects. This inability led the Samburu to vacate the northern and eastern parts of their domains and concentrate themselves for safety from Turkana and Borana raids. Thus, a major rinderpest outbreak in late 1914 took as much as sixty percent of Samburu cattle, by official estimates.[11] The consequences of the colonial administration's weakness were even more tragically evidenced in December 1915, when Aulihan Somalis launched a major raid on Samburu who had moved with their herds eastward towards the Lorian Swamp. Fifty-four Samburu lost their lives in the attack, and the Somalis snatched thousands of cattle and small stock. When a British officer and a party of Samburu *murran* attempted to follow the raiders, the Somalis turned and routed their would-be pursuers in what another colonial official described as "rather a bad show."[12] Such deprivations inflicted upon the Samburu by the Turkana and Aulihan clearly demonstrate their vulnerable position during the early years of colonial rule. Indeed, manpower shortages and budgetary constraints led the junior administrative official over the district to spend much of his time devoted to his duties as transport officer for the NFD during the First World War and even several years thereafter in addition to his regular responsibilities.[13]

By the end of the war, Samburu herds were congested on the north bank of the Ewaso Nyiro as well as grazing on the plateau. They could not move north because Turkana were occupying lands formerly held by the Samburu, and the government prevented their movement southward.[14] Nairobi's initial solution to this problem was to force the Turkana out of the NFD in 1921, and then move the Samburu northward accompanied by a King's African Rifles (KAR) patrol. Not only would this keep Leroghi free for exclusive European settlement, but the Turkana and Samburu would be kept separate, an idea which fit in well with the colonial conception of keeping distinct ethnic groups under separate administrations. The loss of nearly half of the Turkana cattle, however, from starvation and with grazing restrictions noncompliance on the part of the Samburu defeated this scheme.[15]

Adding to the woes of the Turkana were the first recorded incidents during the colonial period of Samburu so-called "spear-bloodings." The practice was later described by a British field administrator as a "tradition which demand[ed] that the warriors must prove their manhood by some exploit before winning a wife."[16] In some cases this could be done by killing a lion or wild animal; in this event, by the murder of several stragglers from among the evicted Turkana as well as six Elmolo further north. The Samburu were just then preparing to initiate a new *laji*, the Kiliako, and some members of the out-going Merisho age-set of *murran* were apparently responsible for the killings.[17] The official response to these "spear-bloodings" was the execution of two Samburu for the Turkana murders (a third was killed earlier in an escape attempt), and the imposition of a collective fine of two thousand small stock on the Samburu for the Elmolo killings. The stern reaction on the part of the NFD administration, in the colonial view, "undoubtedly had a profound effect" on the Samburu.[18]

The "spear-blooding" incidents were soon forgotten as the authorities' attention soon shifted to growing tensions between the Samburu and white ranchers in the Rift Valley and White Highlands. At first, the conflict was reflected in vociferous settler complaints concerning Samburu "trespasses" and the potential spread of animal disease from "native" livestock to European herds.[19] It did not take long, however, before settler grievances crystallized on the coveted grazing on Leroghi. A handful of wealthy Europeans were eager to obtain the plateau and, with the support of settler political organizations such as the Laikipia Farmers' Association, they pressured Nairobi to grant them the land. These whites, including prominent politicians such as Lord Delamere and R. Berkeley Cole, put forward a host of historical, economic, and legal arguments to gain Leroghi and get the government to remove the Samburu from the area.[20]

Although their case was decidedly weak, indeed some of their claims were outright manufactures, the Europeans soon succeeded in getting the backing of influential members of the Kenya government. These ranged from local administrators to the colony's chief veterinary official and other key department officials in the Secretariat such as the Chief Native Commissioner (CNC) and Commissioner of Lands. Eventually, Governors Sir Robert Coryndon and Sir Edward Grigg added their support to the designs of the settler capitalists.[21] On the other hand, those with service in the NFD administration and Samburu district generally took the side of the Samburu, as did the maverick Deputy-CNC, Oscar Watkins.[22]

Consequently, the Samburu occupied a politically weak position from which to defend their claim to Leroghi. One of the most striking features of the controversy was that the voiceless Samburu would not be able to articulate their position until the final act in the land dispute. In the interim, they would have to rely on outsiders to put forward their case.

By 1930, the grazing on the plateau had become vital to the livelihood of the Samburu. Government officials estimated that there were 6,574 Samburu with nearly 115,000 animals on the plateau. This constituted perhaps half the population, and local field administrators were convinced that the Samburu would lose much of their stock if uprooted for the sake of giving Leroghi to European settlers. Moreover, moving the Samburu would be very costly, require the dislocation of neighboring pastoralists, and was sure to create hardships, as the experience of the forced Turkana move in 1921 had clearly demonstrated.[23] The issue was finally decided more by nature than by man when a severe drought led three-quarters of the Samburu to take refuge on Leroghi in 1933, having suffered the loss of one-in-five of their animals. This misfortune occurred at the time when the Kenya Land (or Carter) Commission was deciding the fate of the plateau, and had the paradoxical effect of influencing the commissioners in their decision to grant Leroghi to the Samburu.[24]

Meanwhile, tension mounted over the purported "lawlessness" of Samburu *murran*. During the 1920s, this had manifest itself in occasional stock thefts from European farms (termed "raids" by the settlers) as well as from neighboring Turkana, Pokot, Rendille, and Borana. In June 1933, relations with the Samburu were further strained with a second outbreak of "spear-bloodings" that continued into the following year. This time the killings were done by Kiliako murran anticipating their promotion to become elders and hastening to prove themselves.[25] As these incidents were directed mostly at Gikuyu youths or other African herders who were working on European farms in the Laikipia and Nanyuki areas, they became tied up in the bitter dispute over Leroghi. Of even greater significance, the mysterious death of Theodore Powys, a young white ranch foreman, in north Laikipia in 1931 became linked to the Samburu "spear-bloodings." Although the evidence against the Samburu in the Powys's "murder" was circumstantial, rumor was sufficient to convince Europeans of their culpability.[26] Moreover, this occurred within a settler community that felt betrayed when the decision of the Carter Commission became public.[27]

Yet, settler agitation, the fear of white vigilantism over the alleged "ritual murder," and criticism that the frontier administration was not doing its job would have profound consequences for the Samburu.[28] Already during the investigation, a British official had beaten two uncooperative Samburu youths, used Kenya's Witchcraft Ordinance to deport Ole Odumo (an *oloiboni*) or ritual leader, for obstructing the probe, deposed a chief, and imposed a fine under the Collective Punishments Ordinance of 1930 for shielding those guilty of "spear-blooding."[29] It is ironic then that in April 1934, Governor Sir Joseph Byrne wrote the head of the East Africa Department at the Colonial Office a private and confidential letter in which he declared that Samburu "unrest" had become the most absorbing issue in Kenya.[30] Six months later, Governor Byrne declared that the Samburu were "in a disturbed state" and tightened the colonial grip by dispatching police reinforcements and a KAR patrol. Meanwhile, Nairobi decided to remove the Samburu from the purview of the NFD for administrative purposes.[31]

The year 1935 witnessed the Kenya government's consolidation of control over the Samburu once and for all. A KAR patrol, divided into two detachments, moved through Samburu domains for six months beginning in February, overawing the pastoralists by seizing hundreds of cattle, confiscating spears, forcibly shaving the *ol-masi* (or hair of *murran*), and beating a few recalcitrants with hippo hides into the bargain. The Samburu were initially placed under the direct authority of a district officer and George Brown, a no-nonsense DC, who earned the nickname "Hammer of the Samburu," for his rigorous suppression of the pastoralists. Brown appointed new headmen over the Lokumai, Pisikishu, Loimusi, Lngwesi, and Longieli sections, reasoning that these men could "not be worse" than their predecessors.[32] The formal transfer of the Samburuland to Rift Valley Province was completed in April when the area was merged with Laikipia to form Laikipia-Samburu District.[33] Rumuruti became the headquarters of the new district and Samburu Sub-District's *boma* was located at Maralal. H.E. Welby, the Rift Valley PC, of course, was pleased with the new set-up. Echoing the annual report of the Samburu officer-in-charge, Welby declared that the new arrangement obviated the problem of "misunderstandings" with NFD officials, expedited decisions on matters affecting both settlers and Samburu, and would cut costs as well.[34] With the Samburu seemingly cowed and his job apparently done, Brown recommended that the levy be withdrawn.[35]

Nevertheless, the subjugation of the *murran* was by no means complete as stock thefts and "spear-bloodings" continued with five new murders committed between May 1935 and February 1936. Significantly, the killings were now aimed in a new direction, away from white-owned ranches and towards the Turkana. If such troubles continued, British officials feared that the Turkana might act in reprisal, undermining the one accomplishment of colonial administration, the establishment of a rough peace in the frontier region.

It is also important to note that the Turkana killings came on the heels of the acquittal of the Samburu *murran* accused in the Powys case. The Samburu District Officer put much of the blame for these unfortunate episodes on the loss of face the government had experienced as a result of the Powys trial. He declared that as a consequence of the debacle some of the warriors had little regard for law, as the chances were "one hundred to one" that they would be convicted of anything.[36] H.B. Sharpe, the "Hammer's" successor and an official with many years in the Kenya field administration, reacted with a similarly scathing denunciation of the colonial justice system. The Laikipia-Samburu DC wrote his superiors that, "it was obvious that the Samburu had no fear of the Courts in Kenya, as known murderers were exonerated by the courts."[37]

More to the point, Sharpe sent police into Samburu Sub-District to bring the Samburu to heel. The authorities required the

Samburu to pay the expenses of the levy and imposed a collective fine on them for the one incident that could definitely be attributed to Samburu. One Samburu was convicted of one of the later killings, but this time the hangman was cheated when the Court of Appeal reversed the decision. Once again, Sharpe let loose his fury. It is significant that this time he claimed the backing of Samburu elders who, "were very angry about the matter and wished to fine the acquitted man heavily." Sharpe further contended that the elders, "were lost in amazement at the course of British Justice."[38]

Sharpe's claim of support from Samburu elders points to a remarkable change of tack on the part of the field administration in its efforts to control the Samburu. Frustrated not least of all by higher authorities within the colonial system itself, Sharpe searched for other means of authority over the Samburu. The imposition of British rule by the use of brute force, of course, had limitations, and Sharpe looked for more effective means of accomplishing his task by finding allies from within Samburu society. Although he was by no means an anthropologist, Sharpe was aware of the tensions that existed between the age-grades and sought to manipulate them to his own ends. Sharpe, who is said to have possessed a genius for gardening, now cultivated allies from among those who possessed authority among the Samburu because of their seniority, namely, the elders.[39] The DC claimed that the elders were eager for the augmented police force to remain in the sub-district and had even stressed their opposition to any temporary rearmament of the *murran*. The colonial perspective is illustrated in the draft of the 1935 Laikipia-Samburu District Annual Report, by Sharpe,

> It is of particular note that the Elders were not anxious for the extra police force to be removed and it has been kept on until the end of the year at Government expense. It is also worthy of note that when it was suggested that a number of Moran might be re-armed with spears, tempo-

rarily, to destroy Zebra, the elders were most emphatic in their refusal to consider the proposal...

The old men apparently are quite genuine in their desire for a peaceful time but "old age" has not the final say in Samburu any more than in any other part of the world at the present time. Youth look rather askance at age when it is told not to blood spears, not to steal cattle, for age has had its day and it is easy to moralize when the desire to kill and to steal is dead, reasons the Samburu warrior.[40]

Yet, the situation was more complicated than this would imply. From the official point of view, Samburu elders were also partly to blame for the "unrest."[41] They had promised to marry off members of the Kiliako age-grade to aid in the latter's transition to elderhood, but failed to do so. This was because many parents were reluctant to allow their daughters to wed until the girls' elder brothers had become *murran* according to Samburu custom, and, as Spencer has argued, because established elders had more cattle as wealth and social status than their younger rivals (Spencer 1973:154-5). Moreover, there were limits to the power of the gerontocrats. The traditional political system of the Samburu was decidedly decentralized and the estimated 15,000 Samburu were then dispersed through the 10,000 square miles that made up the sub-district.

Sharpe had therefore to seek other allies where he could find them, and embarked on what would be a substantial attempt to restructure traditional Samburu institutions. As part of this exercise in social engineering, the DC sought to coopt part of the leadership of the warriors. Consequently, as the government removed Samburu headmen, it appointed leading Samburu *murran*, or *laiguenak*, in this capacity whenever possible, hoping to exploit their influence for government purposes.[42] A Local Native Council (LNC) was also created in 1936 as a means for the Samburu to discuss local concerns.[43] Composed of twenty-four members, with a *laiguenani* as the leading elected Samburu representative, it was presided over by the DC who could use it as another way to influence the Samburu. Finally, a Samburu Native Tribunal also resumed its functions of administering justice under the supervision of the Samburu headmen.[44]

The 1936 initiation of the Mekuri age-set into *lmurrano*, or warriorhood, and the elevation of the Kiliako to become elders were more important than all these initiatives for restoring the peace. The British compelled the Mekuri to complete a series of ceremonies in a few months that should have taken much longer (Spencer 1973:163). Samburu elders put on a show of acting in conjunction with the colonial administration, but their purported manipulation of customs associated with "spear-blooding" (such as prohibiting *murran* from eating meat in the bush and giving beads to their maiden lovers) were more honored in the breach than in the observance.[45] Yet, of course, the government itself took the leading role in this effort to engineer social changes among the Samburu. One important change dictated by the authorities was that the length of *lmurrano* be reduced to three years, although this too was done with the ostensible consent of the elders. The British intended to watch the new warriors very carefully, but for now they seemed quite under control.[46]

Sharpe concluded his tour in Samburu Sub-District quite satisfied. He wrote that the Mekuri *laiguenak* were "showing a friendly and helpful attitude" to the administration, and added that his policy was one of "getting hold of the young moran leaders and ... giving them a say in things, but at the same time not in any way offending the dignity of the elders."[47] Sharpe recognized that this would require some art, but thought that it could be pulled off. Still, he noted two potential threats to his scheme. The first came from some of the Kiliako who were not satisfied with their lot and some of whom from the Lorogushu had clashed with the new *murran* on Elbarta. The second would be any attempt to cull or destock Samburu herds.[48]

Largely as a consequence of the inroads they had made into manipulating Samburu social and political institutions, some within the colonial administration felt confident by mid-1938 that they could begin to engineer changes in the pastoral economy. Concerned that Leroghi was rapidly turning to desert, soil conservation and veterinary experts concluded that destocking Samburu herds was necessary to preserve grazing before it was too late. They maintained that such efforts would leave the Samburu with fewer, but better, cattle.[49] Fearing competition on the Nairobi market, European cattle-owners represented by the Stockowners' Association recommended a stock tax rather than compulsion to cull the African herds of "uneconomic" cattle.[50] Stronger opposition came from J.G. Hopkins, the Rift Valley acting-PC, who disagreed with the destocking plan and argued that the drastic reductions some officials were calling for would put the Samburu below subsistence levels. The view of the field administration was that only "indirect" methods should be used to cull Samburu herds.[51] In the end, a committee on overstocking appointed by the governor decided that "a measure of compulsion [was] desirable and necessary," and officials thus began a stock census in the second half of 1938. This included the branding of selected cattle for removal from Samburu herds as part of the new policy of destocking.[52]

The Samburu reaction, much like that of the Kamba to a similar initiative in their lands, was predictable.[53] Five years earlier, when Nibelei, one of the Samburu witnesses before the Kenya Land Commission, was asked if he would prefer three hundred healthy cattle to five hundred starving ones, he answered,

> I would rather have a thousand starving ones until God gives us grass, because if a man has a lot of cattle and some die he still has some left, but if a man has a few cattle and they die he has none left.[54]

Taking this perspective into account, it not surprising that it did not take long for the destocking scheme to come undone. A discontented Kiliako core, perhaps composed of the less wealthy elements of the Samburu, was now joined by a much broader following who felt their wealth and even livelihood threatened by the imprudent plan.[55] The field administration encountered no serious problems with its initial attempt to limit Samburu herds. Not much more than a start had been made in culling 8 percent of more than 50,000 cattle on Leroghi when Kenya authorities had to halt the destocking because of Samburu opposition (Chenevix-Trench 1993:98).

The Samburu were upset enough with the plan that colonial authorities organized a *baraza* on the Seya River on New Year's Day, 1939. At the meeting, the government made a number of minor concessions to the Samburu, including a promise not to cull any stock other than a few old bulls until the completion of the cattle census. More significant to colonial policy was the administration's failure to have any of the government-appointed chiefs in attendance at the meeting, as this undermined what little authority they possessed. Stepping into the void, a Lokumai former-chief named Lemondile who had been dismissed back in 1935 declared himself the paramount chief of the Samburu. Lemondile and his followers, termed an "anti-government party" by the British, established themselves near Lake Kisima at the end of March, defying an order that he return to his *manyatta* (or settlement) on the Barsalinga plains. The Samburu opposition put forward a number of demands to the acting-PC, and threatened that if they could not receive satisfaction, they would send representatives to Nairobi to appeal for redress.[56]

Most of the opposition's demands dealt with the new government initiatives and Samburu economic complaints. Lemondile insisted that the census be stopped, that Veterinary Department officials remove themselves from the area, and that the destocking plan be abandoned. Yet their petition went further, calling for an end to grazing restrictions and for access for Samburu herds onto Crown Land north of Rumuruti. The resistance, too, sought the removal of all chiefs associated with the culling plan. Last but not least, the Samburu demanded the reinstatement of the Kiliako *laji*.[57]

Samburu resistance went beyond mere words to deeds. Some of the Samburu headmen were openly threatened, and the

79

Nyaparai chief, Lenguloni, was assaulted by a former tribal policeman. Posts delineating the boundaries of the Forest Reserve and Kisima Veterinary Quarantine were defaced by *simis*, or long knives, and uprooted by recalcitrant Samburu. Twenty-six *manyattas* quitted the district and crossed the Ewaso Nyiro to forbidden grazing areas at Mugogodo. There were five cases of stock theft across the southern boundary on European farms. Finally, members of the Kiliako *laji* began again to wear the garb of *murran*, carry spears, and perform forbidden dances.[58]

The unforseen Samburu reaction led the colonial government to further backtracking and a reassessment of policy. Indeed, by March, the British had been forced to discontinue their census of Samburu livestock. Colonial officials recognized the mistake they had made by responding to Samburu demands without including the chiefs in the decision. On the other hand, S.O.V. Hodge, the Rift Valley PC, concluded that the Samburu saw the administration's concessions as evidence of its weakness and believed that appeasing the Samburu contributed to their growing bellicosity. The logical conclusion of such reasoning was obvious: unless the authorities took immediate "firm action" anarchy would ensue, resulting in another outbreak of "spear-blooding" and stock theft.[59]

Not wanting to reward the Samburu for their truculence, officials in Nairobi refused to meet any of the Samburu demands. Instead, the Kenya government responded to Hodge's request, dispatching a police force of forty *askaris* into Samburuland. Led by Superintendent of Police T.R.J. Ridgway, the constabulary arrived at Maralal in late May and, in Hodge's words, "had an excellent effect especially on the Samburu Moran." The Rift Valley administration informed the Samburu that Nairobi would accede to none of their grievances and, with the help of the levy, extinguished the nascent rebellion within a month. The government imposed a heavy fine on Lemondile and threatened him with "more severe measures ... should he continue to cause trouble." Likewise, the British took measures against those

Samburu who had challenged their authority by taking their herds beyond "tribal" boundaries and by similar acts of defiance.[60]

Thus, the flexing of colonial muscle had apparently led to the Samburu adopting "a more reasonable frame of mind." It is not surprising, however, that the Kiliako were the last to surrender. The Rift Valley PC commented on the fact that the most recalcitrant of the Samburu were "young men who [hid] in the bush and refused to attend meetings." Although these men had eventually to give up their active resistance, it might be added that there was one further minor episode in 1939 when some again defied the colonial administration before their subjugation.[61] Moreover, it should be pointed out that Samburu had won a partial victory since the government had been forced to abandon its destocking plan and three years had passed without the initiation of a new age-set.[62]

Following the reverses caused by the culling campaign, local officials once again searched for "anthropological" solutions to their problems. They remained disenchanted with the performance of the chiefs and found the performance of the LNC (through which they hoped the elders would eventually exercise greater influence) and that of the Native Tribunals unsatisfactory as well.[63] Laikipia-Samburu DCs stressed the importance of getting the Mekuri to marry as soon as possible by summoning elders to Maralal to cajole them and using the LNC as a platform to push for early marriages and the initiation of a new *laji*.[64] Meanwhile, using fines and imprisonment, the administration strictly enforced grazing restrictions as well as its prohibitions of *murran* assemblies, dancing certain dances, the carrying of spears, and eating meat in the bush. Only the Mekuri could wear *murran* adornments.[65] Finally, *il barnot* rituals, which allowed for additional initiations into the Mekuri age-set, were forbidden so that there would be enough youths to create a new *laji* as soon as was possible. The idea was to keep the number of *murran* small enough to facilitate their control by the elders, and thus by the colonial authorities.[66]

The outbreak of the Second World War introduced a new dynamic into the political equation. British hopes to get the Samburu to initiate a new *laji* in 1940 had soon to be abandoned. As the conflict progressed, the Samburu found themselves called upon to contribute to the war effort and subject to growing government demands. Around four hundred Samburu served in the armed forces during World War II, where they gained a collective reputation as first-rate soldiers due to their discipline and courage.[67] Once again, field administrators saw an opportunity to turn recruitment to their own purposes, as service in the KAR would divert the activities of young men "to more useful and lawful channels."[68]

Wartime also affected the pastoral economy. The Samburu were obliged to sell cattle for meat rations, and did so willingly when stock prices were high enough, in spite of official assertions that they were indifferent to money and trade. In fact, in some of the early stock sales they offered more cattle than purchasers were willing to buy, and some were left disappointed after trekking long distances with their animals to market.[69] Yet J. Douglas McKean, Laikipia-Samburu DC in 1943, made no mention of this when he complained about the pastoralists' reluctance to part with their animals:

> The attitude of the local natives, including the chiefs and elders, was consistently obstructive. On every occasion when a sale was fixed, there was not lacking an elder to jump up and say they had no more stock for sale, a statement transparently absurd.[70]

In any event, the Samburu continued to sell significant numbers of livestock throughout the war.[71]

Reviewing the archival records for this period, it becomes obvious that frontier administrators were thoroughly frustrated in their efforts to control the Samburu. With the exception of a couple of chiefs, officials generally considered their agents untrustworthy, ineffective, lazy, and lacking in influence.[72] McKean's remark, "sweeping changes in their ranks would be advocated were it not for the fact that one would not know where to turn for better material," sums up the attitude of the DCs.[73] Likewise, they needed close supervision and were inclined to give out too lenient sentences.[74] From their remarks, one might conclude that the Maralal LNC's greatest ambition was to run a "beer shop."[75] Intended as an instrument to enhance the DCs's authority, it appears that the roles had become reversed and that it was the elders who were manipulating their alien rulers. For example, in mid-1944 when LNC members said they would not circumcise another age-set for another three years, the DC took the position that the government did not think it would accept this "break in tribal custom" because the behavior of the *murran* had not been that bad.[76]

Lest the reader get the idea that all the field administrators had such paternalistic opinions of the *murran*, the comments of George Brown, who had returned to Samburu Sub-District in the middle of the war, are instructive. Brown considered the *murran* an "anachronism" and "a thorn in the flesh of Government." Proper policy in his view should have been to get them no longer to consider themselves warriors, but a "Labour Corps." The "Hammer" then went on to make a modest proposal,

> Although I am very far from being an admirer of the Nazis I do think that their ideas of handling youth are emenently [sic] suitable to the youth of a Tribe such as the Samburu . . . I believe that if parties of Communal Labour were organized on semi-military lines and some time devoted to instruction in Drill and General Discipline (which they would regard as sugar on the pill) such a scheme might have the effect of turning this Tribe from indolence to diligence and a hightened [sic] intelligence.[77]

Fortunately for the Samburu, such suggestions were properly filed away.

The war ended with the colonial administration having made little progress in its efforts in Samburu Sub-District. Hoping to

83

"link up the traditional moran organisation with Government purpose," the authorities appointed returning veterans as paid headmen of the *laiguenak,* and gave them badges to symbolize their
new status. The idea was that the *murran* leaders would "act as
the mouthpiece" of the warriors and serve the government by
helping in tax collection and gathering work crews. The District
Officer required one from each section to report to Maralal each
week, and all of them were supposed to visit the *boma* once a
month.[78] Although the Samburu District Officer claimed modest
success with the experiment, it will come as no surprise that he
found that these *laiguenak* had scant authority over their peers.
In particular, the field officer complained that Samburu *murran*
had engaged in criminal acts, were slow to come out for locust
eradication campaigns, and failed to give adequate help in efforts
to put out a major fire that destroyed sixty square miles of forest
on Leroghi. A second minor innovation was the creation of sub-
headmen in 1946.[79]

That same year, the government returned its earlier policy of
trying to get the Samburu to initiate a new *laji.* It partly relented
on its prohibition against spear-carrying and, using the *laiguenak*
as intermediaries, began to allow married *murran* and former
non-commissioned officers to bear their weapons with a permit.
This relaxation was in accordance of the administration's efforts
to get more *murran* to wed and so hasten the initiation of a new
age-set. Officials became hopeful when the Masula prepared to
accomplish the rituals preceding the initiation of a new *laji.* By
year's end, however, these had not taken place, the Samburu explained, because "the rains and other portents were not correct."[80]

Finally, near the start of the following year, Samburu *laioni,*
or boys and young men due for circumcision, began to seek their
upgrade to *lmurrano.* In September, the Masula conducted the
preliminary ritual with the slaughter of a white ox on Mount Nyiro.
Three months later, the Longieli killed their ox on the Leroghi
plateau. More than twelve years after the advancement of the
Mekuri, rather than three as the British had wanted, the Samburu

initiated the Kimaniki as *murran* in the period between July and August 1948.[81]

As a contingency for possible renewed "spear-blooding" incidents, the administration warned the Samburu repeatedly against such outbreaks at *barazas*, assigned a European police officer to the district at the end of 1947, increased patrols through the district, and prohibited the new warriors from possessing spears.[82] There were no murders nor even a significant upsurge in crime as the British feared.[83] By this time, most of the lawbreaking in Samburu District centered around breaking the grazing restrictions that the frontier administration had sought to enforce more strictly from the middle of the Second World War, particularly on the Leroghi plateau. In the case of such offenses, the government found that it was elders, rather than moran, who were "very often the worst offenders"[84]:

> The Leroghi chiefs and elders cooperate on the whole in grazing control measures, provided that they are not personally affected by having to move their own manyattas. They realise the benefit from the point of view of having a reserve of grass for their cattle, but they have yet to realise the ultimate object of all grazing control is the preservation of their country from deterioration, and continually press for closed areas to be opened too soon.[85]

Thus, by 1948 the *murran* had been pacified and the alliance between Samburu gerontocrats and their British proconsuls had afforded benefits to both the elders and the field administration. Yet the partnership had often been an uneasy one, particularly as revealed by the widespread resistance to the colonial destocking scheme on the eve of the Second World War. The "anthropological solution" to the Samburu question put forward by Sharpe and his successors was not without imagination, nor did it fail to make some important advances from the perspective of the authorities. The relatively peaceful advancement of the Mekuri into elderhood bears witness to this. Still, the sweeping changes that the British had hoped to achieve within Samburu society could not be accomplished. The reason for this lay, as Spencer has so insightfully recognized, in the alien administration's limited understanding of the complexity of Samburu traditions and, thus, the often inappropriate or unsuitable innovations it attempted to impose on the Samburu age-set system and polity in general.

Relations between the British and Samburu would henceforth enter a new era. The issues of grazing regulations and government economic development of Samburu District would dominate relations between Samburu elders and the colonial administration throughout the 1950s and on to independence in 1963. Yet, in retrospect, it would appear that the support of the government had been an important factor in tilting the balance of power within Samburu society toward the gerontocrats at the expense of the *murran*. Consequently, it would be principally the elders with whom the administration would have to contend to accomplish its goals for the remainder of the colonial period.

NOTES

1. The first point is also made by Spencer (1973:172).
2. For similar observations concerning British rule in East Africa, see Graham (1976:1-9) and Liebenow (1971:94) for British rule in Tanganyika; Low and Pratt (1960: 163-78) for Uganda.
3. According to Tignor, this was because wealthy elders bore the brunt of collective fines assessed by the government for *murran* raids. He also notes that such unlawful activities by the warriors invited unwanted scrutiny and interference on the Maasai (Tignor 1976:76, 80-3).
4. See Ludwig von Höhnel (1968:74), Teleki (1889:99), Tate (1904a:223-7, 1904b:92-100), Spencer (1973: 154-7), and Gann and Duignan (1978: 185).
5. Public Record Office (PRO) Colonial Office Original Correspondence Series 533 [C.O. 533]/47, and Partington to Bagge, 11 Sep-

tember, enclosure in the former.

6. Samburu District Annual Report (AR), 1914, L.F.I. Athill, Kenya National Archives (KNA): PC/NFD1/9/1, and Spencer (1973: 159).

7. For the Maasai treaties and moves see Sorrenson (1968:190-209), and Kituyi (1985:20-3).

8. Report of the Kenya Land Commission (Cmd 4556, 1934, London, HMSO:228).

9. Samburu Land Question, u.d., Kenya National Archives (KNA): PC/NFD4/2/3. It is worth noting that when John Patterson had come upon the Samburu in 1907, he had found them south of the Ewaso Nyiro River. See Gamble to Chief Secretary, Nairobi, 12 December 1919, KNA: PC/NFD4/2/1.

10. Northern Frontier District Annual Report (NFDAR), 1916-17, H.B. Kittermaster, KNA: PC/NFD1/1/2, and Archer's Post AR, 1918-1919, T.D. Butler, KNA: PC/NFD1/4/1. The threat of the spread of epizootics such as rinderpest, pleuropneumonia, and East Coast Fever was real, and posed an immense problem in remote areas where there were immense difficulties with transportation, in the days before medicine could be stored by refrigeration (Information provided to the author by E.J.F. Knowles).

11. Uaso Nyiro Post ARs, 1914, L.F.I. Athill; KNA: PC/NFD1/9/1; 1915, A.A.C. Ashton, KNA:PC/NFD1/4/1; and NFDAR, 1914-15, S.F. Deck, KNA: PC/NFD1/1/2.

12. John B.L. Llewellin, Kenya Administration Diary, 1914-1917, 14 December 1915, Rhodes House, Oxford, Mss. Afr. s. 567. See also, NFDAR, 1915-16, H.B. Kittermaster, KNA: PC/NFD1/1/2; and Bowring to Long, 18 February 1918, C.O. 533/193.

13. Archer's Post AR, 1918-1919, T.D. Butler, KNA: PC/NFD1/4/1; NFDARs, 1915-16, 1916-17, and 1917-18, H.B. Kittermaster, KNA: PC/NFD1/1/2. In fact, the NFD officer-in-charge complained that the administration had not been fair in its treatment of the Samburu for the prior five years, and he believed that it was a "marvel" that they had been so responsive to government orders. Kittermaster to Chief Secretary, Nairobi, 20 September 1919, KNA: PC/NFD4/2/1.

14. Kittermaster to Chief Secretary, Nairobi, 20 September 1919, KNA: PC/NFD4/2/1; and Gamble to Naivasha PC, 21 May 1919, KNA: PC/NFD4/2/1.

15. Nevertheless, British officials imposed a number of restrictions on the movement of the pastoralists and reminded the Turkana that they were in Samburu country only by the grace of the government. Samburu District Handing Over Report (HOR), 1 November 1921, E.N. Erskine, KNA: PC/NFD1/9/1; Mahony to Plowman, 21 December 1921, KNA: PC/NFD4/1/4; and Llewellyn to Colonial Secretary, 26 April 1922, KNA: PC/NFD4/1/8/2.

16. Samburu circumcision, DC, Maralal, 29 December 1948, KNA: PC/SP4/2/1.

17. For a similar practice among the Maasai during transitional periods between the circumcision of new age-sets, see Tignor (1976: 75). Samburu age-sets and years of initiation: Merisho (1912), Kiliako (1921-2), Mekuri (1936), Kimaniki (1948).

18. NFDAR, 1922, Major Muirhead; Martin Mahony, diary of service with K.A.R. and administration in the Northern Frontier District of Kenya, 1920-21, 28 March, 23 April, and 21 June 1922. Rhodes House, Oxford, Mss. Afr. s. 487, and Spencer (1973: 159-60).

   The severe penalties inflicted on the Samburu are more understandable when one considers the fact that the NFD had come under military rule towards the end of 1921, as part of a plan to improve administration and cut costs. Unfortunately, from the British perspective, the new system did neither, and the province was returned to civilian rule by September 1925.

19. Yet, right after the war, the NFD PC commented that the arrival of settlers in West Kenya and Rumuruti, increased the demand for passes to trade for Samburu small stock. NFDAR, 1919-20, C.H.F. Plowman, KNA:PC/NFD1/1/2.

20. Samburu Land Question; and Samburu District HOR, June 1924, N.A.S. Lytton, KNA: PC/NFD1/9/1. The subjects of the Leroghi land dispute and the Powys murder which follows can be found in

Simpson (1994:518-73), and Duder and Simpson (1997). See also Spencer (1973: 161-3).

21. Tate to Kittermaster, 16 April 1919, Brassey-Edwards to Chief Secretary, Nairobi, 29 July 1919, Boulderson to Kenya PC, 22 July 1919, KNA:PC/NFD4/2/1, Grigg to Amery, 21 September 1926, KNA:PC/NFD4/2/1, and Samburu Land Question, u.d. KNA:PC/NFD4/2/3.

22. Gamble to Chief Secretary, Nairobi, 12 December 1919, Lytton to Muirhead, 3 May 1924, memorandum on the Samburu grazing question, confidential, u.d. enclosure in Cooke to CNC, 2 June 1924, Llewellyn to Officer-in-charge, NFD, confidential, 13 September 1923[?4?], Lytton to Officer Commanding Troops, Kenya Colony, 30 September 1924, Taverner to Muirhead, 26 December 1924, and Butler to CNC, 5 October 1926, KNA: PC/NFD4/2/1, and Glenday to Gilbert, 15 February 1930, KNA:PC/NFD4/1/6/5.

23. Isiolo District AR 1932, C.A. Cornell, KNA:PC/NFD1/4/2; and Glenday to NFD PC, 15 October 1929, KNA:PC/NFD4/1/6/5.

24. Isiolo District AR 1933, C.A. Cornell, KNA:PC/NFD1/4/2; NFDAR, 1933, V.G. Glenday, KNA:PC/NFD1/1/4; and extract from the Kenya Land Commission Report, KNA: PC/NFD4/2/3.

25. NFDAR, 1933, V.G. Glenday, KNA: PC/NFD1/1/4; NFDAR, 1934, J. Llewellin, KNA: PC/NFD1/1/5; Samburu circumcision 1948, KNA: PC/SP4/2/1. Spencer also notes yet another cause for the Kiliako disturbances, the frustration of murran unable to fulfill their traditional roles as warriors after the establishment of the colonial system (1973: 160).

26. That this interpretation is still accepted, see Curtis (1986: 69), which states that Powys was "speared to death by Samburu Moran at Rumuruti." For the Powys case see The death of Mr. T.L. Powys, 5 April 1934, PRO/C.O. 533/443, Atieno-Odhiambo (1971: 112-3), R. Cashmore "The Powys case: a cautionary tale" (unpublished paper in the authors' possession), and Chenevix-Trench (1993:92-6).

27. There was severe settler criticism concerning the judge and the crown counsel who prosecuted the case against the Samburu. Some

claimed that the government had purposely bungled the case and did not want to secure a conviction, or at least had failed to give it serious enough attention. See, e.g., Laikipia Settlers and Carter Report, East African Standard, 2 June 1934, 47, in KNA:PC/NFD4/2/3; Cole to Bottomley, 18 December 1933; Daily Herald, Morning Post, and Times, 11 December 1933, in C.O. 533/439; minute by Bottomley, 27 January 1934, following a visit by Lady Cole to the Colonial Office; extract from an interview between the Secretary of State and the European elected members of the Legco on 14 February 1934; King to Stapleton, 14 December 1934, enclosure in Glossop to Cunliffe-Lister, 7 January 1935; Cunliffe-Lister to Grigg, private and personal, 10 January 1935, C.O. 533/443; and [Colville] to Colonial Secretary, 13 October 1934, enclosure in Lady Cole to Cunliffe-Lister, 23 May 1935, C.O. 533/455.

28. For settler threats of violence, see Colville to CNC, 26 July 1933; Edwards to CNC, 21 August 1933, KNA:PC/NFD4/2/3; and Pardoe to Lady Cole, 5 and 12 January 1934, C.O. 533/443.

29. The NFD PC admitted that the case against Ole Odumo was weak and that his position was not comparable to similar leaders among the Maasai or Nandi. Glenday to La Fontaine, confidential; and Glenday to CNC, confidential, 18 December 1933, KNA: PC/NFD4/2/3; Collective Punishment Ordinance, Ordinance No. 54 of 1930, C.A. Cornell, 9 April 1934, enclosure in Byrne to Cunliffe-Lister, 6 July 1934, C.O. 533/443; and Cornell to Glenday, Confidential, 18 April 1934, enclosure in Byrne to Cunliffe-Lister, 24 February 1935, C.O. 533/455.

30. Byrne to Bottomley, personal and confidential, 25 April 1934, C.O. 533/443.

31. RVP Ars, 1934 and 1935, H.E. Welby, KNA:PC/RVP2/3/1; and Proclamation No. 100, Colony and Protectorate of Kenya, A. de V. Wade, 13 October 1934, C.O. 533/443.

32. Chenevix Trench (1993: 95), Spencer (1988: 170, n.6), and Samburu District HOR, April 1935, G.R.B. Brown, KNA:DC/SAM/5. As will be seen below, Samburu headmen were weak and much more like their Maasai counterparts than the stronger

Gikuyu chiefs. Cf. Spencer (1973:172-3), and Tignor (1976:87). For a study of the Gikuyu, see Clough (1990). Samburu Sections: Nyaparai, Lngwesi, Pisikishu, Masula, Loimusi, Lorogushu, Longieli, and Lukumai.

33. Technically, however, Samburu District remained part of the NFD.
34. Laikipia-Samburu District AR 1935, KNA: PC/RVP2/9/2, C.F. Atkins; and RVP AR, 1935, S.O.V. Hodge, KNA:PC/RVP2/3/1.
35. Samburu District HOR, April 1935.
36. Laikipia-Samburu District AR, 1935. Chenevix-Trench, who himself served as Samburu DC in the 1950s and is not the harshest critic of the colonial administration, gives an unattributed quote that describes Atkins as "a BNC rowing tough" (Chenevix-Trench 1993: 96).
37. Laikipia-Samburu AR, 1936, H.B. Sharpe, KNA:RVP2/9/2. For the predictable reaction of the white community in Kenya see, for example, Daily Herald, 22 June 1935, C.O. 533/443.
38. Laikipia-Samburu AR, 1936.
39. For Sharpe's personal proclivities, see Chenevix-Trench (1993: 96).
40. Laikipia-Samburu District AR, 1935, C.F. Atkins [drafted by Sharpe], KNA: PC/RVP2/9/2.
41. This point was made by later DCs. One wrote that the 1939 disturbances were "not wholly caused by moran, for certain elders are always ready for intrigue, when they do not see eye to eye with Government." A second wryly commented that the elders "were just as bad in their time," Laikipia-Samburu District HORs, 1 April 1944, M.H. Evans; and 12 March 1943, G.R.B. Brown, KNA:DC/LKA/10.
42. Brown had already begun this as four of his five replacements of chiefs were *murran*. Because no suitable agent could be found from among the Lorogushu, the British appointed, Usambo, a Maasai interpreter, over that section. Thus, by 1936, the only remaining headman from before the disturbances was Lengerassi of the Masula section. See Laikipia-Samburu District ARs, 1935 and 1936; RVP AR, 1935, S.O.V. Hodge, KNA: PC/RVP2/3/1;

and Laikipia-Samburu District HOR, 29 Nov. 1937, H.B. Sharpe, KNA:DC/SAM/5.

Unfortunately for British ends, Sharpe and his successors over estimated the authority of these warrior leaders. Those appointed by the administration were called *laiguenak lolsirkali*, or "spokesmen for the government" and those opposed them, *laiguenak loongishu*, or "spokesmen for the people" (Spencer 1973:174-7).

43. For Spencer's remarks on LNCs, which he refers to as African District Councils or A.D.C.s, see Spencer (1973: 173-4).

44. Laikipia-Samburu AR, 1936; and HOR, 29 Nov. 1937, H.B. Sharpe, KNA: DC/SAM/5. LNCs were first established in down-country Kenya twelve years earlier, and there had briefly been a Samburu Native Tribunal in the late-1920s which had lapsed by 1931. See, Simpson (1994: 278-80).

45. The former was associated with stock theft, and the latter was suspect by colonial authorities who believed that the "taunts of the girls" was behind the disturbances in the early-1930s. See Laikipia-Samburu Monthly Intelligence Report (IR), Oct. 1940; and Samburu circumcision, DC, Maralal, 29 December 1948, KNA:PC/SP4/2/1.

46. Laikipia-Samburu District HOR, 29 Nov. 1937.

47. *Ibid.*

48. *Ibid.*

49. At least one official disagreed with these conclusions, and held that climatic conditions and poor soil were more responsible for the deterioration of land than was overstocking. Cf. "Reduction of Stock, Samburu, Overstocking and Erosion in the Samburu reserve," Colin Maher; and "Destocking Samburu reserve," R. Daubney with "An analysis of the 1935 Samburu stock census in relation to the land and the people," T.B. McClure, KNA:CS/1/5/1.

50. Some notes on de-stocking further to the memorandum submitted to me [Major H.A.D. White] by the Executive Committee of the Stockowners' Association on March 2nd, 1938, KNA: CS/1/5/1. For continued opposition to Samburu competition, see also Dykes to Daubney, 11 December 1939, KNA:AGR/5/2/34; and Daubney

to Baker-Beall [Chief Secretary], 5 February 1940, KNA:AGR/ 5/2/34.

51. Reduction of stock, Samburu, Destocking Samburu reserve, J. Hopkins; and policy regarding stock in relation to soil conservation and land utilization in native reserves, KNA:CS/1/5/1.

52. Reduction of stock, KNA:CS/1/5/1; and RVP AR, 1939, S.O.V. Hodge, KNA:PC/RVP2/3/1.

53. The scheme for destocking Kamba herds and their resistance to it is much more well known. See Munro (1975:220-36), and Myrick (1975:1-26).

54. Report of the meeting of the Land Commission and *baraza* with the Samburu at Kisima on 8th January, 1933 at 10.45a.m., KNA:PC/NFD4/2/3. Also quoted in Spencer (1973: 180).

55. Paul Spencer notes that in the case of the Maasai, impoverished *murran* might downgrade themselves from elderhood by associating with new *murran* and resort to cattle raiding to build up stock (Spencer 1988:94).

56. RVP AR, 1939; Laikipia-Samburu District HOR, 17 April 1939, K.M. Cowley, KNA:DC/SAM/5; and Monthly IR, March 1939, KNA:PC/RVP4/3/1.

57. RVP AR, 1939.

58. *Ibid.*

59. *Ibid.*

60. *Ibid.*

61. *Ibid.* The police levy ended a year after it had begun, although twenty-five constables were kept on under a European officer after its conclusion. Laikipia-Samburu District HOR, August 1940, N.F. Kennaway, KNA: DC/LKA/10.

62. When the scheme went awry, the manager of Liebig's, which had been granted a monopsony for purchasing Samburu beef, pressed the Secretariat in Nairobi to use "some form of compulsion" to ensure the firm adequate supplies, but to no avail. Brinton to Acting Chief Secretary [H.S. Potter?], 10 May 1939, KNA:CS/1/5/ 1. For the continued opposition of field representatives to any such policy, see Cooke to Chairman, De-Stocking Committee, 13 June 1939; and R.C. Turnbull [written by Gerald Reece] to Chief

Secretary, 30 October 1939, KNA:CS/1/3/1.

63. These had multiplied to three with one at Maralal, Wamba, and Baragoi. Laikipia-Samburu District HORs, 15 Jan. 1940, A.C.M. Mullins; and August 1940, KNA:DC/LKA/10; Monthly IRs, July and Sept. 1939, KNA:PC/RVP4/3/1; and AR, 1940, G.R.B. Brown, KNA:PC/RVP2/9/2.

    Spencer states that one reason for the lack of the LNCs' development was that traditional structures for maintaining control among the Samburu were still working adequately (Spencer 1973:173).

64. Laikipia-Samburu District HOR, 15 Jan 1940; and Monthly IRs, Sept. and Nov. 1940, KNA: PC/RVP4/3/1.

65. Laikipia-Samburu Monthly IRs, July and August 1940, KNA:PC/RVP4/3/1; and HOR, August 1940.

66. Laikipia-Samburu AR, 1940.

67. Laikipia-Samburu District AR, 1945, W.N.B. Loudon, KNA:PC/RVP2/9/2; Spencer (1973: 163-4).

68. Laikipia-Samburu Monthly IR, October 1939, KNA:PC/RVP4/3/1.

69. Liebig's acquired a monopoly of purchases in Samburu Sub-District to prevent the "unsophisticated" Samburu from being "exploited by private individuals." Regulations prohibited driving cattle along any motor road because Laikipia settlers alleged that this would spread disease. Cf. Laikipia-Samburu District HORs, 15 Jan 1940; and 12 March 1943, G.R.B. Brown, KNA:DC/LKA/10 with Monthly IRs, Dec. 1940, Jan., Feb., Sept., Oct., and Nov. 1942, KNA:PC/RVP4/3/1.

70. Laikipia-Samburu District AR, 1943, J. Douglas McKean, KNA:PC/RVP2/9/2.

71. Wartime sales of Samburu livestock: 1940—869 cattle; 1941—3,837 cattle; 1942—2,693 cattle; 1943—1,690 cattle and 2,820 small stock; 1944—2,422 cattle and 3,278 small stock; 1945 — 4,347 cattle and 3,767 small stock, see H.J. Simpson, Samburu Sub-District AR, 1946, KNA:DC/SAM/2. The shortfall in cattle in 1943 can be attributed to a famine in the district which required the government to bring in meal and flour bags, see

Laikipia-Samburu District ARs, 1943 and 1944, J. Douglas McKean, KNA:PC/RVP2/9/2.

72. Laikipia-Samburu District HORs, August 1940, N.F. Kennaway; and 12 March 1943, G.R.B. Brown; and 27 March 1945, W.N.B. Loudon, KNA:DC/LKA/10. In late-1941, three chiefs, Legorogoro (Longieli), Lepurkon (Pisikishu), and Lenyokopiro (Lokumai), retired after being convicted for corruption. Laikipia-Samburu Monthly IR, Dec. 1941, KNA:PC/RVP4/3/1.

73. Laikipia-Samburu District AR, 1943, J. Douglas McKean, KNA:PC/RVP2/9/2.

74. Laikipia-Samburu District HOR, August 1940; and AR, 1944, J. Douglas McKean, KNA:PC/RVP2/9/2.

75. Laikipia-Samburu District HOR, 31 Oct. 1947, H.J. Simpson, KNA:DC/SAM/5.

76. Laikipia-Samburu District HOR, 6 August 1944, W.N.B. Loudon, KNA:DC/LKA/10. Yet, half a year later when another DC put forward the idea of introducing a new age-set, the elders on the LNC were of the opinion it would be "premature." Laikipia-Samburu District HOR, 1 April 1944, M.H. Evans, KNA: DC/LKA/10.

77. Laikipia-Samburu District HOR, 12 March 1943, G.R.B. Brown, KNA: DC/LKA/10. A subsequent DC also did not mince words, and wrote, 'the Moran on the whole are a spineless lot, avoid any form of work like the plague and are a perpetual potential source of trouble'. See Laikipia-Samburu District HOR, 31 Oct. 1947.

78. Samburu Sub-District AR, 1946; Laikipia-Samburu District HORs, 23 August 1946, R.O. Hennings; and 31 Oct. 1947.

79. Samburu Sub-District AR, 1946, H.J. Simpson, KNA:DC/SAM/2.

80. *Ibid.*; and Laikipia-Samburu District HOR, 31 Oct. 1947.

81. Samburu District AR, 1947, A.D. Shirreff, KNA: DC/SAM/2; and Samburu circumcision 1948.

82. *Ibid.*

83. The official records listed thirty-three serious crimes in 1948, up from the previous year's total of twenty-six. Such crimes included stock theft, minor theft, and assault. Samburu District AR, 1948, A.D. Shirreff, KNA: DC/SAM/3.

84. Samburu District AR, 1947.
85. Samburu District AR, 1948.

PART II
ETHNOGRAPHIES OF THE POST-COLONIAL

Chapter 3

EXPERIENCING OLD AGE ON
MAFIA ISLAND (TANZANIA)

❖

Pat Caplan

Introduction

In the preface to his book *Anthropology and the Riddle of the Sphinx* (1990a), Paul Spencer notes the existence of a number of anomalies in the anthropological study of aging:

> [T]he problems of youth, the elusive concept of adulthood, the dilemmas of marginality in old age, the existential experience of aging, the entanglement of aging with history, and above all the cultural and gender constructions that shape the life course. (xi)

This chapter attempts to grapple with several of these issues, focusing particularly on the experience of aging as expressed by a number of older residents of Minazini village on northern Mafia Island, where I have been carrying out fieldwork since the mid-1960s. It seeks to respond to the question raised by Amoss and Herrell, "How do people feel about themselves in particular societies, and how do others feel about them?" (1981:19).

On Mafia, the ideal is that when people grow old, they are helped and cared for by children and grandchildren. Indeed, this is one of the reasons often given for having children. Yet older people express very divergent views of their experience of old age, and how they see the past and the present. In this chapter, I present a variety of such views, utilizing as far as possible the words of informants themselves, and I seek to show that, as Amoss and Herrell note, old people are not passive actors but "create the conditions of their own existence within the limits established by factors they cannot control" (1981:5).

After a short discussion on the contexts in which aging has to be viewed, the second part of this chapter focuses upon the life of one particular individual, using her experience of aging not only to discuss how she coped with and adapted to her changing situation, but also to demonstrate that aging has to be seen, as Spencer has suggested, as the outcome of a lifetime (1990b:1).

In the third part, I consider in more detail this view of old age as a period in which a lifetime's investments (cf., Kertzer and Keith 1984:21) in economic, social, and cultural capital yield fruit, or one in which, if no such capital exists, life can be hard and difficult. By economic capital I refer to property (on Mafia this consists principally of coconut trees and animals), and also the ability to continue to generate income. By social capital, I mean investment in social relations, mainly with children and grandchildren, but also with other kin, neighbors, and fellow villagers. By cultural capital I mean the acquisition of specialist knowledge of various kinds: of the genealogies of descent groups; of customary practices such as spirit-possession cults, boys' circumcision or girls' puberty rituals; of Islamic practices such as Sufi order rituals; or the ability to help solve disputes. These three forms of capital are not discrete, since one can sometimes be translated into another, for example, ritual knowledge can generate economic wealth.

Not all old people have equal stores of these forms of capital, perhaps because they did not seek to acquire them during the course of their lifetime, or perhaps because they were unfortunate in trying but failing to do so (for example, not having children, or losing those they did have at an early age). Such circumstances do have a profound effect on their experience of old age. In addition, there are similarities and differences in the ways women and men experience aging.

The Contexts of Aging

The process of aging on Mafia Island has to be seen in a number of contexts. The first one is a cultural ideal, strongly articulated by both old and young, in which the former should remain independent for as long as possible, including living in their own houses, but at the same time they should receive support of various kinds. Furthermore, older people ("the elders" [*wazee*; sing. *mzee*]) are to be respected and are entitled to be consulted on a wide range of issues, such as land allocation, dispute settlement, and the arrangement of marriages. As elsewhere, two stages of old age are recognized, the first being a period in which the elderly can take care of most of their own needs and command the greatest respect; the second stage being when they require considerable amounts of help and are considered to become like children themselves.

The second context is that of historical change. In the thirty years during which I have been conducting fieldwork in this area, life has gotten harder for most people. In a situation of rising prices for bought goods and falling prices for cash crops, rendering assistance to others has become progressively more difficult. Some older people expressed their regrets that the world had changed. In 1994, one old man, Juma, told me,

In those days, everything was in its right place (*yamekaa sawa*). Respect (*heshima*), for example. These days, people talk different kinds of Swahili, but in those days, we all spoke the same language. And people helped each other. In those days, if you called ten people, they would all come if they were well. Today it's every one for himself. If you call six people [to come and help you], only two will come. Their hearts have changed.... That's the way the world is (*dunia, bwana*).

But another informant, an elderly woman called Fatuma, took a more nuanced view:

Oh, each time has its advantages and disadvantages (*kila wakati una wakati wake*). In those days, we had plenty of food, but then we had no clothes and things were not worth anything. Whereas today you can sew your mats, and [with the cash from their sale] you can get yourself clothes and you can buy maize flour. In the old days, there were things, but they didn't have any value attached to them.

The third context is the physical experience of aging, and the high rate of morbidity in this area. As Keith notes in her review of the literature on aging, "the physical facts of old age do not seem to be enjoyed anywhere" (Keith 1980:348) and, indeed, commonly, when meeting an older person, one is told "I ache all over" (*maungo yote yananiuma*). As it will also be shown, people frequently contrast their youth and prime, when they had their strength, with their present state: "I have no strength (*nguvu sina*)." Factors such as health are not within people's control to any large degree, although many engage in health-seeking activities by going for treatment at the government clinic or getting help from local healers of various kinds. Key goals in old age are independence and privacy, respect and attention, and assistance, financial or other, when required.

The Life of Mwanema

Mwanema was entering middle age when I first knew her in the 1960s and was very elderly when I last saw her a year before her death in 1995. Mwanema's attempts to build up various forms of capital for her old age were largely successful until a period towards the end of her life when other factors, beyond her control, intervened.

When I first met Mwanema in the mid-1960s, I estimated that she was in her forties. She was then in the throes of a divorce from her second husband, by whom she had had two daughters. By her previous husband, who had died, she had borne seven children, of whom four were still alive—two sons and two daughters—all of whom were married. Many years later she told me that this first marriage had been very happy, with a husband whom she described as a hard worker who supported her well: "Love comes from giving—if your husband gives you things, you will love him, if he doesn't you won't." In her mind it was very clear. She loved her first husband because he gave; the second didn't do so, and she rejected him.

We became close friends for a number of reasons. One was that the first pregnancy of the younger of her married daughters was a very difficult one, and eventually I was asked to take her to the district hospital in the vehicle of which I had use at that time. She gave birth to a healthy boy who became my *somo,*[1] which meant that I chose his name. Towards the end of my fieldwork, Mwanema arranged an *unyago* (puberty ritual) for her pubescent daughter, a lengthy event, most of which I tape-recorded and later transcribed with her help (Caplan 1976). It was evident from her organization of this large ritual that Mwanema had built up a large stock of capital of all kinds: she had the means to pay for much of the ritual herself and it was attended by large numbers of people. As she was herself an expert on the ritual, she was able to give me a detailed explanation of it, although since it was for her own daughter, she could not conduct it herself, but had called upon a friend and colleague to do so.

On my return to Mafia in 1976 to assist in the making of a film for the BBC,[2] I found Mwanema living in a small hut in the compound of her eldest son. She was busy and involved in a wide range of activities; indeed, it became apparent when we began editing the rushes of the film in London that she appeared over and over again in a wide variety of contexts, and usually in a leading role. With her frequent joking, she perfectly epitomized the "bawdy old woman of ethnographic notoriety" (Kertzer and Keith 1984:38-9; see also Keith 1980:351).

Mwanema by this time was fostering two of her grandchildren and she spoke about this in an interview on camera:

> I've got eleven grandchildren: three from my eldest son, five from my second son, two from a daughter who is married in the next village, and one from my daughter who died. I bring up two of them myself: one because his mother died, so he hadn't got a mother, and I became like his mother myself; the other one's mother is still alive, but she divorced his father and married again. I said, "My grandson isn't going to any stepfather as long as I'm alive—I'll bring him up myself: food, clothes, toiletries, bedding, everything."
>
> It's much easier, of course, to raise a grandchild than to raise your own child. After all, first you have to bear your own child, and then you always have to bath it and massage it with oil, and wash its clothes, and take it with you wherever you go. But a grandchild—you get it when it's already big. I'm getting old now, and I don't have much, but I would go without clothes myself so that I can buy clothes for my grandchildren, and stop them from feeling miserable.

Fostering of grandchildren (or the children of other relatives) is a common practice on Mafia and, indeed, at the time of my fieldwork in the 1960s, no fewer than a quarter of children were being raised by people other than their parents. In some instances, this was because of the death or divorce of a parent, but quite often it was because the person fostering had requested that the children be given to her for upbringing (*ulezi*). Children are viewed as a valuable asset, as well as a cost, and few old couples or elderly women are without at least one grandchild, often referred to as "my legs" (*miguu yangu*), in their household.

On her divorce, Mwanema had gone to live next to one of her sons, at that time a successful shopkeeper. Yet when she was interviewed about whether it was preferable to have sons or daughters, she was quite clear about her views:

> You ask me whether it is better to have boys or girls to bring up. Girls are better—definitely. You bring up a girl, and when she's bigger, she'll pound rice for you, she'll go and fetch water, she'll go and look for firewood, and when you die, she'll wash your corpse. But a boy—he doesn't pound, he doesn't fetch water, he doesn't do anything—except that perhaps he'll dig your grave for you! Girls help you in your work, while boys—perhaps you can send them on errands to the shop, that's all.
>
> And when they are grown-up women are better than men—they have more heart, more sympathy for people. I think that is the way God created them. A man might even snatch food away from his own mother, and go and give it to his wife, while she stays there starving. But a woman, a daughter, would never behave like that. She would remember the day when her mother gave birth to her.

Such a strongly expressed view of sex preferences, I later realized, was one which was held primarily by women. Men wanted sons for a variety of reasons, not least because they thought that sons, because of their access to cash earnings, would be able to provide for them in old age.

At the time of my third visit in 1985, Mwanema was still living in the compound of her eldest son, whose fortunes had, however, deteriorated in the meanwhile as a result of a serious illness from which he had made only a partial recovery. She was still fostering various grandchildren, although my *somo* had by this time grown up and gone to live in Dar-es-Salaam. His mother (Mwanema's daughter) had just had her seventh child, and, as is customary, had gone to her mother's house to do so. The reason for this practice is so that the woman giving birth has a few weeks of rest before and after the birth, and also assistance during the birth itself. In this instance, however, Mwanema herself became ill and was nursed by her daughter, who stayed on beyond the customary 40-day period after childbirth in order to do so.

I asked Mwanema's daughter whether she had been pleased to have a girl child:

A. I'm pleased to have anything. Both have their advantages. A girl is important as you get old. Do you think a man will look after you, wash you, like I'm doing for my mother now that she is sick? A boy goes away, like your somo now in Dar-es-Salaam. That's good too. You need both boys and girls.

Q. Are you getting tired of having children?

A. No, how can I refuse to bring my fellow human beings into the world?

Later, however, she admitted that it was tiring having so many children and I asked her why she didn't give some to her mother to bring up:

A. She's past it now—I have to bring her up. She couldn't manage these youngsters.

Q. Then why not send her your mwali (pubescent girl) to help her?

A. No, I need the mwali to help me. And she will soon be ready for a husband.

It was clear that, by this time, Mwanema was entering the second phase of old age, in which she needed increasing amounts of help. Nonetheless, when I asked Mwanema about her daily routine, it was apparent that, like most old people, she sought to be as self-sufficient as possible,

> I get water myself—three buckets daily. One for washing one for cooking and one for drinking. I go for firewood (*kuni*) every two or three days, sometimes to the beach, sometimes to the fields. I still cultivate myself, but in meadow land. I do my own pounding and cooking, my own sweeping, and airing out the bedding. When I get up I first sweep, then I heat some water, have a bath and make tea. I do some raffia plaiting. Later I cook. If I'm tired, I sleep. If I'm sick, your *somo*'s mother comes and looks after me. She asks her husband's permission and comes and stays until I'm better.

Here, then, is an account of a woman who is still active, but working at her own pace, and feeling secure in the knowledge that she can call on the help of her daughter if she feels unwell. I went on to ask how she managed financially,

A. I make ten mats a year, for which I have to buy the dye, but the children bring me the raffia. I sell them to a trader in the village. And I sell coconuts. I need cash for kerosene, fish for curry, sugar, tea, cigarettes, soap for washing and bathing, and flour for part of the year. And clothes.

Q. Do your children help you in your life?

A. Yes, they do, they give you [me] food and clothes. This (indicating her cloth) was given me by one of my children, and so was this [petticoat].

Q. Is it only men [who help] or do daughters also give things to you?

A. A son will bring you kerosene and kitoweo *(the main ingredient of the curry, usually fish, occasionally chicken or meat), i.e., items bought for cash. Today I got money for soap from one of my sons, and money for kerosene from the other. And the clothes I'm wearing were left by my daughter when she went back.*

107

By 1994, the time of my fourth visit to the village, Mwanema must have been in her seventies, and was finding life harder. She had shifted her residence from the compound of her eldest son (for reasons which were not totally clear to me), and was living in a small hut on the edge of her meadow field, which she still continued to cultivate. Her move may have been connected with the continuing health problems of her elder son and his consequent inability to give her any help. Furthermore, her second son, to whom she was especially close because they were both members of a spirit-possession cult, had died suddenly in the meanwhile and she described herself as "all alone" (*peke yangu*). In fact, this was not quite the case. She had three schoolboy grandsons living with her, and it was rare to find her without a visitor in the form of one of her daughters or granddaughters. All of these, even the boys, would help with tasks which needed to be done, especially the most arduous, pounding rice. She was still cheerful, although she complained a bit of her poverty. Now, she said, she had no sons to look after her, and my *somo*, who used to help out when he came, had not been home for several years. "Who would help me these days? These days my only children left are women. They help me a bit but the one who used to help me most was that one [the son who died]." I asked who gave her clothes— her daughters did.

We remembered the days when Mwanema used to be an expert in the *unyago* (female puberty ritual):

Q. Where did you learn about that?

A. I learnt it by myself.

Q. You mean from going to different rituals?

A. Yes, that's right I used to go to them in the South (of the island).

Q. So did you hold rituals in the South or just here?

A. I just held them here. My wali *(initiates) were from here. (She sings an* unyago *song.)*

Q. So why don't they dance the unyago *any more these days?*

A. They don't dance it these days and I don't have any young people for whom to dance it.

Q. Could you still do it?

A. Yes, I still could manage it. I did it for Binti Hassan, and I did it for my granddaughter all night and all day.

Q. When was that?

A. It was some time ago. It was a time when you weren't here and I also did it for the girl who became the wife of Hatibu, all night and all day. (She sings the song again).

In fact, I was told by many informants that the practice of holding a puberty ritual for girls had almost completely died out, because the Sheiks (Islamic teachers) said that it was forbidden (*haramu*). Women like Mwanema, who had been accorded a good deal of respect for their esoteric knowledge, had thus found themselves undermined.

Nonetheless, Mwanema viewed with some satisfaction her appearance in the BBC film:

Q. Do you remember when we came to make the film here? Did you ever see it?

A. Yes, I did see it.

Q. And what did you think of it?

A. It was good.

Q. You know, people in Europe praised you a lot....
When you watch yourself in the film how do you see yourself?

A. I see it as myself. I recognise myself....Did people in Europe really praise me?

Q. Yes, they said that here was somebody who knew a lot.

A. So why didn't they send me any presents then? (She laughs)

Q. Well, they didn't come here did they? I was the only one who came, and I did bring you a present.

Mwanema died a year later. She had had a relatively fortunate life, by local standards, yet she suffered many bereavements—three children who died at a young age, and two as adults with children of their own—and much grief from the continuing illness of her eldest son, whose health had not responded to the numerous cures which had been sought for him. Spencer notes that the universal experience of old age is a period of loss (1990: 26), but on Mafia Island, with its high rates of mortality, especially child mortality, most people have to cope with loss of loved ones long before old age. Even so, several of her children lived to adulthood and had children of their own. For the middle years of her life, she enjoyed the support of her male and female children and was strong enough to continue living independently, including growing at least some of her own food. She also had grandchildren living with her, initially to support them, but later as companions and helpers in her old age. Her social capital was thus high, and she also had sufficient economic capital to make life a little easier. However, the cultural capital which she had amassed in the form of knowledge of the *unyago* ritual, and which could also be translated into economic capital when she was paid for conducting rituals, dwindled in the latter part of her life, as the ritual fell into abeyance and was even condemned as un-Islamic. In the final period of her life, some of her support disappeared as her favorite son died, and her other son's health deteriorated. Even so, she continued to receive help from her daughters, who had indeed shown that they had 'heart' and "sympathy" and remembered the day when their mother gave birth to them.

In the next section of this paper, I consider each of the three forms of capital in turn, again using the words of informants.

Economic Capital

Amoss and Herrell suggest that "the maintenance of some control over property is crucial to a successful and comfortable old age" (1981:9). On Mafia Island, the most important form of property is the coconut tree, which people acquire by planting, by buying, and through inheritance. Coconuts, whether in the form of copra, as was the case in the 1960s and 1970s, or whole ripe nuts, as during the 1980s and 1990s, provide the main cash crop. Men tend to own far more trees than women, partly because they have greater access to cash for buying them, partly because, under Islamic law they inherit twice as many as women, and partly because men are more likely to initiate planting of new trees (although some couples do plant jointly). Older people are also more likely to have more trees than younger ones.

It is considered important, especially for men, that they should acquire coconut trees during their lifetime. Those who have inherited trees which they have sold off to meet daily expenses are regarded as foolish, trading off long-term security against short-term gain. People who can accumulate a reasonable amount of economic capital during their lifetime are obviously better placed in old age than those who have not, as in the case of Fatuma, the elderly woman quoted in the first section of this article. She lived alone, but close to her brother's son who helped her market her coconuts:

A. I bought a few coconut trees.

Q. Didn't you inherit any?

A. I got maybe ten, but most I bought myself. I would plant rice, [sell some] then buy a cow, which I would sell and buy myself some [more] coconut trees. So now I get a bit [of money] out of them ...

On Mafia, there is no pre-mortem inheritance, and old people are supposed to retain control of their property until they die. However, if they do not have a close relative whom they can trust to arrange for felling and marketing the nuts, they may decide to sell, as in the case of an elderly man called Athman, who was not on good terms with his only son:

> I had a few trees and I used to sell copra. But I couldn't look after those trees, and, as you know, if you don't do that the government can lock you up. So I sold them. There are still a few left, 10, 20, 30, I don't know.

Another instance in which the capital accumulated over a lifetime disappears is when tragedy strikes. Mohammed, a man in his sixties, had sold off his coconut trees because he himself was sick, and then his son had a long illness and was hospitalized in Dar es Salaam (see Caplan 1997 for a fuller account of his life).

Most older people seek to generate some cash income for themselves by a variety of activities. In the case of women, it is continuing to make and sell raffia mats (*mikeka*), although the numbers they can produce each year tend to dwindle. Fatuma, for instance, said that whereas she used to make ten mats a year in her younger days, could only manage four in her old age, but "with the money from that, I can at least get myself some clothes." Men, however, often have to give up some of the activities in which they earlier used to engage, such as trading trips to Dar-es-Salaam or Zanzibar, or casual labor for other people. In their old age, many men take up the making of large mats (*majamvi*), made from borassus palm, or plaiting palm fronds for thatching (*makuti*). In this respect, the roles of men and women tend to converge at this time of life.

Social Capital: Parents and Children

"Children are our wealth" was a frequent saying in the village, and there is an often-expressed ideology that in return for bringing them into the world and supporting them, children should look after their parents in their old age (see Caplan 1995a). Such a statement was made very clearly in an interview in 1976 with Mwahadia, a woman then in her thirties:

Q. I want to ask you about old people here in Mafia. How do they live? On whom do they depend? Like your mother for instance—she is old now, isn't she? So who looks after her? Who does she depend on?

A. Now she's looked after by her own children—me for instance. And the others, my sisters and brothers. There are five of us altogether. She depends on us now—she has no strength left. She can't cultivate. So we women go and take our hoes and do it for her. And the men take their bill-hooks and they go and cut down some forest. We take our hoes and go and plant. We do all this for her, because she is our parent, and her strength is finished. Anyone who fells green coconuts takes one to her. Anyone who buys a kilo or two of flour they divide it with her also; a quarter they will give to mother so she can make porridge. And the men too, if they get some fish, mother should be given some. And they should find ripe coconuts (for cooking) and give some to her. So that we can say that if an old person's strength is finished, then he or she depends upon the children—and the children are people like us.

Q. So, an old person depends upon their children, and they live near to their children?

A. Yes, of course near to their children—where else would they go? You see, it's like this; an old woman like her, she doesn't have any parents—they are already dead. And she herself has become like a child—so we become her parents, because we have to look for food to give her, since she hasn't any means of doing so herself. So we look after her until her strength is finished, and her days are ended, and God takes her, and that's the end.

Q. Suppose someone is old, but not very old, they still have their strength, will they continue to cultivate?

A. Yes, they will continue to cultivate, they will work. They might plait grass, and sew them together and get mats to sell—so she can get money to buy clothes and food for herself. But if her strength is completely finished, then she can't do anything, then she becomes like a small child, and is looked after by her children. You have to cook for her, to fetch water, wash her, wash her clothes, and do every thing for her, you sweep for her, give her food, take her dirty dishes and wash them, keep her food covered, make it all nice, make her bed so that she can go and rest there.

Q. But she still has her own house, doesn't she? She doesn't live in yours?

A. Yes, she will live in her own house. Except perhaps that some people, when they get old, they are sick. So when an old person is sick, whether a man or a woman, if it is your parent, then you take them in provided you are a daughter, for a man can't nurse sick people, only a woman. So you nurse your parent until he or she is well again, and they go back to their own house, and it is finished.

As Mwahadia notes, it is more likely that a sick elderly person will be cared for by a daughter than by a son, and this is borne out in the following interview recorded in 1976 with a divorced woman living with her very elderly father:

Q. This is your house isn't it? Do you stay here with your father?

A. Yes

Q. Can your father cultivate?

A. No he can't, he just sits here. I stay with him and look after him. He's not well enough to do anything these days, so I have to do every-thing.

Q. Who helps you?

A. My elder brother who is here helps me from time to time: he culti-vates and sometimes he goes to the sea and fishes.

Q. Who built this house for you?

A. It was built for me by my cousin—my mother's brother's son. And the fence by various youngsters. When I see them passing, I ask them to do a bit of fencing for me.

Q. Suppose you get married again—would you take your father with you?

A. Any future husband would have to fit in with me, because I want to look after my father until the end of his life.

In this instance, the woman did care for her father until he died soon after the interview, but not all old people are so fortunate. Athman, to whom I have already referred, had married a total of eleven women during the course of his life, but he had divorced them all, or they had died. From these marriages, he had had only one son, with whom he was not on good terms. As a result, he had none on whom he could depend for help in his old age, as he told me in 1994:

A. I haven't eaten since yesterday. Why? Because I didn't cultivate.

Q. Why doesn't your son help you?

*A. You must be joking! That woman he married is not a human being (*si mtu*). She is all over the place (*ovyo tu*).... When you have a child, you love it and the child [should] love its father.... But with my son there is none of that. I put him in the initiation lodge (*kumbi*), I sent him to study with the Koran school teacher, but other people are nicer to me (*wananifaa zaidi*) than he is.*

Q. So who helps you?

A. Not him. If I ask [even for] for salt I don't get it. He says "What's mine is mine and what's yours is yours."

Q. So who fetches water for you?

*A. I go myself, and if I get some flour I make it up (*nasonga*) myself.... There should be love in everything (*kitu chochote ana mapenzi*). (He repeats this twice.) When you come from there [London], you give me a present because we have got used to each other from a long time ago. Some of the people from those days are dead now, only we are left.*

In contrast, Juma, who had also had only one child, a son, was experiencing his old age very differently when I interviewed him in 1994. He too had married many wives, a total of seven, the last of whom had died since my previous visit, and, like Athman, he too was now living alone. His son, however, had had many children by a number of wives. I asked Juma about this:

Q. And is it a good thing to have many children?

A. Yes, children are our wealth (watoto ni mali yetu). If someone doesn't have a child, they will be poor (maskini), and when they die, anyone who is around will have to carry them [to be buried]...That son whom you know has three wives.... by whom he has had sixteen children.

Q. What do you say to that? Are you pleased?

A. Of course I am pleased! They are my people. When they are bigger they will help, while they are small not yet, but they can be sent on errands: "Bring this, go there, fetch that." Should I be angry at having children when I get something (napata) out of it?.

However, the son, with his three wives and sixteen children, lived in another village, and furthermore, he had contracted elephantiasis as a young man, which made walking long distances difficult, so he rarely came to Minazini. Although the old man would go and visit his son from time to time (a journey of some twelve miles which he usually did on foot), Mzee was actually cared for by his step-daughter, Binti Seleman, the daughter of his deceased wife, who had brought this child into her second marriage and whom he had helped to raise.

Q. So who cooks for you?

A. Binti Seleman, I brought her up, I arranged her marriage. By her first husband she had a son, then he divorced her and she married Hatibu and she's still with him. They did have one son but he died.

Curiously, however, he still maintained that it was more important to have sons than daughters:

*A. A boy is better because he builds up the town (mji). He will build.
But a girl, once she is pubescent, you give her to someone [in mar-
riage]. What do you think?*

Q. But isn't it a woman who is looking after you?

*A. How can you have a woman look after you when she has been
given away? Even if she stays here, she is not yours, anything she
does she has to get her husband's permission for. But boys will stay
around and help you. But a woman is not around. She is helping
someone else.*

Mzee meant that sons remain their own masters, and can therefore continue to help their parents, while a daughter's first duty is
to her husband. In his case, the affection between himself and his
step-daughter, which he felt he had earned by "bringing her up"
and "arranging her marriage," ensured her care for him once he
was left alone, a situation in which her husband fortunately ac-
quiesced.

Social Capital: Grandparents and Grandchildren

Relations between grandparents and grandchildren are much more
relaxed than those between parents and children. As in other parts
of Africa, the former are characterized by ritualized joking and
teasing (utani), and by relative lack of restraint in discussion of
sexual matters (cf. Radcliffe-Brown 1952). Quite often, the
woman chosen to give sexual instruction to a newly pubescent
girl is a grandmother, while grandfathers often tease their granddaughters by saying that they are their "wives." In his review of
the anthropological literature on old age, Cohen notes that
Radcliffe-Brown's analysis of joking relations replaces a two-
generational by a three-generational model of "the young and old
in conjunctive alliance with each other" in which parents hand

down tradition to their children, and grandparents are replaced by grandchildren (1994:148).

As has been seen, like most grandmothers, Mwanema had taken on the care of grandchildren; indeed, fostering (*ulezi*) is a widespread institution in Swahili society, an important means of spreading both the pleasures and responsibilities of child-rearing over a wide network. In 1976, Mwahadia described her mother's role in this manner:

Q. Doesn't she bring up any of her grandchildren?

A. Yes she does. One is the child of my sister who died; in fact she has had all her children. First there's that one who married the village official, she used to foster her. That one whom the official married last year. And the second is her sister, she too was with her, and then one called Kombo who is still at home with her. And the last one is called Hatibu, that one who has trouble with his leg, he's lame. Well she brought up all those children.

In this instance, as had been the case with one of Mwanema's grandchildren, the reason for the fostering was that the mother of the children had died, and her own mother took her place. But Mwahadia went on to describe another situation in which a mother might take on a daughter's child:

Q. Suppose you have a small baby and you are suckling it, if you get pregnant again quickly, what can you do? Is there anything to be done?

A. Well, you'll just have to wean the first one, because if you are already pregnant again, and that first one is not yet ready to be weaned, if the baby drinks the milk [while you are pregnant] it will make it sick. So if you have your mother, and she is a nice person and she has a kind heart, then you can leave the child with her; your mother will take that child and bring it up, because if you are already pregnant again, you can't breastfeed a baby, because if you do so you'll ruin the child's stomach, and make it ill. So its grandmother takes it and brings it up.

Even without such emergencies arising, a grandmother or grandparental couple may well ask for a grandchild to bring up. Indeed, one of my neighbors told me rather sadly that both of her children had been taken by their grandparents, so that she herself had no children in the house: "How could I refuse when they asked for them?"

In many respects, according to customary law, grandparents have more rights to grandchildren than parents do. I was made aware of this early in my fieldwork, when a small boy, who had jumped onto the back of my landrover, fell off, cutting his mouth. I immediately went to see his parents, and explained that I had not known what the boy had done until it was too late, but was told that I had to speak to the grandparents because such a serious matter would have to be dealt with by them. Grandparents have a good deal of control over the lives not only of their own adult children (cf. Caplan 1995b for a good example of this) but also over their grandchildren, as is shown in a further extract from the 1976 interview with Mwahadia, who was in the process of arranging a marriage for her daughter,

A. You will go to the elders and say to them ... I have a child, like my daughter for example, now she is in the process of getting betrothed, and an elder, like my old mother, for example, I will go and tell her, "Mother I have come to you because you are my parent to tell you that someone has come wanting to marry your child. So what do you say, elders, will this fiancé do or won't he?" And if there are five elders (grandparents) or six elders, or three or four, then you inform them, "the fiancé is such and such a one, he should be answered, he should be married to our child." But.... among seven elders, from the mothers' and fathers' sides, it is unlikely that they will all agree about an engagement. Half will agree, and half will disagree; they will say, "Oh no, this suitor isn't for us—we don't want him."

Q. So then what will you do?

A. What will you do? First of all, you will send for them, because if there are three suitors, or even four, then the elders will have to decide between them—"This is the one we want." And some will say, "We have decided on such a one, we don't want that one," and they

119

might quarrel about it right there. That's the way old people go on, they say, "We want to send a favorable reply to that one, not this one," others will say, "We want to accept this one, not that one," so even if you have ten suitors, only one will be acceptable to all of them.

Q. But who has the final say, the major responsibility? Is it the parents, or the grandparents?

A. The major decision rests with the grandfathers. With my father and my husband's father. We might decide that we want to choose such a one as suitor, or we might decide we don't want him, so that's that. So if everyone agrees ... but sometimes there are elder brothers, or grandparents, or mothers' brothers and they might not want such a one. But if the grandparents have already agreed, then that'll be the one, they'll marry her to that one.

Consulting the grandparents about the fate of their grandchildren is deemed an important way of showing the former due respect (*heshima*). Furthermore, given that many of them have been reared by grandparents, many grandchildren contribute goods, cash and services to their grandparents when they become adults.

Cultural Capital

Amoss and Herreld suggest that in the study of aging, it is important to establish the extent to which older people monopolize knowledge, especially religious and ritual knowledge, noting that old people are closer to culture than to nature: "more fully enculturated, more fully socialized" (1981:15). On Mafia, as on the rest of the East African coast, two broad categories of knowledge are distinguished (Caplan 1982). Islamic knowledge, which confers respect and leadership status, can be acquired to high levels by relatively young people, although most of the Islamic leaders tend to be middle-aged to elderly, and they are usually male. Customary knowledge (*mila*), on the other hand, tends to be more the province of the elderly, both male and female, who are recognized as having greater stores of knowledge about genealogies, land rights, relations with ancestors, and grave sites than younger people, which gives them the right to make decisions on behalf of others in such areas. Indeed, old people are invariably consulted when it is necessary to contact the ancestors (*kugonya koma*), which is done annually when graves are swept and a *hitima* (Koranic reading) takes place, so that all the names of relevant ancestors will be mentioned and none missed. Similarly, elders are consulted when decisions are made about the annual allocation of bushland, particularly if there is any doubt about who has rights in a particular area. Most older people have greater knowledge of genealogies than younger ones, although only a few are formally recognized as leaders of a descent group.[3]

Most elders have acquired some form of specialist knowledge by the time they reach old age. Mwanema, for example, was an expert (*fundi*) in the *unyago* puberty ritual. Others were experts in the boys' circumcision ritual (*jando*) whether as circumcisers (*simba*, lit. "lion") or as teachers of the complex songs and riddles taught to the circumcised boys. At the very end of my first period of fieldwork, I was called in by my elderly neighbor who said that as I was leaving, he wanted to give me a present, and proceeded to spend two days singing the *jando* songs into my tape-recorder. Both boys' circumcision and girls' puberty rituals are classified as "custom" (*mila*) (see Caplan 1976).

Another form of knowledge which is classified as "custom" is that of spirit-possession cults (see Caplan 1997). Not everyone participates in such cults, even as a spectator, but those who do so have, acquired a great deal of information by the time they are elderly. Athman was one such, who had participated all of his life in the *kitanga* cult. He was able to give an extremely lucid and lengthy account not only of this cult, but also of other spirit-possession cults such as the *mwingo* and the *mkobero* in an interview for the BBC film produced in 1976. He himself continued to participate in the *kitanga* cult until shortly before his death. Athman did not, however, become a shaman—one who controlls spirits—and so was not able to lead rituals or to practice divination or healing and, thus, could not turn his cultural capital into economic resources.

Customary forms of knowledge are, however, less authoritative than Islamic forms of knowledge. People who study the Koran, especially at the higher level of the *madrasa* under the guidance of a Sheik, acquire power in the form of *baraka* (blessing), and they are called upon to lead prayers and Koranic readings, conduct marriages, and take on office in the mosque. This is not a path open to women, as one female informant made clear:

A. Only men can be sheiks.

Q. Why is that?

A. According to our religion only men can stand in front and lead the prayers. If a group of women pray, they all pray together, shoulder to shoulder. But if a group of men pray, they can have one of their number in front. And the Imam (leader of prayers in the mosque) is also always a man.

Nonetheless, there is a form of Islamic knowledge open equally to women and men, and that is through the path of Sufiism. On Mafia, people are followers of both the Qadiriyya and Shadhiliya branches of Sufiism.[4] One woman explained her role as follows:

A. I became an mridi (follower) of a particular branch (ziara) [in the village]. Eventually I was chosen to be the shawishi (flag-bearer), and I am still, but I am gradually withdrawing and getting younger people to take over. I am too old to be going around from place to place, but previously I went all over Mafia to maziara, except during the time when I was having children.

Q. How do you get chosen?

A. We choose among ourselves. People say "I can't do it, I don't know how," but eventually someone is sent off to the Sheik and he says "Do your work. Take no notice of people even if they insult you and make it difficult for you. Just carry on." Then he prays over you and reads a fatiha and that is it.

Q. There are officials of each sex, aren't there?

A. Yes, halifa, shawishi, mrishidi, and aba.[5]

Q. Is there any difference in the rank of men and women?
No, *except that women cannot have a sheik from among themselves.*

Another informant had also been an official of the same ziara, but gave it up because of not being well enough to get to the rituals. Although she had been married to a shaman, she had preferred to prioritize her Islamic knowledge rather than get involved in her husband's spirit-possession activities:

> So I was a halifa and I couldn't dance in spirit rituals (*ngoma*). But it was danced sometimes right in our house. I was really frightened at those times. I could hear people being possessed. I used to go and hide myself until it was finished, then I would come out.

Conclusion

This paper has considered a variety of factors which explain the varying experiences of old age on Mafia Island. To a large extent, this period has to be seen as in the context of a person's whole life. Although some aspects of old age are outside an individual's control—such as their own ill-health, or the illness or even death of a spouse or child—many others can be influenced by the accumulation of various forms of capital (economic, social, and cultural). Viewing old age in this way enables us to consider old people not as passive victims, but as agents, who have strategized their concerns during their lifetimes, and continue to do so in old age. Such an approach also militates against viewing the elderly as a homogenous category, since their experiences are differentiated by gender, wealth, demography, social relations, and levels of knowledge.

ACKNOWLEDGEMENTS

This chapter is dedicated to the memories of Mwanaharusi Binti Nyihaji "Kihubi" and Mohammed Athman "Nymebo," both of whom taught me so much.

Fieldwork and writing periods have been supported variously by the University of London, The Worshipful Company of Gold-smiths, the Nuffield Foundation, the Leverhulme Foundation, and the Economic and Social Research Council. Thanks also to Lionel Caplan for helpful comments.

NOTES

1. Children are usually named after an ancestor or older living relative, and each is then the other's *somo*. Because this child was a boy, he was named after my father.
2. This series of seven films, shot in six different locations around the world, of which Mafia was one, was entitled *Face Values* and was screened in 1978; the accompanying book, edited by Anne Sutherland, had the same title. Some of the film material was later made into another series of short films entitled *Other People's Lives*.
3. These were the people to whom I was directed towards the end of my first fieldwork so that I might obtain the genealogies of each of the six descent groups in the village.
4. On Mafia, people are devotees of the Qadiriyya order, which was introduced into East Africa via Somalia and Zanzibar (cf. Trimingham 1964).
5. The four offices are *halifa* (Sheik's deputy), *shawishi* (banner carriers), *mrishidi* (leaders of the chanting) and *aba* (those who are responsible for organizing the feast).

Chapter 4

Female and Male in Maasai Life: Aging and Fertility

❖

Aud Talle

A Matter of Perspective

Any visitor to a Maasai homestead cannot fail to notice the conspicuous presence of women within the thornbush fence enclosing the homestead (*enkang*). Most likely the visitor will be welcomed inside by a woman, guided by her footsteps through the narrow entrance into her house (*enkaji*), treated to milk or tea upon entering and, if staying over night, offered a place in the house to sleep. Thus, a decade ago I wrote:

> ... by socialising children and domesticating animals, by
> transforming animal products by means of the hearth and
> calabash into food (*endaa*) or by resocialising the
> *ilmurran* (i.e. the young, unmarried men, "warriors,"
> anglicised moran) after their life in the bush, the house
> and its occupants are in many ways mediators between
> "nature" and "culture." The *enkaji* is the most important
> unit of social reproduction and as such is actually the
> embodiment of culture (Talle 1988:196-7).

I also claimed that, in their capacity as managers and owners of
houses, milkers of cows, domesticators of people and livestock,
Maasai women were major upholders of a cultured and moral
world. The reproduction of the social order was as much a female as a male concern.

The same year, in his ethnographically rich and highly read-
able monograph *The Maasai of Matapato: A Study of Rituals of
Rebellion* (1988), Paul Spencer writes in a section on organizational aspects of pastoralism that the fact that women are "*tied
down* to the domestic sphere" (my emphasis) gives them a "subordinate role within the husbandry sector of the economy"
(1988:21). This remark, as I see it, presupposes a hierarchically
ranked dichotomy between the domestic sphere and the rest, giving cultural precedence to that which is beyond the province of
the house. On the same page Spencer continues, saying that "the
women's sphere has a certain autonomy, and forms a separate
economic sector in its own right, subordinate and yet *not wholly
subdued*" (my emphasis).

The last part of that sentence as well as a number of other
passages throughout the book reveal that Spencer and I, in fact,
have made similar observations of Maasai pastoral life. We have
both suggested that women, although ideologically and jurally
subordinated to men (through normative premises to which I return below), are socially and culturally important. In particular,
individual women frequently stand forth as remarkably powerful
persons (cf. Chieni & Spencer 1993; Hodgson 1994). However,
we also differ in perspective. Instead of reducing the "domestic"

to a subordinate position within the Maasai social order, as Spencer seems to do, I prefer to see it as a core site for the regeneration of life, and for the continuity of the cultural order.

The relationship between the house and the "outside" (the cattle corral or the "bush"), representing a prevalent, recurrent duality in the Maasai social universe (cf. Århem 1991), is marked as much by complementarity as by hierarchy. Women and men, juniors and seniors, left and right, the house and the 'outside' are undoubtedly separate and different, but nevertheless mutually dependent and equal (*arisio*) parts which together form a whole, a meaningful unity or "balance." The one cannot act without the other. Nor can any of them grow or prosper in its own right.

Thus, complementarity and interdependence are the points of departure for this chapter which concerns itself with aging and fertility. Therefore, the growing of men into social maturity cannot be accomplished without a feminine mediator; conversely, girls cannot develop into adults without the vitality of young men and the acquisition of male virtues.

To come of age (*botor*, large, senior, old) among the Maasai is to become "fertile," ready to procreate and reproduce life, i.e., to beget children and to increase the number of animals. The Maasai elder with numerous children and a large herd (*olkarsis*, wealthy) is the incarnation of a life fulfilled. Equally, women who have given birth to and raised many children are "wealthy" (*enkitok narikisho*). Men, in contrast to women, continue to increase and "prosper" (*abulu*) even in old age and in that sense they never cease growing (cf. Saitoti 1980).

Among the Maasai aging and fertility, culturally paired, are gendered concepts. The cultural process of maturity, which is notably shorter and less symbolically elaborated for women than for men, may bear witness of an innate "transformative capacity" in women (Arens & Karp 1989, Beidelman 1987). Ageing (*olaji*) as a social and cultural process, and basically concerned with the gaining of fertility, is culturally enacted around the advancement of men through ranked age-grades.

127

During field research among the pastoral Maasai, both in Kenya and in Tanzania, I frequently experienced male informants stressing the importance of female agency in symbolic contexts, as well as in practical life. Typically, after having elaborated on the prerogatives of men in Maasai politics at all levels of decision-making, and on male cultural excellence and moral sophistication, informants would volunteer addenda which unraveled female will, choice, negotiating power, or ritual efficacy, into their accounts. Those added remarks were somehow made to complete the story, I thought. Typically, after often long renditions of age-set values permitting age-mates to have sex with each others' wives, a concluding remark emphasizing the compliance of the woman in question would notoriously follow. Furthermore, the practice of bonding between "warriors" by mixing their semen in the same woman was represented as a privilege not only of the men, but also of the woman. "She likes it" was the comment. The fact that her lover wants to share her with his best friend, and thus seal their friendship through her body, was taken as a sign of his sincere affection.

Finally, female fertility delegations (*olamal looinkituak*), by which women in great numbers tour the country, accumulating livestock gifts as they proceed from homestead to homestead, seeking sex from men across age-set preferences, and thus violating moral norms, are much more than "rituals of rebellion" (Spencer 1988). They are also a demonstration of female power. On these spatial moves, women hold the surrounding areas in awe, claiming animals at will and forcing men to sexual prestations, lest they be mocked for being women "just like themselves." "In the bush the women are terrible," said one informant, alluding to the lack of restraint and creativity of women on these delegations. Whenever they meet a man in their way they run towards him shouting "he may bring me luck" and try to catch him. The only escape for the poor man is to climb a tree where the women will not follow.

In particular the women who have not yet given birth believe that such sexual extravagance may cure their infertility. Precisely due to their sexual excesses, some husbands are reluctant to let their wives participate, but for fear of being reprimanded by age-mates, they have to let them go.

The women themselves remain self-assured about their central place in Maasai life. To them it is almost common-sensical knowledge, too obvious to be verbally elaborated. Although holding husbands in great "respect" (*enkanyit*), fearing their beatings, they remained composed in front of them even at critical times. With a touch of arrogance, I often thought, they obeyed orders, obviously succumbing to the moral legitimacy of elders to exercise control. Similarly, I was often struck by women's relative lack of enthusiasm when acting in rituals revolving around men compared to their own rituals. In a critical article on anthropological representations of the feminine in Nilotic cosmologies, John Burton concludes that "the feminine symbols appear so dormant precisely because the masculine presence was so imposed" (1991:96). The pastoral Maasai, also of Nilotic stock, have frequently been represented likewise.

Curiously, anthropologists more than ethnic Maasai writers (e.g., Saitoti 1980), the former notoriously pursuing models of society, tend to interpret women's withdrawn position when in company of men as an expression of rank rather than difference.

Femininity and Creativity

"A woman is like Engai because she can bear children" (Wagner-Glenn 1992:130). This citation, taken from a study on fertility songs among the Arusha Maasai, neighbors and the close affine of the pastoral Maasai in Tanzania, points to the divine quality of women's natural procreative capacity (cf. also Spencer 1988). Among the Maasai, fertile women epitomize the creation of life (*enkishon*). Their mythical originator *Naiterukop*, a creature or "thing" (*entoki*) possessing both human and divine qualities, has a feminine singular relative prefix, *na-* (literally "she who begins the world"). The feminine gender of the originator is not merely a semantic coincidence, but expresses culturally constituted cognition of the female as "an originating source" (Hillman 1992). In spite of the feminine prefix, however, *Naiterukop* is often, both in the literature and by informants, portrayed in a masculine image.

There are several versions of this originating myth. In one *Naiterukop* is depicted as the first "man" who, by marrying two "women," becomes the founder of the two moieties, to which the five or seven (depending upon sources) Maasai clans belong (Århem 1991, Kipury 1983). Another account is of *Naiterukop* as a woman who descended from the sky and bore two sons, *Maasinda* and *olMeek*. Those two are associated with the origin of the Maasai and the Bantu peoples, respectively (Fosbrooke 1948). *Naiterukop* is even referred to as the one who dropped the hide rope from heaven and let cattle down, giving them to the Maasai and for ever separating the Ndorobo (hunter-gatherers) and the pastoralists (Hollis 1905).

Finally, Naiterukop is one of God's three sons and the one who fathered the Maasai (Saitoti 1980). In the mythological accounts, *Naiterukop* possesses both human and divine, female and male qualities, the two being simultaneous aspects of the same entity. The duality of the Maasai social order was cosmically laid down from the very beginning.

The word for God, *Enkai*, meaning rain or sky, is also etymologically feminine (prefix *en-*). God, however, while still being somehow like humankind (*oltungani*) is "not comparable to a man, a woman or a thing" (Hillman 1992: 354). God is two in one "just like a husband and a wife are one," or like a mother and a father (Wagner-Glenn 1992: 129). Although fixed in some objects (clouds, mountains, sacred groves, trees, sky), *Enkai* does not have a materiality. God is, rather, an essence or life-force that may be invoked by, for instance, individual women's morning prayers and offerings of the first drops of milk from the cows, or by collective prayers for children or by offerings of green grass and prayers at shrines.

Thus, Maasai informants often remained uncomprehending when asked about who God is. "You cannot know God" was a common answer, hinting at the irrelevance of the question, simultaneously conveying that God, who is beyond human comprehension, can neither be explained nor known, only experienced. It is in its inscrutability that God's power lies. God may give you diseases (typically, diseases which are ill-explained derive from God), even disasters such as drought and hunger (particularly if they come unexpectedly or are prolonged), but God can also bless you with rain, animals, and children. The "lucky" ones (*amunyak*, these days the emerging wealthy Maasai elite) are said to be favored by God.

The difference between *Enkai* and *Naiterukop* is somehow blurred; the one may be represented by the other (cf. Hollis 1905). *Naiterukop*, although divine-like, is not as great as God and, by having the ability to produce human issues, *Naiterukop* is a mediator between humans and the divine. In the same vein, women as the procreators of children, symbolically stand between God and man. The reproduction of life, being embodied in the birth of children and calves, the falling of rain and the growing of grass, phenomena enshrouded in mystery, are ultimately the creation of the divine. When Maasai pray, which they often do, and women more frequently than men, the references to God are many and may have both female and male images (Hillman 1992, Wagner-Glenn 1992), again alluding to the uniting or embracing quality or "greatness" (*enkitoo*) of divinity. By analogy women pray more often to *Enkai* in a female image and men through male images.

Semantics aside, the female precedence in Maasai cosmologies, through the figure of *Naiterukop* and the transformative power of *Enkai*, expresses the reverence and respect Maasai have for any procreative capacity. Even though informants may translate and conceptualize a female term with a male image, its etymological roots, given the concrete base of the Maasai language, nevertheless evoke a sense of primordial female creativity. Women are inherently fertile and life-giving, and as the main actors in perpetuating the biological and social life cycle (*olkesen*, Wagner-Glenn 1992:67), they may be likened to God.

As elders, men may also be likened to God. The moral pre-eminence they are endowed with as they age, brings them close to *Enkai*, who is the highest patron of the moral order. Barren women and young men are reversals; a woman who has not given birth to children is "like a wilderness" (Ahr 1991:98). She never matures fully and thus cannot be considered "morally upright" (Wagner-Glenn 1992:148). Young men, still playful and irrespon-sible, will eventually mature and attain the moral composure mandatory for procreation.

Barrenness is, in short, a personal tragedy for a woman, evi-denced by women's sexual excesses on fertility delegations, and their intense and loud voices in collective praying. Their dire fate can only be partly mitigated by adoption of a child from a fellow woman. Thus, spirit possession appears to be particularly preva-lent among infertile Maasai women (Hodgson 1994). Women's love for and nearness to children is ideologically so strong that they are ready to jeopardize the life and well-being of livestock (the means of existence and most precious property) to feed their children. In mythical times both men and women owned live-stock, but through mismanagement, carelessness and favoritism towards their offspring, women lost their animals to men (Talle 1988). Therefore, the cultural opposition between women : men :: children : livestock, is created and recreated at every milking time in any Maasai homestead.

House and Agency

The procreative power of women is practically and symbolically acted out in the house, a physical structure and cultural domain imbued with feminine qualities. To the Maasai, woman and house are so closely linked that semantically and conceptually they can substitute for one another. Maasai elders regularly refer to their wives by the term of the house. Both a metaphor and metonym for woman, the house embodies growth and fertility and, thus, is a place where "peace" (*eserian*, also "well-being" or "prosper-ity," for example in greetings) reigns. No fighting or words of abuse are permitted. Therefore, when husbands beat their wives, or brothers (*moran*) their sisters, they will never do so inside a house, conscious of the fact that the act of beating would contaminate the house which is a sanctuary of procreation.

The Maasai house is small (3 x 5 meters), has an oblong, igloo-like shape, and is constructed of poles, twigs and saplings and plastered with cow dung and mud. It is erected by the woman herself, and she is considered the "owner of the house" (*enopeny enkaji*). As only married—and potentially fertile—women have their own houses (a newly married woman stays with an older in-law until she has built her own house), the occupancy and ownership of houses is a sign of female maturity and is the base from which female agency is most successfully exercised. The house is "like an extra skin" (Carsten & Hugh-Jones 1995:2), at once protective and empowering, giving the woman authority to act. Even in old age women continue to occupy and control separate houses.

Wives of the same husband build their houses alternately, on either side of the gate leading into the homestead. Once a man has separated his herd from that of his father, he marks his autonomy and independence by building his own gate (*enkishomi*, also the term for lineage) in the thorn bush fence. The first wife starts building her house on the right side, the second wife on the left, and so on. Each woman becomes a potential founder of a new lineage segment, but the first and second wife, being the founders of the right-hand and left-hand gate-post sides (*intaloishin*), respectively, take a more prominent position than the younger ones in the segmentation process of the agnatic family (*olmarei*).[1]

Livestock property is channeled through the institution of the house by the transfer of management and utilization rights, which, upon the death of the father, are turned over to the full control of the sons of the house. This means that the animals belonging to the house, as a sub-unit of the family, cannot be disposed of freely, by the husband-cum-father, in spite of his formal control of the whole family herd. In the context of agnation, matrifiliation is

133

important, giving the "house" a semi-autonomous position within the family.

Besides its status as a property-holding group and social institution, the house is a setting of profound symbolic production. Spaces inside the house and in its immediate surroundings are invested with meanings, as people act upon them in their day-to-day and ceremonial activities (cf. Bourdieu 1977). The Maasai house, like the Berber house, has its female and male, profane and sacred, private and neutral, dangerous and safe, dark and light places. In terms of meanings, the spatial organization is not fixed, but is fluid and dynamic, ever changing during the activities of social actors.

The interior of the house is divided into four named sections: the "little bed" (*erruat kitii*), the "big bed" (*erruat kitok*), the sleeping place of small calves and kids (*olale*), and the hearth (*enkima*) in the open place between the two beds. The entrance to the house (*enkutuk aji*, "the mouth of the house") is a dark narrow passage leading into its center, the fireplace area. Rules of conduct and modal behavior circumscribe each of the two major sections, the little bed and the big bed. The little bed is for the exclusive use of the house-owner and is recognized as her private area; the innermost (*kejek*) part of the bed being more private than the front (*dukuya*) part. This is the place where the woman keeps her milk containers, beer pots if she has them, and various personal belongings as well as belongings of her husband. Furthermore, the little bed is the place where a woman gives birth and where she and her youngest children sleep. It is also where the girl sits, well hidden in the darkest corner, but attentively listening to the blessings and words of farewell offered by her father at the last family ceremony the night before she is taken away by her husband. These activities, and many others demarcate this part of the house as female space.

The "big bed," located opposite the little bed or alongside it, is for the husband, the older children, and visitors. It is a place where they eat, drink, gather, and sleep, representing male space inside the house. The big bed is also the place where sexual intercourse is supposed to take place (remembering that the initiative lies with the husband), although the little bed is sometimes used for this purpose. As indicated by the word, the big bed is more spacious than the little bed, and may for practical reasons be used when women deliver. Circumcision of girls is performed at the entrance, but always inside the house. At delivery and circumcision, both momentous events in the life of a woman, the house, acted upon by women and their activities, becomes, in such occasions, a total female space.

Traditionally, the husband does not have a private space within the house or elsewhere, as women *do*, adding of course to the overall "femininity" of the house. Money, letters, photos, clothes, or any other valuables that a man cannot wear on his body, in a purse around the neck, or tucked into his toga, he hands to his wife for safe-keeping. The following incident illustrates the legitimacy and potential of control allocated to women as owners and occupiers of houses.

> A man with three wives had attended a condom promotion meeting held by AIDS workers in the area. At the end of the meeting the participants were given some condoms to bring home and try at their convenience. Upon getting home, the man left the condoms with his senior wife, telling her that they were medicine for the goats (he did not want to tell her the truth lest they get into arguments) and asked her to keep them in a safe place. "But I was very unfortunate," he lamented, because his wife had attended a similar meeting previously without his awareness, so she knew perfectly well about condoms and recognized the packages. She became very upset and asked him whether he wanted to use them on her. If so, she would have to take the case to her family. The husband pleaded with his wife, managing eventually to convince her that he had been given them by the "AIDS people" without an explicit intention of using them.

The purpose and fulfillment of conjugal sexuality is children. Thus, the moral obligation of a husband to impregnate his wife is as strong as the wife's obligation to conceive, no matter how ugly they find, or how much they dislike, each other. The sexual act between husband and wife is always performed inside the house, which, due to its peaceful and safe surrounding, is a propitious place of procreation. In contrast, children conceived by lovers are often referred to as children of the "fireplace" (*oleng'oti*, fireplace outside the homestead).

The woman, referred to in the example above, took great offense at the fact that the husband brought those condoms into her house. Inauspicious for fertility, the condoms would not only pollute the sanctity of her house as a site of prosperity and growth, but potentially they also could deny her the man's semen, which to her is the main benefit of conjugal sexuality, evidenced not least by the demonstrative lack of sexual interest women past menopause show. "What 'profit' is there in sex at this age?" they say, with quite some surprise at my questioning. Accordingly, about this time in their aging process and development cycle of the family, women separate from their husbands to live with one of their sons and his family.

The fact that Maasai women are often more opposed to condom promotion than men may reveal a "secret discourse" (Herdt 1993: 198) acknowledging women's capacity to act as inherent in their faculty of procreation.

Seniority and Maleness

In the anthropological literature, East African pastoral societies of Nilotic heritage provide prototypes of agnatic descent systems (having momentously influenced anthropological theorizing, cf. Parkin 1990), and of age-organized societies, of which the Maasai constitute an exemplary case (Jacobs 1965, Spencer 1965; of less impact than descent on general anthropology, see Parkin 1990; Spencer 1988).

The coining of the Samburu, linguistically and culturally closely related to Maasai but inhabiting a drier area further north in Kenya, as a "gerontocratic society" (Spencer 1965) underscores the political as well as spiritual and moral precedence of older men over young men, and over women, the latter being on a par with junior men concerning decision-making power. The age-based hierarchy between men is simultaneously a gender stratification (cf. Llewelyn-Davis 1981).

Accounts of the Maasai, generally, elaborate on their age organization, vis-a-vis the initiation and promotion of age-sets through the various age-grades: boys (*olayioni.*, pl. *ilayiok*); circumcised men/"warriors" (*olmurrrani*, pl. *ilmurran*), married men/elders (*olmoruo*, pl. *ilmoruak*, e.g. Jacobs 1965, Llewelyn-Davis 1981, Spencer 1988). Moreover, the strikingly colorful Maasai "warriors" and the spectacular ceremonies linked to the ritualized maturity cycle of Maasai men, from circumcision in the upper teens to graduation into social elderhood some fifteen years later, are among the most glorious and elaborated cultural events in Maasai society, collecting people from all over Maasailand and beyond.

Recently, the moran period has been shortened considerably in many areas; emerging systemic changes, however, were already observed several decades back (Fosbrooke 1948). The mustering of resources (slaughter animals, milk, honey-beer) required for the fulfillment of the ceremonies appears to be beyond the means and organizational capacity of the ever pauperized Maasai community. In addition, increased education and modern aspirations among pastoral Maasai have had adverse effects on the continuation of this system.

The age-grade system, privileging seniority, is a structural principle that permeates all social relations in Maasai society and, furthermore, is the conceptual cog on which the normative male hierarchy hinges. Aside from the division of labor, dietary preferences, and rules of appropriate conduct, the system, most importantly, regulates sexual and marriage relations.

Of particular concern is the relationship between married (young) women and *moran*. The latter are prohibited from eating meat seen by married women lest they be polluted; likewise they are prohibited from having sexual relations with them. Even those few *moran* who sometimes get married while they are still in seclusion in their own settlements (*emanyata*, pl. *imanyat*), often refuse to have sexual intercourse with their wives until they have terminated moranhood. Married women, in general, are considered to be "dangerous" for the moran, mainly because sexual relations with such women will make them enfeebled or "lazy" (*ashalu*). Thus, intimate interaction between married women and *moran* is a severe breach of age-set morals and if detected, which happens as they occur rather frequently, is heavily penalized.

There is, however, one exception to this prohibition. In certain cases elderly men send their barren wives to the *moran* settlements to be impregnated. That happens, particularly, when the *moran* leave their "meat-camps" in the bush (*olpul*). During such period, lasting for two to three weeks, the *moran* devour large quantities of slaughtered meat, and they are considered to be very strong and sexually potent. It is said that their sperms have become "hot" (*airowua*), and that their bodies have been invigorated by the nutritious food, coupled with sexual abstinence during the camp period. The "ritualized" sexual confrontation between married women and *moran* on such instances embodies, for the Maasai, a transformative capacity of extraordinary potential.

Despite their physical ability, Maasai men are not considered to be sufficiently mature to control (*aitore*) productive and reproductive resources, such as livestock, women, and children, until they have reached the "elder" age-grade and thereby acquired the self-control, personal discipline, and moral integrity which are are considered necessary to handle those tasks. Conversely, the state of moranhood (*emurano*) is associated with play and leisure, demonstrative virility and fighting courage.

Women are not structurally integrated into the age-set system, since they are not divided into formal, corporate age-groups, but are affiliated with the age-sets into which they are married or the warrior set with which they danced and engaged in sex as young girls. Socially, women get their "age" (*olaji*, is masculine of *enkaji*, house) from men. There is, though, a clear distinction in status between girl (*ndito*), young married woman (*esiankiki*), and mother (*entasat*), a division analogous to the male age-grades. By not being divided into age-sets, however, women are excluded from the control of productive and reproductive resources; they never reach the "age" or the moral maturity whereby they might possess livestock, or have full control of their own bodies and procreative capacities.

Ideologically, then, women never mature to the same degree as men. One educated Maasai woman recounted how her always supportive old father when praising her for her intelligence and courage, which he often did, would end his praise by gazing at her, deploringly stating "but you are only a woman." To him her gender was a limitation to her full growth as a moral person. The generic moral "weakness" of women is primarily associated with their lack of "socialization" into age-set ethics and the *moran* community. The few Maasai men who have not participated in age-group activities are likewise said to be "ignorant" and wanting in the sense of solidarity and male virtues. For such reasons, Maasai school-boys notoriously beseech the company of *moran* during their school holidays.

The hierarchical relationship between senior and junior men is culturally enacted in the "fire-stick" relationship (*olpiron*), established at the circumcision of a boy. When the operation is over, a fire is lit in the cattle corral by elders belonging to the second age-set above the one being initiated. They are the sponsoring elders of the new age-set and will lead, guide, and control the initiates through moranhood and into fully-fledged elderhood beyond their final graduation ceremony. The act of fire-making and the subsequent blessing, whereby the elders claim the initiates as their "sons," express the structural link and emotional tie between alternate age-sets. Thus, the father-son metaphor constitutes anteriority as a guiding principle also in age-set relations.

Fire-making is symbolically associated with copulation and male progenitive capacity, the firestick which is drilled into a soft piece of wood being the male element in the fire-making. Permission to make fire in this specific way is linked structurally with the control of sexual relations and thus fertility. Uncircumcised boys, including the newly circumcised, and women, are not allowed to make fire by firesticks[2] or to initiate sexual intercourse. Maasai men claim that if they allow boys and women to make fire, they will soon be controlled by them (Jacobs 1965). The authority to make fire, a prime transformative agent, symbolically endows elders with the legitimacy to control female procreative capacity as well as the virile powers of young men.

Three important age-grade ceremonies of the male maturity cycle are worth mentioning here: *empolasat* (beginning, initiation into moranhood, after recovering from circumcision), *eunoto* (promotion into senior moranhood) and *olongesherr* (passing out of moranhood). The *olpiron* elders together with age-set leaders are responsible for the timing, procedure, and arrangement of these ceremonies. In terms of practical work, the efforts are quite substantial. A recurrent ritual theme of all age-set ceremonies is the transition from a junior to a senior state, given expressive form in rebirths and fertility symbols.

Despite being at the periphery of age-set politics, women are focal ceremonial figures nonetheless. Their social positions as mothers and wives bring them into the ceremonies at very vital points, for example by mothers shaving their beloved sons at *eunoto*. The removal of hair, always performed by married women, is a central symbolic act in many rites of passage in a person's life (birth, circumcision, woman in confinement, age-set initiates). Maasai women, most significantly by producing and nurturing offsprings, are "natural symbols" of prosperity and growth. In age-set ritual contexts the "feminine," representing the capacity to multiply, expresses fertility in a very fundamental way. For example, newly circumcised boys wear female ornaments (*surutya* brass coils worn by women who have given birth, likening the young men to women in confinement) as a sign of

140

their initiation into reproductive status. The official at the *moran*'s retirement ceremony, *olongesherr*, is called *losurutya*, the one with *surutya*, an emblem of fertility and growth, which is a ritual position of deep respect (Fosbrooke 1948:40; Jacobs 1965). The cattle corral surrounding the ceremonially built house, *osingira*, at the *eunoto* ceremony contains only female animals. Irrespective of the powerful blessings of *olpiron* elders, for men to advance and to be reborn as age-set members and reach maturity, such ritual action must be enacted by a ceremonial female.

Growing by Bodily Marking

Circumcision (*emurata*) for boys and clitoridectomy for girls (also *emurata*) are momentous events of their maturing into social and gendered persons. As soon as the operation is done, the boys are called to wake up, "you are now a man." A girl who dies before she is circumcised, is referred to as *endorrop sesen* ("short body"), a designation emphasizing her bodily (and moral) immaturity. Until the surgical intervention has been done on their bodies, both boys and girls are irrevocably "children."

Maasai tend to look upon all men who are not circumcised the Maasai way as "boys." For example, non-Maasai, collectively known as *ilmeek* or *swahili*, categorically remain "children." In an uncircumcised state, the male person is "unclean" (*entorrono*, "bad") and prohibited from involving himself in sexual relations with circumcised women. Females, on the other hand, may have sex even when they are not circumcised, but they must not reproduce, and, as "children" should not give birth to children. Should a girl become pregnant before her circumcision she is operated upon and married away immediately, not necessarily to the one who impregnated her.

After circumcision and initiation into moranhood, the legitimate sex partners of the *moran* are prepubescent girls from ten years and onwards. The *moran* and the girls meet to sing, dance, and have sex in houses (*eosoto*) of the homesteads (before, more commonly, in the settlements of the *morans*) specifically assigned

141

for this purpose, or at shady places in the bush. The *eosoto* house belongs to one of the *morans'* mothers, who continues to occupy the house also when the young people assemble. In fact, she plays a supervisory and advisory role at these meetings.

Labeled as "play" (*aiguran*), the penetration or opening of a girl, is considered to be the work of the *moran*. It is usually done gradually, beginning when the girl is still quite small, but not consummated till she is considered sufficiently mature. The decision as to the girl's readiness for penetration is taken by the mothers in collaboration with the *moran*. Depending upon her physical constitution and the size of her body, the adult women, who check the girls, will direct the *moran* as to how far they may penetrate in a given case. The girls, on their side, comply with being penetrated, not without fear or anger sometimes, but because they know that the making of their "hole" (*audo*, euphemistically "door," *enkishomo*) opens their way to birthing, and finally, social adulthood. Most commonly, girls are penetrated by their chosen boyfriends, but if a girl does not have a boyfriend and is considered big enough for penetration, it will be done forcefully on her. Three or four of the *morans* hold the girl while another penetrates her. The mother, also participating, sometimes helps to hold a stubborn girl (*ndito sero* literally "bush girl" indicating lack of domestication in a moral sense).

It is the responsibility and work of the *moran* and their mothers to ascertain that a girl is properly prepared for marriage, most importantly that her virginity is broken. Traditionally, a virgin bride is sent back to her natal family and her father will have to compensate the husband with a heifer for the misdemeanor. Amongst the Maasai a virgin bride is looked upon as an awkward phenomenon. Her bodily "defect" signals lack of proper upbringing, which is an embarrassment to her own family. By not having a "door" (*meeta enkishomo*), she is considered a "child," an immature person who is not ready for marriage or procreation. To send such a girl is a great offense to the elder who has married her.

Among the Maasai, as noted, the door or gate into the homestead is a male symbol of maturity and independence. The opening of the girl then could be seen as an inscription of male attributes which is a precondition for growing. A bride's virginity may also signify that she is what the Maasai refer to as an *esinoni* (male *olosinoni*), that is a person who has no luck with (or interest in) the opposite sex. The destiny of such a person is not bright within Maasai society, as sexual willingness both on the part of men and women is conceptually linked to the capacity of producing children.

Maasai elders voice strong views against penetrating virgin brides. They hold it to be the work of the *moran*, an age-grade which is closely associated with puerile behavior, playfulness and irresponsibility. In their adult and responsible position it would be highly immoral for elders to impregnate "children." They would not only go against fundamental moral preferences, but in the act they would become *moran* as a result, reversing the age-based order, from which ultimately the wider social order is constituted.

The Maasai have a rationale for women's early sexual debut. They claim that the semen (*olkirati*) of the *moran* helps. In fact, according to the Maasai, semen is almost a prerequisite for girls, in order to gain 'health' and develop their breasts (working on an analogy between semen and mother's milk), which is the major physical sign for the timing of their circumcision and subsequent growing into maturity. "You have become fat because of our sperm," the *moran* tell the girls. Male vigor and vitality, contained in the semen of the young energetic *moran*, do not only enable barren women to conceive, but also it also helps girls to mature and achieve fertility.

Circumcision, the excision of clitoris (*emuoo*: "horn") and labia minora, is the last step in the "opening" or maturity process. By paring away the outer flesh, the female genitals get an "open" look, a bodily mark differentiating between a fertile female and a girl. Girls are a sign of infertility; in prayers women ask *Enkai* to bring them out of the girl (barren) status (Wagner-Glenn 1992). When a girl is excised her marriage is already arranged for, and she is brought to her husband's home within a few months after the surgical intervention.

As newly circumcised, the girl (*enkaibartani*, "the one who is looked after," synonymous to *olaibartani*, newly circumcised males) is dressed in black cotton sheets, smeared with fat, wearing dark blue ("black") beads and a cowrie-shell wreath (*olmariasian*) around her head, all insignia of fertility, and she leads a rather secluded and protected family life. Her wreath has chain strings in front, partly covering the upper part of her face and protecting her from other's gazes. Being in a vulnerable state, a newly circumcised girl should not be "seen." She spends most of her time with the married women of the homestead and is not permitted to attend the dances and meetings of the *moran* anymore, but she may associate herself with the newly circumcised young men, who are in the same kind of liminal state as herself.

Elderhood and Fertility

After *eunoto*, the promotion ceremony to senior *moran*, the young men return to their family homes and begin to prepare themselves for the ritual of "drinking milk" (*eokoto ekule*), which in many places among the Maasai is performed in the house of the *moran*'s mother. It is at this event that the young man, for the first time since his circumcision several years before, sits down alone and drinks milk without the companionship of age-mates. The milk-drinking ceremony is primarily a blessing of maturity and, consequently, symbols of seniority, such as placement at the right hand side, and the display of dark blue (or black) colors, have a prominent place in the ritual (Talle 1988).

Besides the young man, the major actors in the ritual are the mother and the mother's brother (of the alternate age-set). Once, I drove a *moran* more than 100 kms to fetch his mother, who had run away from her husband's homestead a few years back and had since lived in the homestead of a half-brother. Her participation in the ritual was seen as imperative. The mother willingly followed us, now reassured of her strengthened position in her husbands's homestead by her son growing into independence.

At the milk-drinking ceremony, the mother's brother prepares the "milk" (i.e., a mixture of fresh and sour milk, honey, beer and water) to be drunk. The following morning, he also gives a blessing of prosperity and luck to his sister's son, in the cattle corral, and after the drinking ritual.

Because mothers' brothers are basically benevolent towards their sisters' children, their blessing is held to be very effective, in much the same way as their curse is said to be extremely potent. The mother shaves her son and sprinkles "blue" (i.e., blessed) water onto his cattle, while the father's participation is less visible in the ritual. Milk and mothers are inseparable concepts; women nurse children and milk the cows. After this ceremony the senior *moran* is socially mature enough to marry and to begin to orient himself towards family life again, but now as the potential procreator and head of a family.

However, before a man can count himself as a proper elder within the age-set system, further ceremonies are obligatory. He must also be released from the prohibition against eating meat alone and against eating meat in front of women. The most important of these is the *olongesherr* (cf. above), which formally promotes the *moran* age-sets into the junior elder grade and is, in fact, the final age-set ceremony of any significance. In his position as junior elder, a Maasai man has reached the height of his structural power and may now become *olpiron* or sponsoring elder for a younger age-set.

Olongesherr, also called *enkang olorikan* ("stool homestead"), is the ceremony when a man receives his personal branding iron (*olmishire*), which is the sign of the extensive property rights to livestock bestowed on him as a full-grown and responsible Maasai man. On this occasion he also acquires the right to wear a tobacco container and a flywhisk, as well as other attributes of male seniority.

Before a mother and father are able to circumcise their first child, two important ceremonies must be performed to mark their stage in the aging process: the transfer of *inkishu enkapute* ("cattle of the in-laws"), and the *olkiteng loolbaa* ("steer of wounds"). The *inkishu enkapute* is often referred to as the formal marriage transaction and is what Maasai informants often mean by bridewealth. A woman for whom these cattle have been paid is called *esainoti*, meaning she has been properly married according to customs. The *inkishu enkapute* normally consists of three heads of cattle (two heifers, one steer) and a young ewe, and some honey, but the composition may vary slightly from one local area to another and between families.

The transaction is obligatory and the "goods" should be transferred to the woman's kin before the first child is circumcised. It cannot be put off till the circumcision of a younger child, but has to follow the succession of birth, or the family may face misfortune. The distribution of the animals among in-laws of the husband is more or less prescribed and it follows principles of agnatic descent, matrifiliation and seniority. The transfer is accompanied by a minor ceremony, *errikoto oo nkishu* ("taking away with livestock"), in which the woman is married to her husband for a second time. After the transfer of these animals, the marriage can never be formally dissolved. Any children born to the woman after the "cattle of the in-law" have been delivered belong to the husband and his lineage, irrespective of whether the woman actually remains with her husband or not or whether the husband is dead or alive. By this transaction paternity is irrevocably sealed.

As the agnates of the wife drive the animals away from the homestead, the woman sits outside on the branch (*oltim*) which closes the gate to the homestead. She is dressed in ceremonial clothes and her body is ritually smeared with fat and ochre. She carries three milk calabashes on her back (the same number as when she married for the first time) and holds a bamboo stick in her hand.

This ritual is something of a duplication of the first marriage ceremony, but with significant differences. The sitting on the *oltim* indicates that this homestead and its lineage are the woman's permanent home. The calabashes are the symbol of prosperity (that she will have them full with milk), and the bamboo stick symbolizes honor (elderhood) and signifies that she will have animals to rear (the stick is a main attribute of a livestock owner and is usually carried by men). After this ceremony the woman is recognized as a mature and responsible person. Her adult status is expressed by masculine attributes: the branch which closes the homestead gate (a male area in the homestead) and the stick.

Socially, the ritual of "taking away with animals" may be compared with *olkiteng loolbaa*, which is obligatory for men before they circumcise their first child. An unblemished, black steer is slaughtered outside the homestead and a ritual is performed whereby the man is "born anew," cleansed of his former "mistakes" and sins, and reincorporated into family life. Among other things, he is seated on the stomach of the slaughtered animal with his senior wife, an act efficaciously signifying husband and wife as equal parts of one whole (this is generally how Maasai evaluate husband and wife as parents).

There is another aspect of this ceremony in particular which interests us here. That is the ritual fight between men and women for the roasted meat of the beast. The right and left side of the steer are divided between men and women respectively, but, before they may begin to eat the meat, the age-group into which the man and the women have married begins a mock "fight for the meat skewers" (*aurro ilmodat*). Everyone tries to take as many skewers, as possible, and it is customary not always for men to win, emphasizing the fact that some women are very brave and courageous when fighting men. Women and men are considered equal in this situation, hence they may fight each other with sticks. The contextual equality between women and men in this particular ritual is based upon the acknowledgement that they are both parents of the child being circumcised, and in that capacity they are held to be of equal status, members of a pair.

The rituals of *errikoto oo inkishu* and *olkiteng loolbaa* convey a change in social growth for women and men, respectively. They are becoming full adults as parents, but also members of the domestic unit. They have reached the final destination of their gender positions in terms of social status. The "taking away with cattle" ritual emphasizes affinal relations, in which the married woman is a mediating link and conveys rights of descent to her progeny, which are vested in her husband's lineage. Therefore, through this ceremony, the woman takes an important step away from her own family in the direction of that of her husband and sons.

The "steer of wounds" has a ritual focus on age-set and gender relations. The man is released from the ties of his age-set and moves more towards the domain of family life, so that the structural inequality between husband and wife gradually becomes weaker as they mature as parents.

Conclusion

In Maasai culture, aging is represented as a fertility process, codified in concepts of growth and prosperity. The ability to procreate and multiply, cosmologically expressed as a female quality, is gendered masculine through the organization of hierarchical age-sets. Nevertheless, it must be enacted through female bodies and feminine symbols. As sponsoring elders, men "give birth" to men, and as *moran*, they "create" procreative females. Women, inherently fertile, similarly can only age and mature through a bodily and symbolic inscription of male attributes. Thus, it appears that the complementarity between Maasai women and men surfaces particularly clearly in rituals of aging.

NOTES

1. Normally, Masaai men do not have separate houses within the homestead, but circulate among their wives' (or "mothers" in case of unmarried men) houses. Wealthy men, however, have begun to build their own modern houses within the homestead. This practice, which I have discussed elsewhere (Talle 1988), has proven to have profound consequences for female-male relations

as well as spatial organization.

2.   Women, however, rekindle and make fire by matches. They may also make fire by firesticks, if for instance they come upon a dead or sick animal in the bush, which must be slaughtered and its meat roasted. It is the ritual firemaking (*airpun*, "to originate") that is prohibited for women.

Chapter 5

Youth, Maturity, Aging, and Ancestors in the Society of Masks

❖

Laurel Birch de Aguilar

Paul Spencer can rightfully claim to have contributed significantly
to the literature on two important topics: age and dance. Yet the
two remain separate themes as exemplified in his two books,
Society and the Dance (1985a), and *Anthropology and the Riddle
of the Sphinx* (1990a). Taking these two topics together, I support Spencer's assertion that "society creates the dance, and it is
to society that we must turn to understand it" (1985:38). I would
further add that concepts about age are interpreted and constructed

in social contexts, and that the dance re-interprets and re-constructs those concepts of age within society.

If masked performances are society, and not merely its symbolic parallel, as Kasfir (1988) suggests, then masks and the study of masks should reveal insights into society as much as society reveals insights into masked performance. This essay examines the premise that masks are the visible images of ideas and concepts in society and, particularly in this essay, ideas and concepts about age. Not only age, but social roles, hierarchy, historical changes, levels of knowledge, and initiation associated with age are all enacted and made apparent in masked performance.

Paul Spencer lays out theoretical considerations in the development of age as a theme in anthropology. He emphasizes age as a social process rather than a static condition. We all age, and we all experience aging. In this "life course" of changing relationships, roles, and positions of authority, he sees a process which "provides a changing and hence ambiguous element that lends itself to various levels of interpretation ..." (1990b:2). I suggest that masked performance is also subject to various levels of interpretation. Interpretations about age in masking are varied and complex. In this essay, certain aspects of masked performance are like mirrors of society as masks, performance and the social process of aging comment upon one another, adding one level of interpretation on to another, leading to a larger understanding of aging in Chewa society.

Age is not a tangible thing. There are signs associated with aging, and social constructions which are triggered by certain "coming of age" processes. People who grow old change in appearance, and children grow up and mature, associating adulthood with physical bodily changes. These signs of age are present in all societies and, as suggested by Baxter and Almagor, "age-grading, whether formally marked by a rite of passage or merely tacitly recognized, is probably universal" (1978: 1). But how we conceptualize "age" is significantly different from one social context to another. In the case of the Chewa masked performance in Malawi, social processes of age extend from pubescent maturity, child-bearing and rearing, senior statuses in society, and elder status, past death, and recognition as an ancestor. Age and maturity, wisdom and teaching in life, do extend into a stronger, more powerful presence in death.

Background

The Chewa people in the central region of Malawi are mostly rural people, living in villages under the authority of a local Chief, and a regional Paramount Chief. Villages consist primarily of female kin, mothers and their children, daughters, aunts, grandmothers, all related to an ancestress; and their husbands who marry into their wive's villages. The ancestress may be living or dead, but the village is usually no more than five generations deep in memory of one single ancestress. Chiefs are most commonly a brother or son of the eldest woman, or women in the village. As in all kinship systems, this is an idealized model, and actual practices vary depending on individual circumstance.

Malawi is located near the equator, but the central region rests on a high plateau at the base of the Rift Valley, making the climate quite temperate and even cool, with dramatically defined seasons of rains and dryness. These seasonal changes mark the seasonal activities of masked performances and are part of the construction of knowledge in masked initiations and creation mythology.

Masked dances are prepared in the dry season for the most elaborate events: the remembrance of those most senior people who have died, and the initiation dances for girls and for boys. Masked dances are also performed for the death of any initiated member of the community, which, of course, can occur any time of the year and may be quite sudden.

Nyau Society

Young people are initiated into the *Nyau* society, a name with a wide semantic range, including all those who undergo initiation, the society of which individuals and whole communities are members, the mask, the masked dancer, the performance event, all associated with the secretive knowledge.[1] Only those initiated into *Nyau* may participate in the masked performances known as *Gule Wamkulu*, the Great Dance, ("Great" as in mature, fully grown, full in stature and, correspondingly, of age).

Nyau seems to be both noun and adjective, descriptive and substantive, at the same time, in the same sentences; for example:

> Those *Nyau* people. It is a *nyau* (pointing to a masked dancer). They practice *Nyau*. He is one of them—he is *Nyau*.

Initiated members of *Nyau* can identify one another from different village regions a hundred kilometers apart. With shared knowledge learned in initiation (certain gestures, hummed rhythms, and secretive words associated with everyday objects), *Nyau* members can easily identify fellow members in any town. This seems to be particularly true for young and middle-aged men who migrate from different village regions to the towns for work. Urban non-members have described this secretive communication as something they see happening and have expressed fear that a group of *Nyau* members may approach them and learn they are not members.

Nyau is also a term which identifies individuals and whole villages as those who claim to maintain the religious practices of their ancestors, as opposed to those who have adopted Christianity as their primary religious practice. Villages have been split by these identifications, with separate graveyards for Christians and *Nyau* members. People identify *Nyau* with religious practices concerning masks and masked events, ancestors, *mzimu* or spirits of the deceased, secretive knowledge and initiation and, indeed, concepts of age regarding these practices.

Initiation: Experience, Knowledge and Maturity

People may be initiated into *Nyau* at any time of life. The most common initiation in a *Nyau* village is at about the time of puberty. A young man undergoes several days in the wooded graveyard, secluded from the village (Birch de Aguilar 1996), and a young woman will undergo a much longer period of time between the initiation house in the village and a secluded place in the fields or in rock shelters in the mountains. The masked dance performed at the conclusion of training the young person acknowledges that the initiate is now an adult and is entering the society as a mature person. A grown man or a woman with children and even an elderly man or woman who has not been initiated may still be referred to as "young," not mature, and one who "has not grown." Initiation marks maturity, the fact of growth, the ripening like the maize, coming into full stature in life (*kukulu, kukula*). As I was told over and over again, those who have been initiated into *Nyau*, through the approaching and touching and even entering inside the dreaded and feared masks, have experienced an event no one outside *Nyau* has ever experienced.

Two masks are central to the initiation event. For the boys, that mask is known as *Kasiyamaliro* (to leave the funeral behind). For the girls, that mask is *Njobvu* (elephant). Initiation is partly about maturing bodies and the learning about sexual matters to promote fertility and potency and to encourage socially proper sexual conduct. Boys learn about women; girls learn about men.

The large antelope mask is made in female form[2] for the initiation of boys into adulthood. The *Kasiyamaliro* mask form for initiation is that of a mature female, a mother. Boys enter into the antelope mask form, which is likened to the womb. The mask is described as beautiful, a womb, a pregnant woman; it is mature rather than youthful or very elderly. The form is like a mature woman; strong, intelligent, potentially dangerous, sexually potent and ripe, a mother and ancestress, requiring proper respect,

155

the source of food and sustenance, and—being white-colored—the source of all life.

Girls are initiated through the grasping of the elephant's tusks. *Njobvu* is associated with the power of chiefs, the leaders of society and defenders of the village against enemies (including witches and the supernatural), standing in full stature of life. The mask is described as masculine, virile, sexually potent, very strong, potentially dangerous, intelligent, dark-colored, and powerful. *Njobvu* is the highest mask form in the hierarchy of masks, is like an ancestor, and commands respect. It represents maturity, knowledge, and the ability to father many children.

In initiation lessons, the adolescent boy or girl learns to respect those who are older and in more senior positions. Though they, too, may now be physically and knowledgeably capable of producing children, the mask forms in their initiation represent women and men who are older than they, who are more mature than they, who have already borne or sired children, who are in positions of authority and respect, and are their teachers and leaders.

Masked Dancers and Age

Only men make and wear masks. Only women answer the songs of the masked dancer. The most senior men, such as the chief and the *Wakunjira* who organizes *Nyau* events; and the most senior women, such as chiefs,[3] and the *Namkungwi* or teacher and advisor to the chief, may be present in either the boys or the girls initiations, and are formally instructed in both male and female knowledge.

The hierarchical structure of mask genre[4] is easily translated into the age of the dancer. Those men who are newly initiated wear masks which are lower in the overall hierarchy of mask genre. No young initiate would be allowed to perform *Njobvu*, which is reserved for chiefs. Men wearing the mask genre *Chadzunda*, I was told, must be more than thirty-five years in age (the average life expectancy of a rural Malawian in the 1980s was mid-forty). Masks made of cloth, feathers and/or hide were acceptable for younger men, and young initiates wore costumes of cloth or feathered masks, with banana leaves or rags covering the body. The carved wooden masks were worn by those with resources to own one, and only certain genre depicting youth were allowed for younger men.

Antelope Masks: Three Generations

Age, status, and specific roles are all criteria of the relative importance of mask genre. Masks depicting youth are less important, authoritative, powerful or respected, than those which depict maturity.

Among the woven antelope mask forms, *Kasiyamaliro*, both male and female, are considered mature. Their movements involve great skill and even elegance. On the other hand, the smaller versions of *Kasiyamaliro*, which perform in the night dances, are described as reckless, aggressive, aimless, energetic. These are most likely to lose control and rush into the crowds of people, scattering people and knocking over chairs of the honored guests (including my own) and senior people present. The "young" and "youthful" mask forms were half the size of the tall mature forms. Dancers in the mature forms stand to dance, while the smaller forms required the dancers to either bend the back over, squat or even crawl.

For certain very elaborate occasions, such as the remembrance of the death of a male chief or female *Namkungwi*, a larger version of *Kasiyamaliro* is made. One remembrance performance I witnessed contained a dozen dancers in its length of more than twenty feet. This mask is known as *Chimkoko* (literally translated as "the large banana bunch," but having a secretive translation as well), the greatest of the antelope and animal forms. The performance of this mask required the ability of those within to move as one: forward, undulating, stopping, stepping backward, and moving forward, undulating again. The movements were described to me in comparison with the mature and youthful forms.

Chimkoko is the *agogo*, the grandmother, the ancestress or the ancestor, the great elder who moves with caution, slower, more deliberate, with great skill.

Carved Masks: Society, Age and Role

Masks are made according to certain canons or rules. Each genre of masking is recognizable because certain formal elements are present. In making the masked image of age, certain genres are invoked, each of which appeals to certain social conventions which make the concept of age recognizable.

One mask genre, *Chadzunda*, depicts the village chief. The formal elements which clearly indicate this mask form include the color, which is black; the costume which includes chiefly elements such as the fly whisk and animal hide (preferably leopard, but commonly serval or even civet); and (perhaps most important visually) the defined signs of age, such as carved wrinkles in the forehead, the appearance of baldness, and white or grey hairs.

The visible masks are only one sign of age; Movement is another, intended characterization yet another. The dancer's expert movements reveal intentions without sound. Satire, humor, promiscuity, anger, rivalry and conflict, as well as age are indicated by even the most simple and subtle gestures. The flip of the hand, the toss of the head, all reveal insights into the dancer's intended characterization.

Performative elements also indicate the *Chadzunda* mask genre, including the way the dancer enters the dance space, specific drum rhythms associated with this mask genre, and particular dance movements. *Chadzunda* enters the *bwalo* or dance space without guidance or permission, unlike most other lesser mask genres. A common dance performance by *Chadzunda* masked dancers involves a mock rivalry and fight, the chief defending the village, fighting a rival chief, though the characterization may also indicate the frailty of age; Rangeley (1949) points out how one dancer of a chief's mask pretends to be an old deaf man.

When a cluster of these formal elements are present, the audience can easily recognize that the masked dancer is depicting *Chadzunda*, a chief. Each *Chadzunda* is created with the intention of portraying age as one of the criteria of this particular form: a middle-aged and aging man, mature, and in a position of authority.

The person who controls the village community is not only the chief and his wife, but the senior ancestress and *Namkungwi*. The eldest grandmother is the focus of any Chewa village. Those who live in the village are her female relatives—sisters, daughters, granddaughters, and nieces—who bring their husbands to live with them. The chief, who is most often male (though not necessarily so), is the eldest grandmother's brother, son, or grandson. The husbands who marry into the village respect the elder grandmother as the ancestress, and work for her in her gardens proving themselves as worthy sons-in-law, earning the right to remain in the village—or, in some cases, to take one's wife with him to live elsewhere, if she chooses to accompany him.

The ancestress is important in age due to her ability to form an extended family into her own village. Her descendants form a village in her name, and her daughters and granddaughters will live in the village with her, inheriting the right to choose their own chief. Only senior mature women related to the common ancestress are chosen to be present in the selection of a Chief for their village, and that selection meeting occurs in the house of the eldest grandmother.

The senior grandmother, the ancestress, is portrayed in the dance in either youth or age, but in either case, the mask is made in her presumed likeness after her death. The formal elements of the female mask include the color red, as opposed to the black color of the Chief's mask, and in the case of respected senior women, the mask is made with scarification marks. Scarification marks are signs of belonging, identity with a specific group, and becoming a social person, one who has been taught, rather than one who knows nothing (Vogel 1986). The mask will be crowned with feathers and animal hide, and the expression will be one of serious demeanor.[5]

A woman is depicted in youth, as one mask-maker (mask-makers are male) said, to remember her beauty; but also to remember her when she was in her child-bearing years, a time of great importance and reverence for Chewa women. The bearing of children is a mark of wisdom, a passage of female knowledge and experience, and a sign of having achieved maturity.

Those senior women who become *Namkungwi*, the eldest grandmother, and the chief's wife all receive specialized instruction in both male and female knowledge in order to assume these important roles. Those who teach this secretive knowledge are those most senior chiefs, *Namkungwi*, and *Nyau* leaders who have shown the greatest ability to interpret cosmology and the ways of society. Men who have achieved elder status (roles of age and wisdom) hold leadership positions in the organization of masked performances (*Wakunjira*), and those who become chiefs are also given special instruction in both male and female knowledge.

Those men and women who have assumed the most responsible, demanding, and socially recognized roles of power, hierarchical control, and knowledge are also those men and women who have attained their status at least partially through age. The ancestress and the elders are specifically age-related social roles, while the roles of chief and *Namkungwi* are given only to those chosen by the most senior (and older) women.[6]

Age, Youth, and the Immature

Age and position also indicate the social tensions between youth and the keepers of position, status, comparative wealth, respect, and authority. Age and behavior associated with age may be more important than social position, in certain instances. The social role of chief is usually marked by the portrait of a deceased chief being rendered into the mask genre *Chadzunda*. In one particular case, a chief died, and his portraiture was rendered into a more youthful mask genre known as *N'gan'gandi*.

A man was selected to be chief at a relatively young age, and he died as a mature but relatively young man. He was known as a very handsome man, well-liked by the women. Though he held the social position of chief in life, his character was thought to be more closely related to the sexually attractive, virile and potent but also less powerful mask genre *N'gan'gandi*. *N'gan'gandi* was interpreted by the man who made this particular portrait mask as being like an eldest son of the Chief, or younger brother of the Chief, neither in line to be Chief themselves.[7]

Regardless of the man's senior social role, his age and behavior placed him in a more youthful role after death. Unlike the black color of *Chadzunda*, his mask was red, less dangerous or powerful than a male, and more closely associated with the women, with whom he was said to be very popular. Unlike the signs of age and respect with carved wrinkles and the fly whisk, this mask depicted a fully mature, handsome man rather than old or aging. The masked dancer wore bright clothes, and even a woman's skirt, and the dancer performed near the women, teasing and flirting.

The youthful *Kadyankhadze* (*kadya*, to eat; *Nkhadze*, a tree with a stinging, poisonous sap) is a mask of a chief's sister's son who is the likely successor of the Chief in Chewa society. *Nyau* members described *Kadyankhadze* as one who barges into the dance area unannounced, chasing off the other dancers, and with a toss of his head shakes the feathers from his face, revealing the carver's intended visage of the determined, pitiless, and wild young man who shows no respect to his elders. *Kadyankhadze* is portrayed as a young man who is out of control, untamed, pushing to take over the chieftaincy before his time.

The male dancers' movements may very convincingly portray a seductive young woman, whose promiscuity is a sign of lack of respect, or maturity, or knowledge. Most often this young woman is dressed in Western clothing, wearing Western hair ornaments and hairstyles, things which are financially out of reach of the village woman. In contrast, the dancer wearing a female mask with traditional costume whether in age or youth, indicates a woman who has been initiated, is mature, and (as I have been told over and again) is therefore "beautiful" (*kongololo*) regardless of age.

In a popular performance, the dancer wearing a mask of a British man from the colonial period (though the same mask may be interpreted as any number of European foreigners), performs his very aggressive dance, and reaps the laughter and cries of people as one hand "speaks" in front of his lips, and the other hand "speaks" behind his back at the same time. This mask is also associated with youth, those who may exercise power but have not experienced knowledge nor achieved maturity through initiation.

Older characters may also portray behaviors which are not socially correct. The old woman, *Kachipapa*, dresses in dirty clothes and speaks in a loud and vulgar manner, gesticulating and carrying a dirty basket of ash on her old, bent back. Another masked dancer I saw wore a simple cloth mask with very long ears. The dancer moved in a bumbling manner, holding a hand to an ear and pretending not to hear. The dancer occasionally scratched himself, and pushed out his pelvis in an exaggerated sexual movement which caused immediate laughter. His deafness and (as indicated to me) sexual impotence were signs of age as well as of a lack of the qualities associated with maturity and seniority. Both characters, though senior in age, were immature, silly, laughable, ridiculous.

Other mask genres depict age, but are also ridiculed. These mask genres portray various undesirable behaviors and socially undesirable conditions. Among these are the loud and vulgar woman, the dirty, the drunk, the bad-tempered, and the man who does not work so his wife has no clothes. Other masks without faces or features of faces may depict the diseased, the maimed, the insane and the stupid. The social misfit or the outcast who does not belong are also portrayed in this way.

Age and the Role of Observers of a Masked Performance

Observers and the observed, society and the dance, are mirrored in that people are placed hierarchically around the dance arena just as masks and masked genres are understood to be in a hierarchy of age and role. The eldest male members of the *Nyau* society sit together near the point of entry for the masked dancers. These men, the elders, circle the *bwalo*[8] before the masked dancers perform, clearing the way for the coming of the spirits. Their age is visibly obvious, but not all elderly men are included in this group. The elders hear the songs of the dancers, discuss the suitability of new masks, dances, and innovations prior to performances. Their influence is related to their activities and knowledge in *Nyau* throughout their lives.

Most dances begin with a line of men and a line of women dancing. The men are those older men in senior roles: chiefs and *Nyau* leaders. The women are older women in senior roles: chiefs, chief's wives, *Namkungwi,* and senior leaders. These same women perform together as the group of women nearest to the most senior group of men. The women answer back the words of the spirits, the masked dancers. Male Chiefs sit together, and male elders sit together, nearer the women.

From these gendered groups, people arrange themselves in the *bwalo* according to their age and social category. Older women are nearer to younger women, to adolescent women. Those who have babies are nearer the children. Mature older men active in *Nyau* and village affairs are nearer the senior men, who are in turn near younger men, and then adolescent boys, followed by male children. Those men, regardless of age, who have not been initiated, are told to stand with the uninitiated pre-adolescent boys, near the children, which is the place which is furthest from the masked dancers.

Placement of individuals who are honored guests, outsiders, or people from other village regions unfamiliar with the senior people is decided by the chiefs in consultation with the senior

Nyau leaders, and the individuals are placed according to perceived hierarchy.

Masks, Spirits, and Death

Through the study of mask forms, the importance of age and the association of age with power, respect, wisdom, knowledge, and teachings, and even the association of age with closeness to God and the spirit world, becomes more evident. To be a chief, elder, the senior grandmother, chief's wife, female chief *Namkungwi* (teacher of wisdom) is to assume a stronger and more vital strong role in the spirit world as well as the physical world of the living. As Baxter and Almagor have suggested, "some (cultures) ... recognise a post-life grade of ancestorhood" (1978:1).

Ancestors and those who were considered wise, well-respected, and powerful in life are also communicating values and morality in the *Nyau* dance in death. The *mzimu* returns to the living as a leader and teacher as the person was in life.

Masked performers are spirits, in the transformed time, place, and ritual conditions of the masked performance.[9] Certainly the mask-maker's portraitures are (most commonly and ritually correctly) of senior people who have died.

Masks depicting youth, recklessness, sexuality, humor, and satire are far more numerous than portrait masks in the dances. These mask genres are spirits, but are spirits without portraiture. They are generic characters rather than the specific image of an ancestor, and may be understood as less powerful *mzimu* (cf. Colson 1962). Particularly the young do not attain the status of an ancestor after death. However, those with the most powerful spirit presences are those who possess the attribute of age. Masks associated with the social construction of age are depicted as being in senior roles—being dreaded, respected and even feared, commanding and teaching others, having great wisdom and knowledge, and leading *Nyau* in all its manifestations.

According to the Chewa, the spirit of a senior person is more powerful—and potentially more dangerous—than that of a younger person. The senior person, with greater knowledge of and closeness to the world of masks and therefore the world of spirits, is regarded as a person with far greater potential to either harm or help the living community. These people must be properly buried and appeased by their relatives and the *Nyau* community. These people have a stronger *mzimu* spirit presence than others, and these people are the ones who become ancestors.

The actual age of a person is only part of this understanding of being an ancestor. The actions, behavior, social roles, bearing of children, and ability to command respect as an active *Nyau* member during one's lifetime have bearing on one's presence as an ancestor in death. Recognition of a person's strong *mzimu* is acknowledged in the *Nyau* funeral performance, and the remembrance performance on the anniversary of that person's death.

In the funeral of a *Namkungwi*, the *Kasiyamaliro* came to the house of the deceased and, it was said, captured the spirit from the body, carrying the spirit safely to the grave. The *Chimkoko* was being prepared in the graveyard, a sign that the woman was a great and mature grandmother—in role as well as in age—and would become an ancestor, capable of affecting the lives of people in the village. Her image would be a likely one for the maskmakers to re-create in the form of a respected carved mask, to be re-united with the living as a powerful spirit presence.

On the day of the burial, the senior women staying closest to the body of the deceased announced that a young initiated woman would be given the name of the deceased *Namkungwi*, because her *mtima* (or character) possessed virtues which were worthy of the one who had died. Masked dancers cried for the loss of their mother, a universal mother of all in the village, and they cried for another to take her place. Two young girls (aged nine and ten) were given a kind of initiation of endurance, introduced into the adult world, staying up all night with the most senior, elder women near the body of the deceased and being near the feared masked dancers who represented presences of others who have died. In the burial procession the two young girls and the initiated woman with the name of the deceased were carried on the shoulders of the elder women, following the body of the deceased to the grave-yard.

I would suggest that these actions—masked dancers (spirits) calling for a new mother, the naming of a woman of child-bearing age, and the vigil of two young girls by the body of the deceased—are signs of renewal and regeneration, of regenerating the qualities of this senior woman in two younger generations. These signs of regeneration are also signs of respect, esteem, and honor for the deceased *Namkungwi*, and the expectation of a continued life cycle.

Coupled with this regeneration, respect, and honor was the compelling need to appease the *mzimu* of this powerful woman. This *mzimu* could either return in anger to punish or return in benevolence to guide and help in unity with the living and the dead, depending upon the proper actions by the *Nyau* leaders and masked dancers in her burial.

In another example, the burial of one the great supporters of *Nyau*, Chief Mkuzi, lasted more than five days.[10]More than 500 dancers were present, as reported to me by an assistant who went to the funeral in 1993, some months after I left. Chief Mkuzi's image is most likely to appear on a mask or more than one mask, since he was well known by mask-makers, dancers, and *Nyau* leaders throughout the region. Even in death, Chief Mkuzi will be present during the masked performances in the *bwalo*, wielding his power in the world of the dead, affecting the world of the living. He will be revered as an ancestor. His powerful *mzimu* will be evoked every time his image returns to the *bwalo* to perform, and he will be present among the living even when all those who knew him have also died.

This relationship of the *mzimu* or ancestor coming back to guide the living is most clearly detailed in the interpretation of a pair of masked dancers in Njombwe village. John Kadzundila, a student who conducted this research on my behalf, related the story of two well-known masks resembling animals called *Chimbano* (great teeth). One is taller than the other and leads the dance, followed by the smaller one. I was told that the taller mask represented the great ancestor who first founded the village. Because he was one of the first to settle this area near Kasungu after the time of the Ngoni wars, he laid claim to surrounding lands and organized immigrant villagers into *Nyau* sub-chieftaincies. In his death, he is remembered as the founder, the ancestor, the leader, and the most senior Chief—all recognized in this mask form.

The smaller version of the same mask, which performs as a partner to the first, represents the current chief of the village. In the dance performance, the great ancestor leans on the chief, as if he is teaching, guiding, leading the present chief. I was told the pair of dancers are interpreted by elders as the deceased ancestor spirit advising the living chief. The living, current chief dies and is replaced by the next one, but the taller mask, the ancestor, remains the same. The most powerful presence in life is still the most powerful presence even in death.

The social construction of age, even past death, is thus made visible in masks. Youth and age are both present in masked forms, but the most senior carved masks are of those senior people who have been acknowledged as leaders in life and are then acknowledged as ancestors in death. As Adorno (1984) suggests, the visual image and the non-visual are both present in art, and in this sense I suggest the masks of the Chewa visibly exemplify the invisible social concept of age in life and in death. The visual mask of an ancestor is also the visual image of the invisible qualities of maturity. Age is much more than physical aging; it is the acceptance of responsibility, of socially acknowledged respect from others, and of the role of guide and teacher to those who are "younger" in maturity and knowledge.

Life Cycle and Aging

As Stuart Thompson (1990) suggests, the life cycle of agriculture in Taiwan is symbolically related to the process of aging. Among the Chewa the life cycle of maize, the primary food crop, is the metaphor by which the human life cycle is explained. This metaphor is further exemplified in the construction of the large antelope mask, which is covered with the dried leaves of maize husks. While the entire exegesis of this cycle is too complex for this chapter, the basic elements relate to the process of aging, death, and regeneration.[11]

Maize begins new life in the soil as a germinating seed. The soil is likened to a woman's womb, and the presence of the supernatural being which creates all new life in the soil is considered female. The rains, which begin in November (spring in Malawi), are likened to sperm falling from the sky, where the supernatural being is considered male. The fertile soil then gives birth (like a woman giving birth) to a new cycle of life as the seedling emerges from the earth. The seed is nurtured and cared for by the farmer and the rains and grows to maturity. It is then cut, the food is provided and shared, and the husk leaves are discarded in the rubbish pit.

From the rubbish pit, the dried, white-like leaves are gathered secretly by *Nyau* members and are carried into the place of graves, a forest grove. Here, in the place of the dead, the leaves are woven together to create the large antelope animal forms which lead the funeral processions and the remembrance dances. The antelope mask is given life, movement, dance, form, in the season of coldness and dryness. As the spring approaches again, the air becomes hot and dusty with lack of rains. In early spring, the grasses are set on fire and the ash is spread over the fields as fertilizer. With the first rains, the air cools, the ash goes into the soil, and the new seed germinates.

Metaphorically this cycle of life embodies *Nyau* concepts about religion, cosmology, creation mythology, seasons, masking, and aging in human life. As the spirit of the deceased senior and aged person is taken into the womb of the antelope mask for burial, the spirit then enables the regeneration of new life from the soil. The antelope mask itself, made of the dead maize leaves and the dried grasses, dies at the end of the dry season. It is burned, and a bit of the ash is eaten by new initiates. The ash is spread in the graveyard grounds, with the hope of renewal and new life coming from the fertile soil with the new rains.

Regeneration is possible for those who have lived fruitfully, meaning those who have borne children, lived long, and provided food, labor, service, and knowledge to the community of the living. Even in the time of death (the cutting of the maize), those who have aged and matured, ripened into full stature in life, and contributed to the well-being of society provide the food (the maize grain) which enables the community to live and regenerate itself again.

Conclusion

Age, aging, signs of age, roles associated with age, are construed socially, as I suggested in the beginning of this essay. Physical signs of age, such as wrinkles and grey hair, are re-enforced by association with roles high in the hierarchical structure of masking and village society. An example in this essay is the mask *Chadzunda*, the Chief. Actual physical age, however, is only one criterion of understanding regarding those who have assumed the status of an aged person. As Spencer notes, "not all older people are respected" (1990b: 8).

One critical point in this discussion is that seniority, which includes age, is completely denied to men and women of any age who have never been initiated. The uninitiated are to the *Nyau* community like children who know nothing. In the social construction of age as a sign of maturity, those who have not been initiated have not matured. Age then, among the Chewa, is more deliberately associated with experience and knowledge: levels of understanding, involvement in *Nyau* activities, relationships with people, and possession of qualities of good character and behavior.

More than this, initiation in *Nyau* signifies a member of a community, and an identity apart from others. One who has been initiated has accepted certain obligations and privileges, including the obligation to perform the *Gule Wamkulu* for the benefit of the deceased and the whole well-being of the community; and the privilege of having others perform the *Gule Wamkulu* for you, assuring your own unity or harmony with the spirit world, and regeneration of life.

Those who have been initiated have attained a certain status in Chewa society which allows them to become involved in *Nyau* practices, to which they were formerly denied access. Higher levels of knowledge are attained by those who achieve the most senior status. The greatest wisdom is shared by those senior people who have received knowledge of both male and female initiation. The female *Namkungwi* possesses male knowledge and in a sense becomes an honorary male in certain ritual situations.[12] Her age, past child-bearing, releases her from her gender, and she assumes knowledge of both males and females, which is otherwise strictly separated. Male Chiefs may enter the girls' initiation house and are also instructed by the *Namkungwi*.

To what extent a person has achieved his status of age, wisdom and maturity in society is made clear in death, beginning with the kind of funeral ceremony the person receives. The funeral of a child or uninitiated person, or a person who has not achieved his or her full status in age, is far different from the coming of *Nyau* from all over the central region, who are inspired to come to the village of the deceased Chief or *Namkungwi* in order to honor that person in death.

Those people who have achieved a senior age in all respects are believed to have a strong and potentially dangerous spirit, which is rendered into the status of ancestor in another elaborate performance of *Nyau* for the funeral anniversary or remembrance of the deceased person. In this performance, the *Chimkoko* circles the *bwalo,* signifying both the leaving of the funeral behind and the presence of the deceased person in the *Nyau* dance once again. The dead have returned to the living, and the unity of the most senior, powerful, aged, and strong members of the community of the living become the most senior, powerful, aged, and strong members of the community of the dead.

Ambivalence, the balance between a pacified spirit and a spirit which may cause damage to the community, is ever-present. The senior aged person is potentially dangerous in that they may choose not to provide food in death; they may choose not to aid the regeneration of life from the soil. On the contrary, they may choose to attempt to render the land fruitless, infertile, barren, if the spirit is not satisfied, not in harmony with the living. Unhappy deaths, deaths attributed to witchcraft, deaths in violent circumstances, or deaths of people in angry relations with others may cause great harm. Therefore, the attribute of age as well as good character and the other values associated with the most senior people is so vitally important. To have lived long is one sign of having lived peacefully and well.

As the dead are reunited with the living in those moments of performance, the songs of the masked dancers become the words of the spirits. Songs are heard and rehearsed, and are accepted by those same people of maturity and age among the living who will be revered as ancestors in death. The masked dancer's words—admonitions, warnings, praises, reminiscences, pleas and proverbs—are selected, approved and often even sung by the most senior elder men, and the spirits are answered by the most senior elder women. The voices of the spirits are the same voices of those in line to be the future spirits; those who have achieved initiation, knowledge, wisdom, respect, experience, authority, and, indeed, age as in years of life.

NOTES

1. The closest translation I have found for *Nyau* was given to me by those who were raised in the village, but received an education outside the village (information further verified in Scott)1929: "*Nyau-nyau,*" to make the skin crinkle, or writhe or wrinkle, as, for example, when in extreme fear; cf. Heatherwick 1951.

2. All masks are gendered, and the large animal mask constructions can be made in the form of female or male animals. In initiation of boys, the female form is required.

3. Women may be chosen as Chiefs. In a formal meeting of Chiefs in the Bunda region which I attended in 1992, five of the 64 Chiefs present were female.

4. Mask genre refers to mask forms which are recognized by formal elements and naming and dance rhythms known from one village area to another. There are more than twenty such forms which are well known, and are understood to be more or less important in relation to one another. A hierarchical structure is presented in Birch de Aguilar 1995 and 1996.

5. These formal elements are changing; the color red is not exclusively female, though it is most often associated with the female masks, and the use of hide and feathers is changing as more new masks are made with modern materials with a trend toward increased realism, such as hair in place of feathers.

6. In Chewa rural society, a senior group of women choose their own chief, and a Namkungwi is selected among the same women (Aguilar and Birch de Aguilar 1993).

7. By custom, the Chief's sister's sons are likely successors rather than his own sons or brothers.

8. The *bwalo* is the cleared ritual space or performance space for *Nyau*. Each *Nyau* Chief has his own *bwalo* which confers his right to hold a *Nyau* event in his village (Birch de Aguilar 1996).

9. For a more detailed consideration of how, and in what sense they are spirits, see Birch de Aguilar (1996).

10. *Nyau* funerals usually begin the night of the death, and the deceased is buried the next day, or the day after, allowing people time to arrive. The funerals of senior *Nyau* leaders will last three days: two nights of dancing, and a third day for the funeral ceremonies. Five days of dancing is a tribute to Chief Mkuzi, who was known throughout the central region.

11. See Birch de Aguilar (1996) for a more complete analysis of the Chewa life cycle.

12. The *Namkungwi* may dance with the male masked dancers in public performances, which no other women may do. She is present in the graveyard for the boy's initiation, and instructs adult male dancers in tradition, proper attire and behavior for the dance.

PART III
AGE IN THE POST-MODERN STATE

Chapter 6

In Search of Discipline: Generational Control, Political Protest, and Everyday Violence in Cradock, South Africa, 1984-85

❖

Michael S. Tetelman

Introduction

In early 1985 an African township in the small rural Eastern Cape town of Cradock gained international acclaim for its heroic and innovative anti-apartheid resistance campaigns. The township was officially named Lingelihle, an isiXhosa word loosely meaning a "worthy effort." One year before, this township launched the longest school boycott in South Africa's history and inspired townships across the Eastern Cape to initiate similar protest. Later in 1984, Cradock's activists created a grass-roots structure known as street committees. Townships nationwide adopted this structure, which underpinned anti-apartheid opposition (Lodge and Nasson 1991:74-5; Mufson 1990:110-3).[1]

Like other townships that resisted apartheid in the mid-1980s, Lingelihle was racked by violence. As an Eastern Cape newspaper decried in early 1985,

> What is the Government doing about this Karoo town, where violence and upheaval has become part of everyday life? Has it abandoned the African township of Ilingelihle to the ongoing trauma of petrol bombs and rubber bullets, of teargas and murder, of boycotts and bannings?[2]

On one level, the *Eastern Province Herald* was right to frame the violence as a by-product of resistance, state repression, and confusion. The state veered between conciliatory and coercive tactics to break protest. Younger Africans, especially males, engaged in violence against the state and against suspected black collaborators in order to assert their personal and political agency. Older black protest leaders relied on these violent tactics to destabilize the state, but they later tried to curtail violence to regain control over younger residents. Sympathetic white organizations and media also used images of state violence to capture moral currency for the struggle.

Like the *Herald* article, most studies of township resistance in the 1980s demonstrate that its attendant violence was a recent phenomenon, occurring in the wake of state repression and intensified protest campaigns. In this vein, these studies also show that inter-generational conflict increased dramatically in the late 1970s and mid-1980s (Bundy 1987; Carter 1991; Chikane 1986; Jochelson 1990; Sitas 1992).

While the scope of township violence certainly grew during this turbulent and tragic time, there is another side to the story.

178

Most of the writing on 1980s resistance focuses on revolt in larger metropolitan areas. With a few exceptions, these studies have failed to connect deeper historical patterns of violence, inter-generational conflict, and modes of discipline to the protest and everyday violence of the 1980s. In smaller townships one might more easily discern the impact of prior protest campaigns and mechanisms of generational control on resistance and violence in the 1980s. In Cradock, for example, leaders employed forceful and often ingenious means to control younger people from the 1930s onward. In the 1980s, older township activists adapted many of these disciplinary devices to mobilize and control younger residents.[3]

This chapter poses several questions about the relationship between inter-generational relations, politics, and violence in Cradock during 1984–85: how did the activists' use of long-standing disciplinary practices affect political protest; how did younger Africans appropriate and reshape these modes, histories, and images of discipline and resistance; and how did the state's efforts to stunt protest affect the multi-valent deployment of discipline and violence.

Discipline, Social Upheaval, and Political Protest, 1930-1983

Cradock has a long history of blending generational and patriarchal control with political protest. Its black Anglican clergyman from the late 1920s to the late 1970s, Canon J.A. Calata, was committed to developing and controlling younger people. In the early 1930s, many older black elites, and Canon Calata in particular, were deeply concerned over what they perceived as pervasive generational conflict in Cradock's so-called "old location." Elders also feared the increasing sexual independence of younger unmarried African females.

Calata and other black elites drew upon a complex mix of ideologies and cultural practices in their quest for social control. Steeped in Cape liberalism, Cradock's black elites formed a rich variety of youth clubs fashioned on British lines. These organizations included scouting movements for boys and girls, church choirs, drama groups, and active school sporting teams. Calata made his church, the St. James Mission, the hub of many of these projects. By the late 1940s, Cradock's "location" enjoyed a thriving network of these clubs. On the other hand, young Africans were subject to indigenous modes of generational control like circumcision school for males and female initiation practices.

Elders also used physical forms of punishment to control younger residents. Cradock's African teachers were as renowned for their strict discipline, such as the caning of students, as they were for their stellar teaching. Further, from the early 1930s onward, older African men formed neighborhood networks to control younger men. These networks cooperated with the municipality, especially to control the so-called "faction fighting." With the municipality's blessing, these networks employed corporal punishment. Calata was also known for his use of corporal punishment, both toward young males and females, particularly when upholding puritanical norms of sexual chastity (Tetelman 1997, chap. 1).

Calata was as committed to political change as he was to shaping the location's youth. He served as secretary-general of the African National Congress (ANC) from 1936 to 1949. In 1949 younger ANC Youth League organizers like Walter Sisulu and Nelson Mandela ousted more passive Congress leaders like Calata and A.B. Xuma from leadership. Calata remained on the executive board, but now focused on local protest (Carter and Karis 1977:16-7; Walshe 1970).

Calata's impact on younger residents paid political dividends. He made St. James the site of potent local anti-apartheid campaigns during the 1950s. Calata founded the Congress Choir, a Cradock-based group formed of parents and children that galvanized the Eastern Cape. In the early 1950s, several of Calata's younger club-goers and congregants formed a local branch of the ANC Youth League. Working in close contact with Calata and a cadre of older ANC women based mainly in St. James, these younger men underpinned Cradock's protest movements. Cradock was a linchpin of ANC protest until the early 1960s, when the state imprisoned many of these organizers and removed its African residents to the new township known as Lingelihle (Tetelman 1997, chap 2).

The move to Lingelihle increased inter-generational conflict, as it did in townships nationwide. The architecture of the new townships, with their emphasis on smaller houses, caused younger men and women to leave their parents. Worsening economic conditions debilitated indigenous modes of sexual control. For example, the practice of bridewealth declined. On another level, Cradock's social institutions that once fostered inter-generational co-operation had now weakened. Younger residents withdrew from church groups, scouting movements, and state-sponsored rugby clubs as police informers and security agents penetrated these clubs. Finally, the imposition of Bantu Education undermined the authority of African teachers, both in Cradock and nationwide (Tetelman 1997; chap 3).[4]

Yet this rupturing was not just an endogenous phenomenon. The emergence of Black Consciousness (BC) inspired many of Cradock's students and young school-leavers to further transform social and political relations within the township. Younger residents, particularly males, formed BC-oriented study groups and pushed their elders to switch their allegiance to BC-affiliated rugby clubs. The Soweto uprising of 1976 and the subsequent killing of BC leader Steve Biko galvanized Lingelihle's students and younger residents to launch a brief but potent protest against the state in late 1977. As parents and older teachers looked on in fear and astonishment, students and young school-leavers burned township schools, the homes of security policemen and suspected student informers, and state buildings like the township's post office.

While some elders supported this action, most saw the protest as a subversion of their authority. So too did the state; it arrested several of the young protest organizers. Overt confrontation disappeared until 1980, when students affiliated to the ANC-oriented organization COSAS (Congress of South African Students) joined a nationwide school boycott lasting several months. Once again most elders did not support their action, and students failed to sustain their campaign (Tetelman 1997: chapter 3).[5]

In the early 1980s, two of Lingelihle's younger African teachers were determined to ameliorate conflict. Like Canon Calata, both these teachers had extensive political exposure. One was Fort Calata, Canon Calata's grandson. He was galvanized by his grandfather's activism and participated in protest in Cradock during the late 1970s. Fort began to teach in Cradock in the early 1980s. The other teacher, Matthew Goniwe, participated in Calata's local clubs as a child. In 1958, at the age of ten, he was arrested with the Congress Choir. Goniwe's older brother Jaques was a local Youth League leader who joined the ANC's exiled armed guerrilla unit, *Umkhonto we Sizwe* (MK). Several years later, Jaques and other exiled Cradock activists were killed. In the mid-1970s Matthew joined a Marxist cell group in the Transkei and was jailed. He was released from prison and began teaching in Cradock in 1983, at Lingelihle's junior secondary school known as Sam Xhallie. He later became its acting principal.

These two teachers were distraught at the socio-economic conditions in the township. While poverty was endemic, their fears centered around what they perceived as pervasive inter-generational conflict and a shattering of sexual norms, especially in the wake of the 1977 and 1980 protests. Drinking, drug-taking, teenage pregnancies, and the apathy of most of Lingelihle's teachers alarmed the two teachers (Tetelman 1997: chap 4).[6]

Fort Calata and Goniwe appropriated long-standing modes of discipline to restore generational control. They used corporal punishment freely. Goniwe stood by the school entrance and sjamboked students for arriving to school late. The two teachers constantly visited the homes of their students to inform parents of their children's progress. Student tardiness and absenteeism plummeted. Goniwe and Calata also held weekend workshops for students on civic responsibility and familial respect. In early 1983 Goniwe convened a meeting of parents and educators, which led to the formation of a club run by adults for students. The club was named the Cradock Youth Association (Cradoya). It organized students and recent school-leavers in drama, sports, and music. Teachers and other black professionals saw Cradoya as apolitical and joined it.[7]

Before Cradoya could flourish, local and national political events subsumed the township. In August of 1983 the ANC-aligned United Democratic Front (UDF) was officially launched. It resolved to oppose the state's plan to establish a separate parliament for Indians and Coloureds. Black townships had also formed associations formed to deal with residents' material grievances, like rental increases. The UDF rapidly incorporated these organizations to generate an explosive new front of anti-apartheid opposition.

Local grievances galvanized Lingelihle most. In the late 1970s, the state created elected black municipal councils to administer African townships. However, the government committed almost no funds to township development. In 1983 the state pressed Cradock's council to institute steep rent and service charge increases, despite the township's dilapidation. In June of 1983, Canon Calata passed away. Calata's funeral allowed UDF leaders to link the movement to the ANC and inspired Lingelihle's residents to criticize state policies with increasing volume; now the township needed a coherent strategy to challenge the state effectively.[8]

Goniwe provided this leadership. He organized a civic association of older residents known as the Cradock Residents' Association (Cradora) to oppose the rental schemes. Goniwe's adroit use of Congress themes, slogans, and images drew many older residents. As the state ignored Cradora's demands, its membership boomed. Black councilors balked at implementing the increases, saying that Cradora had rallied support against them. The police tried to disrupt Cradora though disinformation campaigns, which only strengthened the civic. In December, with the launching of the UDF in the Eastern Cape, Cradoya announced that it had become a political protest body. Cradora and Cradoya established strong links with other Eastern Cape civics, and they were poised to topple black local government.[9]

Launching the Boycott

In November 1983, the state again tried to stifle Cradora. The Department of Education and Training (DET) ordered Goniwe's transfer to a nearby town. While the DET stated that the transfer was not politically motivated, Cradora organizers believed otherwise. Residents considered a host of options, including a school boycott.[10]

Cradora leaders had a powerful base with which to launch the boycott. Many older students were fanatically loyal to Goniwe. The core group of boycotting students had studied under Goniwe at Sam Xhallie and admired him as a teacher, friend, and political leader. These students formed the nucleus of Cradoya and a local COSAS branch.

Unlike the 1980 boycott, parents and elders also pledged their support. Older residents were galvanized by Goniwe's commitment to restoring inter-generational cooperation and sexual chastity through time-honored disciplinary methods. His sensitivity to their material grievances and his adherence to Congress politics also appealed to elders. One student boycott leader, Madoda Jacobs, relates:

> The parents were with us in the schools boycott and with the youth outside because the boycott was a community issue and because we were informing them. People trusted him (M. Goniwe) and loved him because of what he was doing.

Older women were steadfast supporters of the boycott. Two women in particular, Nonyanga Sibanda and Babise Soga were active ANC and Cradora organizers. They launched an intensive campaign amongst parents to forestall the transfer, and they succeeded. As one Cradoya organizer recalls,

All women marched to the DET offices demanding that
Matthew must not be transferred to Graaff-Reinet because he was born and bred in Cradock and must not
transfer his skills.

In a mass meeting in late 1983, some two thousand residents
voted that Goniwe refuse the transfer. By early 1984, the DET
dismissed Goniwe; students, parents, and civic leaders agreed
on a school boycott.[11]
One organizer expressed serious reservations about this decision: Matthew Goniwe. In light of the conflict following the 1980
school boycott, Goniwe feared the violence and generational conflict that might re-occur. He begged protest organizers to let him
find other employment, but they insisted he support the boycott.
He reluctantly complied.[12]
The school boycott happened with lightning speed. In early
February a delegation of parents reported that they again had failed
to change the DET's decision. Secondary school students demanded the right to form a Student Representative Council (SRC)
to push for Goniwe's reinstatement. Two Cradoya members, who
had been elected "Head Boy" and "Head Girl" prefects, con-
fronted the acting secondary school principal about Goniwe's re-
instatement and the SRC. The principal refused both conditions.
Some 1600 students at the high school and junior secondary school
walked out of their classes. The boycott soon spread to the primary schools. Parents pulled the primary school students out of
school, for police had entered Sam Xhallie and *sjamboked* boycotting students. By March 18th five thousand students were now
boycotting classes.[13]
The boycott quickly attracted wide publicity and new political alliances. The Progressive Federal Party (the liberal white
opposition party in Parliament) pressed the government to nego-
tiate with the boycotters. For the state, the re-instatement issue
was becoming a larger political quagmire than had been anticipated.[14]

Internal Conflict and Negotiation: March to November 1984

The state met the boycott with hard-line tactics. Cradock's magistrate invoked the Internal Security Act and banned meetings by Cradora and Cradoya for that day. Police entered Lingelihle on a massive armed patrol. They encountered two roadblocks. The SAP fired teargas at residents, allegedly after residents stoned their vehicles.[15] Several days later, Cradoya and COSAS organizers held a mass meeting of students in a church hall. Police fired teargas into the hall. As students poured outside choking, police fired rubber bullets at them. An African school inspector appealed to the police to stop the assault. Some residents hurled stones at the inspector, whom they thought was collaborating with the police. One struck his head, and he required ten stitches.[16]

All possibilities of resolving conflict now disappeared. Police patrols raced through Lingelihle. On 30 March the Minister of Law and Order, Louis le Grange, banned public meetings for three months. The police then detained Goniwe, Fort Calata, Mbulelo Goniwe (a nephew of Matthew Goniwe and a Cradora organizer), and Madoda Jacobs.[17] Cradoya's top leaders may have been disciplined and stressed non-violent tactics, but the remaining leadership had little control over such a large assemblage of younger people—especially unemployed school-leavers. Both they and Cradoya's students would begin to participate in violence, especially as police raids became constant.

Tactics by the security police to sow dissension sparked the rebirth of inter-generational conflict. Besides recruiting more informers, the police looked to undermine a Cradora executive member and teacher named Nozana Nqikashe. He was one of the few teachers who remained with Cradora once the police had responded with force. The police spread a rumor that Nqikashe had withdrawn in protest. Nqikashe was a good target for the security police. He had already angered younger activists for criticizing the school boycott at a mass meeting. As one Cradora organizer recalls, "When people are for a thing, it is dangerous to

186

be against it. His folly was to be outspoken." In this tense and confused atmosphere, organizers believed the rumor and pulled away from Nqikashe. Students and school-leavers stoned Nqikashe's house, and he warded them off with a pistol. He left Cradock and did not return. In a performance reminiscent of the 1977 protests, a crowd of people burned Nqikashe's home.[18]

Violence skyrocketed in early April. Residents appeared at the local trial of Fort Calata's wife, who had been arrested for wearing a "Free Mandela" T-shirt. The crowd sang freedom songs and marched to Sam Xhallie. Some ten students had not observed the boycott and were studying within the school grounds. The crowd tried to chase the students out of the school, and as they did so police arrived. The police fired teargas as the crowd, now numbering about one thousand, pelted them with stones. The police arrested seven young residents on public violence charges. Several days later, the nephew of a principal stabbed a student boycotter to death. The police did not bring the alleged murderer to court.[19]

Cradock's black councilors bore the brunt of the escalating conflict. This was not a recent phenomenon. In 1980 young BC-oriented school-leavers had driven the councilors from a public meeting and then burned the township's beerhall to protest rent increases and inadequate township facilities. The councilors did not suffer overt threats for the next several years, but with Cradora's formation in late 1983 they came under renewed pressure. By early 1984 councilors begged regional officials to give them hand-guns due to "intimidation of the various opposition parties ... and the threats of violence." The council's chairlady, Doris Hermaans, stressed that the councilors "had reason to fear for their lives" but they were still "determined to serve the community ... to the best of its ability" (Tetelman 1997: chapter 4).[20]

The councilors' fears materialized. In mid-April, a small crowd *toyi-toyed* in front of Hermaans' home. Two days later, younger people stoned her house. Residents hurled petrol bombs at Hermaans' home following the stabbing of the boycotter. Police guarded her home, and the six councilors installed wire fencing around their houses. The security police then orchestrated a bombing of a Cradora executive's home, which prompted younger residents again to bomb Hermaans' home as well as those of a councilor, a teacher, and several policemen. Hermanns' mother, who suffered from heart trouble, died of cardiac shock.[21]

For Hermaans, her mother's funeral confirmed that her own life hung by a thread. In a show of solidarity for their beleaguered colleague, black councilors from other Eastern Cape townships attended. "Absolute chaos" pervaded the funeral. Angry crowds tried to overturn the hearse and pelted it with stones. The police were called to guard the mourners, who quickly buried the body. As one resident recalls, "People wanted to burn the corpse"; residents also brought buckets filled with feces to denigrate the coffin. One of Hermaan's relatives fired his pistol in the air to repel the demonstrators. The police arrested several protesters. Hermaans was shattered. She recalls: "It was not a funeral, it was a circus ... I was a nervous wreck."[22]

Older civic leaders were in a dilemma, as on the one hand, violence was producing results. The council system was destabilized. In late May, an official informed le Grange that the regional administration board was witnessing "the destruction of what has been achieved over a number of years." The official begged le Grange to visit Lingelihle and use "more stringent police action against the agitators of unrest." While supporting the official's call for more enforcement, Cradock's black councilors pressed the state to impose uniform rents. Officials refused to acknowledge that Goniwe's transfer or the rent scheme was the cause of protest.[23]

On the other hand, with Goniwe and Calata in detention, older civic leaders feared they could not control the increasing violence by younger residents. Thus they requested the magistrate to allow them to hold a public meeting which would ask both police and young protesters to end the violence. The magistrate refused. In all likelihood, the state did not want Cradora to be seen as the restorer of social order, for this would further discredit the black councilors and the police.[24]

In the face of the state's intransigence, civic and youth organizers maintained pressure. Cradora launched a consumer boycott on June 16, to commemorate the Soweto uprising and to protest police abuses. Organizers claimed that 95% of Lingelihle's residents observed the boycott. The school boycott also continued. By the end of May only seven out of 4,500 students attended class.[25]

Cradock's protests now captured national attention. Non-governmental organizations (NGOs) and parliamentary opposition leaders pressured the state to release the detainees and end the meeting ban. The media seized onto Cradock as a riveting linchpin of resistance. The English press depicted Cradock's protests and the state's use of force as a David-and-Goliath-like struggle against a merciless state.[26] Black political organizations also took up Cradock's cause. The UDF organized a solidarity rally that focused on Cradock. The UDF's president, Rev. Alan Boesak, knew Cradock's value in promoting the struggle. He visited Lingelihle with a swarm of journalists, though police did not allow the press to enter. Police later forbade Boesak access to Lingelihle, but he ensured that the press stayed interested in Cradock.[27]

Money was as important as media pressure. In July, Cradora organized another consumer boycott. Africans in nearby towns also boycotted Cradock's white-owned businesses. Cradock's officials and businessmen fretted that "adverse publicity" would destroy Cradock's tourist trade and plans for growth. The town clerk begged the state to solve the school boycott.[28]

The state was at an impasse. Its hard-line tactics had failed. National and regional-level resistance had also snowballed. In September, the Vaal Triangle exploded in massive protest, as had the Eastern Cape. Officials did not want rural townships like Lingelihle to become more politicized. Pretoria then switched tactics. The court acquitted most Cradock activists accused in the public violence trials. In early October, le Grange lifted the public meetings ban. Cradock's students and the UDF sensed the state's weakness. They announced that the school boycott would continue until the state released the detainees (Lodge and Nasson 1991:65).[29]

Pretoria finally buckled. In early October it released the Goniwes and Fort Calata. Goniwe returned to a hero's welcome. Priests, nuns, journalists, residents, and parliamentarians streamed into his home. Mayoress Hermaans, who lived on the same street, shut up in the tense isolation of her guarded home, watched the endless procession of visitors, wondering what would befall her next.[30]

Internal Conflict and Street Committees: November 1984 to February 1985

Goniwe and Calata's release energized civic and youth organizers. A journalist wrote that "even the smallest children no longer waved a friendly greeting. Instead skinny arms are now raised in a clenched fist salute—the political symbol of power to the people." Cradock's activists extolled the image of unbreakable unity among Lingelihle's residents. At a mass meeting held one week after their leaders' release, a Cradora organizer boasted that even apolitical residents had become drawn into protest due to the harshness of the police.[31]

Opposition leaders nationwide exulted. A small township had defeated the might of the South African state. Boesak waxed eloquent about Lingelihle's unity and unwavering commitment to undermine apartheid,

> The inhabitants are living in a constant state of fear because of police actions, detentions and harassment. Yet the unity and solidarity between the school boycotting children and the older community members is a remarkable achievement.[32]

Lingelihle and the UDF enjoyed a symbiotic relationship. Local activists depended on national publicity to pressure officials, and they looked to the UDF for resources and new strategies. On the other hand, Lingelihle's images of generational unity underpinned the UDF's project of establishing itself as a legitimate opposition party. Themes like inter-generational co-operation also tied neatly into older ANC discourses espousing discipline and the inclusive nature of struggle. The image of school boycott further connected with past protest. And Lingelihle could serve, for publicity purposes, as a microcosm of the fierce resistance that was emerging in the rural Eastern Cape.

Civic organizers now had the momentum to dislodge the black councilors. A rumor spread that councilors were "dishing out houses" in return for money. Two councilors resigned in October, once residents accused them of corruption. One councilor collected children and drove them around Lingelihle in his pickup truck. He instructed them to shout "Amandla" to show everyone that he was now politically correct.[33] Hermaans held on to her position, though her life had become a living nightmare. She states: "In November 1984 the toyi toyis were continuing. By that time I had deteriorated. They gave me so much drugs I would sometimes go to bed with my eyes wide open." Goniwe met secretly with Hermaans to persuade her to resign. Finally, on 4 January 1985 the council did so. In a poignant moment of discipline, reconciliation, and capitulation, Goniwe and Calata instructed young activists to remove the barbed wire and corrugated iron from Hermaans' home.[34]

Lingelihle's council was the first in the Eastern Cape to resign as a bloc. Officials promised that they would hold new elections, but no one came forward. The council's resignation marked one of the most critical rejections of apartheid to date. The state had spent years promoting local black government. This domino had fallen, and it galvanized organizers in other towns to plan the destruction of their councils.[35]

Beneath the image of a politically solidified township, however, lay a different reality. Goniwe and Calata faced a township unlike the one they had left in early 1984. Parents and elders still supported the school boycott, yet the violence of the past eight months had exacerbated internal divisions.

Local institutions like churches were ripped apart. Congregations that did not participate in protest experienced reprisals. According to oral testimony, activists deliberately scheduled mass meetings that conflicted with church services, forcing people to leave church. Others recall how Goniwe and Fort Calata had alienated many clergy, for Calata in particular had lashed out at passive or compliant clerics. In the Anglican church tensions between protesters and non-participants skyrocketed. Several of the councilors had been leading congregants. Younger activists labeled and threatened some older church women as informers. Female activists like Sibanda angered older congregants by violating patriarchal norms. She addressed them from the pulpit, although women were not supposed to speak from there. And most of Ascension's clergy refrained from political protest, which drew the ire of civic and youth activists.[36]

More broadly, the violence of the past eight months had alienated elders. Some felt that in light of the state's violence, the protest campaign was undermining younger people. They also complained that crime had skyrocketed, and that sexual mores had regressed. One Cradoya activist recalls his grandfather's anger directed toward Goniwe during the unrest:

> "He's doing nothing. He's finished with his studies and would put us in hell". Once kids came running from Nxuba from the police, shooting them and with dogs in their hands. When the students came to my grandfather's house, he said, "Go back out! You know what you are doing". Thus I had to get my friends to fetch my things and my bed, and I went to stay with my father.[37]

Civic protest had repelled many older men. They had become frustrated by the increasing power and bravado displayed by younger activists. The word "comrade" had gained universal currency. Many youth, males and females alike, insisted that all residents use this term. While the use of the term "comrade" enabled activists to promote solidarity and a linkage to broader opposition, it also enabled younger people to challenge traditional terms and boundaries of generational and gendered relationships.[38]

Finally, some civic leaders felt that the increase of violence had hampered Cradoya and Cradora's foundation for success: its inclusivity. Goniwe in particular feared the growing lack of accountability and self-criticism. One confidant of Goniwe recalls that he "was not happy with the Stalinism creeping in. People were not being flexible .... democracy was the watchword. It was right for people to express their views."[39]

Civic leaders needed to restore their authority over younger activists and to incorporate disaffected elders. In late 1984 Goniwe organized Cradora into a set of structures known as street committees. Organizers divided Lingelihle into seven zones, each comprising about forty activists. Organizers held public meetings in these zones. Each house voted for a street committee representative. The street representatives selected area organizers who in turn answered to a Chief Organiser. This officer liaised with the Cradora executive. Cradoya soon established a similar structure.[40]

The street committees drew upon older protest strategies akin to the Mandela Plan (or M-Plan) which ANC leader Nelson Mandela had devised in the early 1950s. Cradock's structures later became popularly known as the G-Plan. This cell-based structure briefly appeared in Cradock during the early 1960s, when Jaques Goniwe was active in Cradock's protest. Matthew Goniwe had also been in an underground study group during the 1970s, so he was familiar with forming these structures (Tetelman 1997: chap 2, 4).[41]

The street committees succeeded on this political level. They protected civic leaders from police harassment, for activists maintained a low profile and remained centered in their local neighborhoods. The committees disseminated and gathered information about meetings and residents' grievances. At their peak, street committees ensured that the township was assembled for a meeting two hours after Cradora's leadership determined the meeting time (Lodge and Nasson 1991:74).[42]

The street committees also looked to redress inter-generational conflict and thus regain the support of elders. The committees were strikingly similar to older disciplinary networks. Middle-aged men became street and area committee representatives, which persuaded them to take a renewed interest in political organizing. Unlike disciplinary networks of the past, many older women also underpinned the committees, particularly at the street level. Younger residents formed their own street and area committees.[43]

The committees quickly swung into action. They handled domestic problems, like arguments among families, akin to informal courts. They also tried to control crime, and youth committees worked to reduce drinking among younger people. On Christmas Day of 1984 the UDF called for a "Black Christmas." Street committees organized patrols that ensured that no one was drinking. Journalists reported that crime and drinking had been stamped out, and that residents sang freedom songs and chanted slogans. For a brief time, the committees worked. Older men and women recall that the committees helped reduce domestic violence and crime.

The street committees were so appealing because they drew on longer histories and symbols of social control. By placing elders in positions of authority, the committees redrew generational boundaries which had become blurred during the past eight months, as well as assuaging elders' anxieties about the loss of sexual chastity. Finally, the committees and their informal courts provided a system of collective justice that had been lacking in the township. The Community Council had been empowered to hear disputes, but its ability to dispense justice had been eradicated by the resurgence of political protest.[44]

Cradora demonstrated other administrative skills within Lingelihle. In the wake of the councilors' collapse, Cradora supervised the payment of pensions to eliminate the forced payment of bribes to officials. With the assistance of NGOs like the

Black Sash, Cradora established an advice center and a literacy program, and it revived a creche. Thus, on both an organizational and symbolic levels, the specific street committees—and Cradora more generally—ameliorated much of the inter-generational conflict that had emerged during much of 1984.[45]

Activists extended their influence beyond Lingelihle. In early 1985, Goniwe and Cradoya organizers traversed the Eastern Cape to organize civics, street committees, and youth associations. Goniwe's reputation spread far beyond the region. One Sowetan activist recalls: "Leaders like Matthew Goniwe in Cradock shot into national prominence because, viewed from afar, it seemed that all they had to do was press a button for whole townships to move into action. But behind that mobilization were solid organization and careful consideration, techniques that Soweto markedly lacked at this stage." For the UDF, which was weak in rural areas, Goniwe's commitment and skill were critical to extending the range of their opposition (Lodge and Nasson 1991:265).

By January 1985, Cradora and Cradoya leadership regained the authority they had lost within Lingelihle. Moreover, Goniwe had survived detention to establish structures of unrivaled effectiveness throughout the Karoo, structures which were now linked into a national UDF network. It was his finest hour.

Death Squads and the End of the Line: February to July 1985

The state did not toast Goniwe's success. Le Grange attacked Goniwe for "spoil(ing)" Cradock and surrounding areas. In late January, the state fired its first shot. Cradora planned a rally to launch itself officially and to commemorate the school boycott. The UDF's national president was to speak, and civics from around the region were to attend. Cradock's magistrate banned the rally. Privately, he admitted to Cradora leaders that "he had got instructions from above." Cradora appealed to the Supreme Court, but the magistrate submitted an affidavit that public order would be jeopardized if the rally occurred. Cradock's chief of security police also warned that the UDF would incite Lingelihle to commit violence. The presiding judge upheld the ban. Police celebrated the decision with a *braai* and then allegedly taunted residents.[46]

Violence quickly followed. A small group of residents burned the home of an African constable, one of the few who still lived in Lingelihle. The constable was stabbed to death that night. Residents also bombed several teachers' homes. The following morning, while on a manhunt for the constable's killers, police shot teargas into the Dutch Reformed Church as its congregants held a service. In the most brazen act of violence, police shot a young man, Thozi Skweyiya, while he ran into a house. They dragged Skweyiya into a Caspir; he then died.[47]

The violence drew a massive outcry from sympathetic whites. The *Herald* published editorials excoriating the state. PFP members rushed to the activists' aid. They collected affidavits about Skweyiya's death and called for a judicial inquiry. Senior officials responded with vitriol. Le Grange criticized the Progressive Federal Party for ignoring violence committed by black opposition. The deputy minister of Health and Welfare, who had been Cradock's Mayor, retorted that Cradock's whites were ready to go to war with Africans. The Deputy Minister saved his most scathing criticism for Goniwe, claiming that he used a "Marxist technique to stimulate unrest and to intimidate and victimise people."[48]

Protest throughout the Eastern Cape now moved at a break-neck pace. In early March, the Eastern Cape's UDF Regional Executive elected Goniwe as their rural organizer. It confirmed the UDF's commitment to strengthen their rural branches. By April, black local government had crumbled. Protest also covered the Eastern Cape's urban townships. In February concerted attacks began on P.E.'s councilors, and activists initiated consumer boycotts. On 21 March the police killed 20 blacks and wounded some 27 others in Uitenhage's Langa township. The government had declared war on the townships.[49]

As the intensity of protest and state violence increased, the

UDF and civics suffered new challenges to their control. The UDF national executive lamented that

> In many areas, organizations trail behind the masses, thus making it more difficult for a disciplined mass action to take place. More often there is spontaneity of actions in the townships.

Goniwe responded to the intensified level of repression. He and other Eastern Cape activists began transforming ANC underground structures into military units, with links to MK headquarters in exile.[50] Goniwe also initiated a small political study group within Lingelihle. He focused his efforts upon a cadre of loyal younger Cradoya and COSAS activists. Goniwe saw this group as the one reliable mechanism to maintain discipline amidst rising unrest.[51]

Goniwe and other civic leaders were deeply concerned about the township's "ungovernability." With the renewed cycle of police violence and response, the street committees and civic leaders again watched their control over younger residents slip away. Younger residents, particularly males, appropriated emergent Charterist and "people's power" discourse to fit their agendas. School-leavers who had been active in the 1977 protests and who had been marginalized in Cradoya had gained a power base through the use of violence and the school boycott. These younger men linked Congress-oriented revolutionary discourse, such as MK songs, to their own struggles.

By March, attacks on suspected collaborators skyrocketed in Lingelihle. Younger school-leavers loosely affiliated to Cradoya killed a Ciskeian police officer while he was visiting family. This officer had helped quell student protests in Lingelihle during 1977 and was unaware that residents remembered his past. The group attacked the policeman with stones and then lit him on fire. According to one observer, "they wanted to show the other informers and police how they were operating." The *Herald* compared the killing to "Mau Mau tactics," no doubt evoking fear among whites that the specter of death lurked at their very doorsteps.[52]

For teachers, early to mid-1985 had become a nightmare. Two African principals had seen their homes petrol bombed. One left with his family and moved to King Williamstown. A younger teacher, who had been a Cradora executive member, had become alienated from protest politics due to the renewed spate of violence. He decided to leave Lingelihle "(w)hen they were burning people's houses, necklacing, and it was just done randomly. You don't know who's next, and I thought thugs had taken over and I must pull out."[53]

The DET's hard-line policies placed the teachers at more risk. In mid-March it decided to close all of Lingelihle's schools. The DET looked to transfer teachers to other school districts. In a mass meeting, students vowed to continue the boycott. Younger activists responded by burning the homes of teachers who planned to transfer.[54]

Many parents and elders now felt the boycott had gone on too long. Students who did not want to commit violence were being coerced into doing so. Inside the households, children challenged their parents. One resident recalls that "mothers could not control their children." Student pregnancy rates were rising. Parents tried to persuade students to return to school, but they refused. A Cradoya activist recalls: "you find five hundred students now just staying at home and not going to school ... They began running away from a lot of things, just sit and smoke dagga and trying to avoid pregnancy."[55]

Nevertheless, those dissenting from the boycott had little ability to voice their demands. Boycotting students and young school-leavers intimidated those students and parents who advocated returning to school. Parents began enrolling their children in homeland schools. A Cradoya organizer admits that the community was very hard on parents taking students out. Students themselves known to be outside were fearing to come back.[56]

Goniwe also wished the boycott to end. Yet he had little power over younger, more militant protesters. As Fort Calata's sister Peggy Calata relates,

> And now the children were out of control. Matthew could
> have controlled the children, but the children were say-
> ing to them, "You don't listen to us. You keep on saying
> we must go back to school and we are telling you we are
> not going back to school ... What kind of leaders are you
> who don't listen to us. We want you back. As long as you
> are not back, we are going to do our own thing. Period."[57]

After prior school boycotts of 1977 and 1980 had met with failure, younger boycotters had little incentive to cede their political
leverage or the personal power they had accumulated. For Goniwe,
he had seen his anxieties expressed at the onset of the boycott
come to pass. Students had rejected his authority.

Yet the dimensions of the conflict were not just merely inter-
generational. For example, Goniwe and Fort Calata clashed over
the use of violence. While Calata wished to end the school boycott, he encouraged youth to use violence in the face of state repression. Calata was also tough on suspected collaborators. At
mass meetings, Calata openly denounced them. Goniwe would
stridently object, especially when residents attacked the property
of those whom Fort singled out.[58]

Goniwe renewed his call to conclude the boycott. In April,
some 1,500 students and parents agreed to end the boycott, despite criticism of the decision. Students were to return in mid-
April.[59] The day before students were to return, parents and children looted and burned the township's liquor outlet. Goniwe was
furious and *sjamboked* several students. A crowd of younger
people attacked Goniwe with rocks, welding rods, and knives.
While students returned to class, the attack on Goniwe confirmed
that many younger people had broken away from organized political struggle and were shaping their own notions of resistance
and authority.[60]

The Eastern Cape security forces were under their own pressures. Pretoria demanded that they stifle the UDF. The security
police decided to deploy the most stringent counter-revolutionary tactics. On 8 May, three prominent civic activists from Port

Elizabeth disappeared and never returned. Later it was discovered that they had been taken to a police station near Cradock, where African and white security policemen had tortured and killed them. The security forces next trained their sights on Cradock's civic leaders. An inquest report later noted: "The security police and the army were engaged in what was regarded as counter-revolutionary strategy. Matthew Goniwe was a thorn in the flesh of the security forces and he was at times referred to as an enemy of the state." The security forces did not see that Goniwe's authority had become tenuous or that he was one of the only leaders left who could restore social order in Lingelihle.[61]

Early in 1985 police had informed Goniwe that "a better more sophisticated police officer" would be coming to Cradock to "sort them out." The police installed Major Eric Winter as the local security police commander. Winter had been in the Koevoet, an elite military unit specializing in guerrilla warfare and assassination. Winter's presence worried Goniwe. Matthew's brother recalls the fear that hung over Cradora's leadership:

> When he (Winter) arrived here, he came to our house. He sat with Matthew in this house. He said he wanted this place to be quiet. Winter stayed in town, and Matthew was worried about that. He said he doesn't know how this man works ... The PEBCO Three disappeared and Matthew was concerned about that ... he was worried because people in P.E. are not making a noise about this disappearance and the security guys are going to act again.[62]

Goniwe was correct. On 27 May, the police and security forces launched a massive raid upon Lingelihle. A helicopter flew overhead at dawn telling residents to stay in their houses and attacked Goniwe for failing to provide Lingelihle with services. Police distributed pamphlets that described Cradora and Cradoya as terrorist organizations. Saracen troop carriers, Caspirs, and other police vehicles raced through the township. Several infantry battalions supported the operation. An informant hidden in a police van identified activists suspected of unrest. The police arrested residents for public violence, stocktheft, and housebreaking. In a poignant juxtaposition of defiance and malnutrition, children burned the pamphlets while clamoring for the ration left-overs that the security forces handed out.[63]

On 7 June, the Eastern Cape's security branch sent a telegram to the senior officer at the State Security Council in Pretoria. The telegram called for the "permanent removal from society" of Matthew and Mbulelo Goniwe, as well as Fort Calata. The Eastern Cape Command convened with the P.E. security police and Winter. They arranged an assassination, tapped Goniwe's telephone, and waited to strike.[64]

On 27 June Goniwe, Calata, and two other activists left for P.E. to attend a UDF meeting. Goniwe had phoned to arrange the meeting. Cradora leaders met with regional UDF organizers that evening and prepared to return to Cradock. Goniwe promised that he would only stop for police roadblocks. The four Cradock men never returned. On the 28th, Goniwe's car was found burned and gutted outside of P.E. Goniwe's family alerted the media about the missing men. Residents launched a school and consumer boycott to force the police to locate the bodies. On 29 June, searchers located two of the four bodies. On July 2nd, searchers found Goniwe and Calata's corpses. All four men had been tortured, shot, stabbed, and their bodies burned.[65]

Expression of outrage at the murders soon followed. The police denied responsibility. They claimed that conflict between the UDF and a rival opposition party known as the Azanian People's Organization (AZAPO) caused the murders. UDF leaders scorned that suggestion. They emphasized that the state was responsible for the killings, given the sophistication of the assassination.

The funeral of the "Cradock Four" was to take place in mid-July. Unrest and police violence tore through Lingelihle until the funeral. Vigilante groups attacked suspected collaborators. One resident spoke of "hitmen" who killed and destroyed the property of those who did not protest. Police fired teargas and birdshot on crowds stoning private homes. Organized political protest like the street committees had vanished.[66]

The funeral signified a brief and final moment of peace. Fifty thousand people from across the country attended, as well as representatives from sympathetic countries. It was a quiet, disciplined, and yet angry funeral. Speakers denounced the state and announced that a State of Emergency was imminent. Matthew's wife Nyameka was unsure what lay ahead. She noted that only a few qualified leaders remained in the township, and the murders damaged the street committees. She expressed some optimism, stressing that "(s)omehow, some of the beautiful things he stood for will continue."[67]

Those "beautiful things" did not come to Doris Hermaans or to Lingelihle. Cradora activists placed Hermaans at the front of the funeral, to represent a collaborator made good. The police were not impressed. They destroyed her home with a bomb. Residents came forward, donating clothing and food. The SAP did not look kindly on this charity, either. They shot residents with pellets as they convened in front of Hermaans' smoldering, ruined home. For the next five years, violence and terror subsumed Lingelihle.[68]

Conclusion

Cradock's civic and youth leaders inspired a heroic, determined and meticulous protest campaign. Goniwe's innovative efforts at social control and his sensitivity to material grievances sparked mass protest in 1983; the creation of street committees to stunt violence and internal conflict briefly restored political direction and social control in late 1984. These achievements, however, were no match for subsequent state repression and internal conflict. Ironically, when Goniwe and Fort Calata's authority in the township became most tenuous, the state assumed precisely the opposite. The murders of the "Cradock Four" ignited a cycle of intensified violence and repression that ended only with the ANC's unbanning.

What then is the relationship between everyday violence, inter-generational relations, and politics during this two-year period of resistance? As Begona Aretxaga has argued in reference to the use of hunger strikes in Northern Ireland, "historical memory plays a deep role in political legitimacy. Historic actors do not play in an atemporal space or in a symbolic vacuum." Just as Irish hunger strikers drew on long-standing cultural precedents, so too did Cradock's activists skillfully appropriate conventional techniques of generational control as well as prior political discourse, symbols, and strategies. Cradock's leaders produced at transitory but critical moments compelling visions of social order and political power that appealed to a wide range of historical memories, held by youth and elders alike. In so doing, leaders like Goniwe not only made Cradock a powerful site of local anti-apartheid opposition, but the township became a critical component in regional and national struggles (Aretxaga 1993).

In 1995 President Nelson Mandela came to Cradock to honor the four dead activists, to recognize them for their pivotal role in opposition politics. And after an inquest dating back to 1989, the state has ruled that the security police had staged the assassinations. The diverse, kaleidoscopic memories of violence, heroism, betrayal, and passion live on—continuously retold, reconstructed, and contested in this small Karoo town.[69]

ACKNOWLEDGEMENT

This paper was originally presented at the annual conference of the African Studies Association, San Francisco, California, 23-26 November 1996.

NOTES

1. See Anonymous, "Building a Tradition of Resistance," *Work in Progress* 38 (August, 1985):4-8, and A. Sparks, "South African Unrest Spreads to Country," *Washington Post* 11 March 1985.

2. "Government Must Act on Cradock", *Eastern Province Herald*
    7 February 1985.
3. For a study that links longstanding modes of discipline to the
    "people's courts" of the 1980s, see Scharf and Ngcokoto 1990.
4. For a broader discussion of removals and their social consequences
    in South Africa, see Surplus People's Project 1983, Mayer and
    Mayer 1970, (chap 19:294-318), and Pinnock 1985. For a dis-
    cussion of Bantu Education, see Diseko 1992 and J. Hyslop, "As-
    pects of the failure of Bantu education as a hegemonic strategy:
    school boards, school committees and educational politics 1955-
    1976," unpublished paper presented to the History Workshop,
    University of the Witwatersrand, February 1987.
5. For a broad discussion of the Soweto uprising, see Kane-Berman
    1978, Hirson 1979 and Lodge 1983: (chap 13).
6. See also testimony presented by Gilbert Skweyiya for the Delmas
    Treason Trial, I2.39, vols. 411-2, pp. 23, 938-23, 943.
7. Testimony by G. Skweyiya for the Delmas Treason Trial, pp. 23,
    942-23, 945; Jo-Ann Bekker, "A Diet of Shaka and Beer Made
    the Kids Hungry for Change," *Weekly Mail* 24 April 1987; per-
    sonal interview with Thembikile Boss, 30 December 1994; per-
    sonal interview with Nomsa Frans, 21 December 1994.
8. Mandla Tyala, "More than 3,000 at Burial of Calata,' *Eastern
    Province Herald* 27 June 1983; personal interview with Nomonde
    Calata," 27 December 1994.
9. Testimony of G. Skweyiya for the Delmas Treason Trial, pp. 23,
    946-23, 954; minutes of the fourth ordinary meeting of the
    Lingelihle Village Council (hereafter the "LVC"), 12 April 1984,
    vol.10, pp. 675-6; personal interview with Gladwell Makhawula,
    11 February 1995; personal interview with Mopo Mene, 14 Feb-
    ruary 1995.
10. "Teacher Transfer Not Linked to Politics, says DET," Eastern
    Province Herald 17 January 1984; "Report to the N.E.C. on events
    in Cradock," submitted by Cradora organizer and used as evi-
    dence for the Delmas Treason Trial; personal interview with N.
    Frans.

11. Personal interview with Andile Sindelo, 12 March 1995; personal interview with Madoda Jacobs, 16 December 1995; testimony by G. Skweyiya for the Treason Trial, pp. 23, 957-23, 959.

12. Personal interview with G. Makhawula, 11 February 1995; personal interview with Di Bishop, 20 July 1995.

13. Personal interviews with M. Jacobs; personal interview with N. Frans; personal interview with G. Makhawula; testimony of G. Skweyiya testimony for the Delmas Treason Trial, pp. 23, 964; "Pledge not to transfer Goniwe 'Broken,'" *Eastern Province Herald* 24 August 1984.

14. "Cradock Boycott Meetings Banned," *Cape Times* 26 March 1984.

15. Isabel Koch, "Cradock schools due to reopen," Eastern Province Herald 27 March 1984; "Cradock boycott meetings banned," Cape Times 26 March 1984; J.-A. Bekker, "State separates trials for 22 on "violence" charges," *Eastern Province Herald* 2 August 1984.

16. Personal interview with N. Frans; personal interview with Nonyanga Sibanda, 23 August 1993; "Violence "could extend boycott," Cape Times 27 March 1984; "Teargas was used at Cradock-witness," Eastern Province Herald 3 August 1984; "Teargas was used "after police were stoned", Eastern Province Herald 7 August 1984.

17. Bernie Jongbloed, "Four Cradock detentions confirmed," *Eastern Province Herald* 2 April 1984; "Wife says detainee is without his tablets," *Eastern Province Herald* 2 April 1984; "Goniwe fine," Suzman", *Argus* 6 April 1984.

18. Personal interview with Fred Koni, 28 February 1995; personal interview with T. Boss; personal interview with N. Frans.

19. "Police stoned as 1,000-strong crowd is dispersed at Cradock," *Eastern Province Herald* 12 April 1984; J.-A. Bekker, "Policeman tells of shots at Cradock crowd," *Eastern Province Herald* 16 August 1984.

20. Minutes of the third ordinary meeting of the LVC held on 8 March 1984, vol. 10, pp. 558-9; minutes of the fourth ordinary meeting of the LVC held on 12 April 1984, vol.10, pp. 675-6.

21. Interview with Doris Mbanjwa (Hermaans), 20 December 1994; testimony of G. Skweyiya for the Delmas Treason Trial, pp. 23, 971-23, 972; Barney Mthombothi, "Troubled towns. Death, Fire-Bombs and Terror: Residents Find Themselves Locked in a Town ship at War with Itself," *Sunday Tribune,* 29 April 1984.

22. Interview with E.M. Ralawe, 28 January 1995; personal interview with D. Mbanjwa (Hermaans), 20 December 1994; personal interview with Daisy Bounce, 3 January 1995; "Jail for three guilty for stoning funeral," *Eastern Province Herald* 17 October 1984; confidential memorandum from LVC Chief Executive Officer G.J. Barnardt to Minister of Law and Order L. le Grange, 29 May 1984, as enclosed in minutes of the sixth ordinary meeting of the LVC held on 7 June 1984, vol. 10, pp. 945-51.

23. Memorandum from Barnardt to le Grange, 29 May 1984; minutes of second special meeting of the LVC held on 11 June 1984, vol. 10, pp. 966-7.

24. Testimony of G. Skweyiya for the Delmas Treason Trial, pp. 23, 972-23, 973.

25. Testimony of G. Skweyiya for the Delmas Treason Trial, pp. 23, 973-23, 974; "Le Grange visits Cradock," *Cape Times* 29 June 1984; Mono Badela, "Free Our Leaders, Say Students," *City Press* 8 July 1984.

26. Mandla Tyala, "Savage Calls for Swift Government Action on Goniwe," *Eastern Province Herald* 21 July 1984; M. Tyala, 'Police used *sjamboks* in house raid – claim," *Eastern Province Herald* 2 August 1984; J.-A. Bekker, "Violent unleash" unnecessary—witness," *Eastern Province Herald,* 9 August 1984.

27. "Solidarity rally today," *Eastern Province Herald* 21 July 1984; "Boesak angry about cancellation of service, *Daily Dispatch* 22 September 1984; "Boesak visits Cradock with television crew," *Eastern Province Herald* 10 August 1984; J.H.P. Serfontein, "Cradock: angry focus on the South African realities" *South African Outlook* October 1984.

28. M. Badela, "White Shops Boycotted Over Meeting Ban," *City Press* 29 July 1984; "Unrest taking its toll on white business,"

Eastern Province Herald 2 October 1984.

29. "Cradock Meetings Ban Lifted," *Eastern Province Herald,* 2 October 1984; "Lifting Cradock meetings ban 'no solution'", *Eastern Province Herald* 6 October 1984; M. Badela, "Now free our leaders," *City Press* 7 October 1984.

30. "Three Cradock Leaders Freed, Returned Home," *Eastern Province Herald* 11 October 1984.

31. J.H.P. Serfontein, "Cradock: Angry Focus on the South African Realities"; M. Tyala, "Cradora Backing Grew in Unrest- claim," *Eastern Province Herald* 16 October 1984.

32. J.H.P. Serfontein, "Cradock: Angry Focus on the South African Realities."

33. Personal interview with B.V. Ralawe, date not recorded; personal interview with D. Mbanjwa (Hermaans), 20 December 1994.

34. J.-A. Bekker, "'Rejected' Cradock Ilingelihle Council resigns en masse," *Eastern Province Herald* 5 January 1985; "Entire Village Council Resigns," *Cape Times* 7 January 1985.

35. "Victory for Cradora," *City Press* 13 January 1985; "Ilingelihle Resignations Draw Mixed Reactions," *Eastern Province Herald* 8 January 1985; interview with M. Jack, 6 August 1995.

36. Personal interview with N. Calata; personal interview with A. Sindelo; personal interview with Chester Kholiso, 28 November 1994; personal interview with Michael Adams, 29 November 1994; personal interview with Bonakele Makasi, 1 December 1994.

37. Personal interview with M. Mene; personal interview with anonymous, 10 August 1995.

38. Personal interview with G. Skweyiya, 24 February 1995.

39. Personal interview with Lungisile Ntsebeza, 3 February 1995.

40. There is confusion over the origin of Cradock's street committees. Mufson (1990:111) implies that the committees were operational in late 1983, in conjunction with CRADORA's founding, and that the idea for them came entirely from Cradock. Almore Cupido writes that CRADORA borrowed the idea from the Grahamstown Civic Association (GRACA) in late 1984; see untitled and unpublished paper on the biography of M. Goniwe.

Lodge and Nasson (1991:81-2), however, suggest that the street committees emerged in late 1984. Skweyiya supports Lodge's chronology, noting that the street committees were solidified by January 1985. See testimony by G. Skweyiya for the Delmas Treason Trial, pp. 24, 035-24, 040.

41. See also personal interview with L. Ntsebeza; Patrick Laurence, "Chicken Farm" Trial," *The World* 28 February 1977.

42. Also personal interview with G. Makhawula, 11 February 1995.

43. Personal interview with V. Bounce, 3 January 1995; personal interview with Khnyelwa Ralarala, 14 August 1995; personal interview with M. Mene.

44. M. Badela, "Dignity Kept Cradock from reveling," *City Press* 6 February 1985; personal interview with Vulindlela Bontsi.

45. Anon., "Cradock: building a tradition of resistanc"; M. Goniwe, undated notes, Matthew Goniwe Papers, Manuscripts and Archives, Yale University, New Haven, CT; personal correspondence with Janet Cherry, 28 July 1996.

46. "Sunday's Cradora Rally Banned by Magistrate," *Eastern Province Herald* 1 February 1985; Juliette Saunders, "Cradock Meeting Ban Upheld," *Eastern Province Herald,* 4 February 1985; Statement by G. Makhawula for the Delmas Treason Trial, file S6. 6.

47. Statement of G. Makhawula; statement of Mb. Goniwe; statement of M. Jacobs; statement of J. Ngabeli; statement of A. Pikinini (all submitted to the Delmas Treason Trial); J.-A. Bekker and D. March, "Two Dead After Cradock Violence," *Eastern Province Herald* 4 February 1985. Saunders and March write that Jacobs died in the hospital, while Makhawula claims that he died in the Caspir.

48. J.-A. Bekker, "Allegations will be raised in Parliament," *Eastern Province Herald* 6 February 1985; "Cradock unrest: 'no Comment' report denied," *Eastern Province Herald* 7 February 1985; Patrick Cull, "MP calls for probe into alleged police misconduct," *Eastern Province Herald* 14 February 1985; "PFP want police conduct probed," *Cape Times* 14 February 1985; "Le

Grange lashes out at malcomess," *Eastern Province Herald* 14 February 1985; I. Koch, "Morrison attacks PFP over Cradock unrest," *Eastern Province Herald* 15 February 1985.
49. J. Seekings, "The UDF in the Eastern Cape and Border regions, 1983-85," unpublished manuscript chapter and Mufson (1990: 82-90).
50. Louise Flanagan, "Goniwe's secret work in ANC underground," *Weekly Mail* 2 to 8 July 1993.
51. Personal interviews with M. Mene; personal interview with Mtutu Ntombela, 3 March 1995.
52. Personal interview with Zukise Frans, 21 February 1995; "Cradock Bodies 'looked like Mau Mau victims,'" *Eastern Province Herald* 19 March 1985.
53. Personal interview with T. Boss; anonymous interviews.
54. J Hyman, "Bid to Set Fire to Cradock Teachers' Homes," *Eastern Province Herald*, 20 March 1985.
55. Personal interview with Kaizer Duka, 17 March 1995; personal interview with A. Sindelo; personal interview with D. Bishop.
56. Anonymous interviews; personal interview with A. Sindelo.
57. Personal interview with Peggy Calata, 27 August 1995; personal interview with D. Bishop.
58. Personal interview with N. Calata; personal interview with F. Koni.
59. "School boycott in Cradock called off," *Eastern Province Herald* 9 April 1985; "Let's build on this good sense," *Eastern Province Herald* 10 April 1984.
60. "Report that Goniwe was Badly Injured is Denied," *Eastern Province Herald* 17 April 1985; personal interview with Fannie Ferreira, 12 December 1994. Ferreira served on the Cradock municipality and claims that he demanded the crowd to stop attacking Goniwe. A more reliable report comes from a personal interview with D. Bishop, who asserts that Matthew's wife, Nyameka Goniwe, confirmed to Bishop that the attack had occurred.
61. Inquest (into the death of the "Cradock Four"), #cc 7/93, finding by N.W. Zeitsman, Judge-President of the Eastern Cape Division, presiding officer at the inquest, pp. 19-20.

62. N. Goniwe, "Statement to First Hearings of the Truth and Reconciliation Commission," 17 April 1996; personal interview with A. Goniwe, 28 December 1994.
63. "Classes Suspended in Cradock," *Star* 23 May 1985; I. Koch, "Cradock's Raid: "Some" Arrests," *Eastern Province Herald* 28 May 1985.
64. Mncedisi Saliso, "Goniwe Killings: Officers Blamed," *Eastern Province Herald* 8 February 1994; M. Saliso, "Inquest court on tenterhooks," *Eastern Province Herald* 10 February 1994.
65. TRC testimony by N. Goniwe; J. Cherry, "Briefing notes" on Cradock presented to the TRC (draft copy, July 1996).
66. J. Nel, "Township Resident Fed Up With 'Unrest'", *Eastern Province Herald* 20 July 1985.
67. J.-A. Bekker, "Goniwe a "Moderating Influence"," *Eastern Province Herald* 22 July 1985.
68. Personal interview with D. Mbanjwa (Hermaans).
69. Inquest (into the death of the "Cradock Four"), #cc 7/93, finding by N.W. Zeitsman, Judge-President of the Eastern Cape Division, presiding officer at the inquest.

Chapter 7

STREAMS OF CONTESTATION: AGE AND POLITICS IN MAASAI LAND CLAIMS AND CONFLICTS

❖

John G. Galaty

Word blew like dust through the market of the small rift valley town of *Ewuaso oon Kedong,*' "the river-of-bee-hives." Ewuaso herders had been accosted by a group of armed men, *young* men, or, rather, older boys, from an age-grade of later teenagers often glossed, not inappropriately, as "warriors." These *Il-murran* from Mosiro, the group ranch immediately to the south of the Ewuaso ranch, sought to prevent the herders from watering livestock at the wells along the border between the two localities. In the market town, a comparable set of young men from Ewuaso quickly gathered, readying themselves for a counter-attack to defend what they saw as their group's rights. But before they could move to the site, news came that the police had established control, so with a mixture of relief and regret, the would-be champions of the locality drifted home. A wind rises, becomes a swirling sand devil, then subsides. The state prevails.

Local Maasai politics always seems to involve a ready mix of talk and violence: often talk, then violence, but just as often violence, then talk. After the deed, talk puts a sort of "local construction" on the event, framing, highlighting, justifying, and reinterpreting it to certain aims and purposes. Never simply acts of force, violent deeds are practices which have force not despite but because they signify. For the young men /older boys from Mosiro, their attack on a herd that belonged to the Senior Government Chief of Keekonyokie location, of which both Ewuaso and Mosiro form a part, was defensive, for the ingression of his herd into Mosiro locality in early June 1994 was a concrete sign of his claim to land in the area. To have allowed his herd access to the wells, given ongoing conflicts, would be to concede his right not only to water but to land.

Named after its terrain, *osero*, a place of dry bushes, a sort of "wilderness," Mosiro benefits from the flow of the Ewuaso Ng'iro down from the slopes of the rocky *Osoit le Mosiro*, but its lowland plains have served as wet season pasture for several Maasai groups.[1] The locality has long been a site of contestation for several reasons. The construction of artificial wells, boreholes, and dams has furthered the ongoing process of establishing land claims throughout the ostensibly vast expanses of Maasailand, so areas such as Mosiro have gradually become sites of semi-permanent habitation. Accordingly, at the historical moment of vulnerability when Mosiro group ranch is undergoing subdivision, legally registered members and outsiders alike position themselves to make claims on parcels of its land. Land law hovers over the region like an unavoidable cloud, but it meets a second, irrepressible mist rising from the land, that of customary claims. In the confusion of claims, the force of law often seems pitted against the

212

perceived legitimacy of local rights. In neighboring Lodariak (another locality in Keekonyokie division), hundreds of absentee title claimants technically own land that they have been forcibly prevented from occupying, or even visiting, since their claims are viewed as illegitimate (not to mention illegal) by local Maasai who are the actual residents of the region (Galaty 1994a). Law, legitimacy, and justice do not always flow into the same stream.[2]

The Group Representatives Act stipulates that in the case of subdivision group lands were to be divided equitably among its registered members. But in fact vast discretionary powers have been vested in the land committee of each ranch, or were deemed to have been so by officers in the Ministry of Lands who have overseen (and often benefited from) the adjudication process.[3] Prior to the events of June 1994, a major scandal erupted when it was discovered that Mosiro was in the process of being given away from under the feet of its members, due to collusion between Ministry of Land officials and the secretary of the land committee in allocating Mosiro land to outsiders. I received the following account of the affair:

> As the surveyors were busy helping the committee, they got close to the Secretary for their own convenience. They introduced rich non-Maasai men, as well as their own relatives, to the committee members. This was aimed at efforts to acquire "Maasai" land in the area on the part of the ranch beneficiaries. Most of these people were Kikuyu.
>
> The committee members were heavily bribed, and the rich men managed to acquire pieces of land. They then started pressuring the committee to quickly organise plans for getting title deeds to the land illegally. The presence of politicians in the area made all these events to be undertaken secretly.
>
> When the Ministry of Lands helped the members process the title deeds, it was discovered that the names on the list were a mixture of Maasai as well as non-Maasai names. With the adjudication of Mosiro still incomplete,

the Ministry began giving out the title deeds, which was basically illegal. Complaints from knowledgeable people who were from other parts of Ngong confirmed these illegal transactions. Eventually, the District Commissioner looked over the matter and stopped the whole exercise.

I have described elsewhere (Galaty 1994a) how the adjudication was annulled by the district commissioner in the presence of the vice-president of Kenya, who is the member of parliament for the Kenyan constituency where the localities in question lie.[4] But local Maasai were left shaken by the threat of being dispossessed by outsiders and locally powerful individuals, through machinations beyond their control and comprehension. Now, a year later, in June 1994, violence threatened to erupt that would pit one Maasai group against another rather than insiders against outsiders.

Lending drama to the episode, the district officer ordered the Sub-chief of Mosiro arrested for allegedly having incited the young men to act against the Senior Chief's herd. The Sub-Chief knew that the Senior Chief and other prominent Keekonyokie Maasai (who were not, however, from the Mosiro locality) had staked out large individual ranches in the area, for which they anticipated receiving title deeds and over which they were now beginning to assert rights.[5] The ox's horn always precedes the ox; in this spirit the presence of the Chief's herd marked his claim.

With anthropology's center of gravity lying somewhat lower to the ground than that of the state, its narratives tend to be woven out of episodes of actual experience, ideally conveying something of the texture and pattern of the socially real in cultural practice. But today we are convinced that the path of the local, although tangential to the long gravel and earth road proverbially built only yesterday, also transects global space. Do we then envision the people we know as "local characters," acting out parts in dramas, written elsewhere, about transnationalism, dependency, and postcolonialism? How do we accommodate both aspects of our twofold cognizance, that people everywhere participate in a

214

single world of global force and import but pursue projects of local scale, designed with home-grown definition, value, and shape? To make manageable this conundrum in anthropological identity and method, I would try to refashion it by first working upward and then downward to join the strands of cultural locality to those of state and globality without allowing either priority over the other.

Throughout history, peasant wars have been fought against the backdrop of precisely the sort of erosion of land rights as this episode reveals. And the significance of this momentary eruption of aggression, and the emotion behind it, gains added contrast against a backdrop of two simultaneous events. The first is the widespread experience throughout Keekonyokie Division of corruption in land allocations and a longer history of drastic land loss by Maasai. The second is an eruption of ethnic clashes across the Rift Valley region, born of a backlash against long-term rural migration to Maasai and Kalenjiin territories from Kenya's Central Province, which, in the context of incipient multi-party elections and democratization-from-above, was seen as a crucial factor in the national struggles during the 1992 Kenyan General Elections. International pressure and the implementation of a structural adjustment program in Kenya have helped accelerate the sub-division of group holdings, initiating the sort of local opportunism that invariably accompanies enclosure. Given that it is an enclosure of a collectivity, the sub-division process may seem to outsiders to resemble privatization of a socialist cooperative, but since group ranches were in fact domains under private title, the process in fact represents a dissolving of the assets of an agrarian freehold corporation, which are then allocated among the diversity of its owners. But international pressure for democratization has also strengthened national ethnic blocs, thus lending a sense of high drama to the usual local squabbles over land.[6]

"Global forces," yes, but with local faces. The assumption held by a congeries of Chiefs, Sub-Chiefs, Councilors, Mayors, and local businessmen and politicians from Kajiado District, in which Keekonyokie division lies, that *they* above all deserve the fruits of "development," is surely what class formation is all about. It is unlikely, however, that the progressive appropriation of land wealth in Maasailand could be accomplished without the sort of factional strife that is rife there. In the recent past, a subtle alliance between Kikuyu and more wealthy Maasai supported the rise of the incumbent Vice-president of Kenya from national to local prominence (an interesting reversal of the more conventional political career, which stemmed from his being a nominated member of parliament, appointed minister of finance, who subsequently sought office), and this alliance was cemented through the distribution of illegal allocations of land carved out of pastoral group holdings and through officially sanctioned purchases.

Politicians from the two major Maasai Districts (Kajiado and Narok) have often been at odds with one another, and most recently a powerful minister from Narok has quietly garnered support in Kajiado from those who oppose the Vice-president's faction. The former has also become the public advocate of preserving the integrity of Maasai land, while the latter has been increasingly associated with the erosion of indigenous land rights. One reason for the quick arrest of the Mosiro Sub-chief was that he was seen as acting on behalf of the Narok parliamentarian, by inciting local protest against appropriation of land by members of the Vice-President's faction. It has been thought that the Narok Parliamentarian was biding his time, accumulating embarrassing evidence that might ultimately be used to topple his prominent opponent. But his hand would be strengthened if protest broke out against irregular land allocations in the Vice-president's own constituency. Thus local strife was generally construed as an act of high politics, perhaps the initiation of a wider mobilization against a sitting Vice-president.

But events have subsequently shown that a few weeks can be a lifetime in politics. In late 1996, shifting political strategy, President Moi demoted the parliamentarian from Narok in a shuffle of ministerial posts, clearly signaling his support for the Vice-President. One reason was another outbreak of violence between

Keekonyokie and Purko, which occurred in a dispute over a boundary between two group ranches. Although both ranches had largely been subdivided among their members, a spring along the side of the escarpment had been left undivided, due to the fact that everyone in the area, including herders from both ranches, depended on it for water. For years, both Keekonyokie and Purko herders had shared use of the spring. But recently the Purko had begun to move in, claiming the area, saying that the Keekonyokie would just seize the land, get a title-deed, and sell it, like they had sold much of the rest of their land. It was said that the Purko came to settle in the area only after the Keekonyokie had been subdividing their own land. The Keekonyokie then told them to go to their own side, back to Mosiro, ending the shared use of the resource that had previously been the case. But when Keekonyokie tried to move into the area, there was an armed clash, resulting in several Keekonyokie being killed. Then government forces came in to stop the violence.

The minister from Narok District, a Purko, was publically blamed for the outbreak of violence, since the area concerned was technically in Keekonyokie. Not only was it seen from the outside as another case of Purko expansionism, but also as illustrative of the politician's "tribalistic" chauvinism, here splitting two groups of Maasai. However, it was suspected by some observers that the vice-president, a parliamentarian from Kajiado, may have quietly instigated the affair by encouraging the Keekonyokie to move into the area, in order to embarrass his political opponent. The episode was in fact immediately followed by the demotion of the Narok politician, and this may lead to a weakening of those who oppose allocating Maasai land to outsiders and those who seek reversal of illicit allocations through the courts or through legislation.

But even these specific manifestations of national and international factions and forces rest on a locally-defined structure of relations and interpretations. For instance, why should Keekonyokie officials try so blatantly to appropriate land in Mosiro, and why should they be so resented when they do so? A

217

bit of administrative history may shed some light on this question. When the boundary between Kajiado and Narok was established, efforts were made to contain most Purko Maasai in Narok;
Kajiado was primarily occupied by the Osilalei Maasai, but the
Keekonyokie, long allies of the Purko, straddled the boundary
between the two districts, one of its localities (Oike) lying in Narok
District along the western Rift Valley escarpment. And the Mosiro
locality in Keekonyokie, which adjoins a part of Mosiro in Narok,
is administratively part of Keekonyokie; it was, and is, in fact
occupied by "ethnically" Purko Maasai. As I was told,

> The Purko who inhabited the area (of Mosiro) originated
> from Oldorko le Losokon in Narok. Their migration into
> this area was instigated by a drought that occurred in
> Narok. When they got to Mosiro, they found the area
> sparsely populated and decided to settle permanently.
> They were also encouraged to settle down by constant
> showers in the area. Clashes arose among the Loodokilani
> and Purko people which were finally quashed by the gov-
> ernment.[7] The Purko stayed on even after this instability.
> By this time, Mosiro was a group ranch belonging to the
> North Keekonyokie, and it seemed to have swallowed
> up the Purko as from the beginning.

The people of Mosiro might publicly proclaim that they were
Keekonyokie, which administratively they are, but they also are
known in fact to be Purko, a reality they view more with pride
than denial. Here, in the microcosm of a sub-ethnic administrative locality, we can see the more global implications of joining
nation and state. Ethnic distributions never quite match the political and administrative structures they define, but rather generate
around identities a complex set of social anomalies and paradoxes of ethnic affinity and residence, namely non-resident nationals (who live elsewhere) and non-national residents (seen,
justifiably or not, as having come from elsewhere). In Mosiro,
land rights that clearly rested with its local and indigenous inhabitants were seen as flawed by the Keekonyokie, who could assert

that its Purko residents should "return to Narok" Though traditionally allied in relation to other Maasai groups, Keekonyokie
and Purko are nonetheless opposed segments of the highland
Maasai. Throughout the twentieth century, in particular during
the post-Independence period, this latent opposition has been re-
inforced by its congruence with district boundaries and distinct
political interests, in particular over land. The local premise that
Purko residence in Keekonyokie section is illegitimate is strengthened by the fact that Mosiro leaders not only ignored but abetted
the corrupt process of land allocation, which would have left the
ordinary Mosiro Maasai landless. From the point of view of
Keekonyokie leaders, if Mosiro leaders wish to give up their land,
who else should benefit from it but they, who represent the location as a whole?

If the rough structure of Maasai sectional relations bears on
this local clash, so does the processual nature of the Maasai age
system. Today, the politicians in power are largely from the *I-
Seuri* age-set, who have just completed the long ritual task of
inaugurating and socializing the age-set that, in a pattern of dual-
stream alternations, lies two behind them.[8] Relations between
sponsoring and sponsored age-sets are usually marked by ambivalence; in particular, with the maturation and growing independence of the younger group, deference and respect come to
be mixed with episodes of revolt. During the last five years, the
widespread and probably accurate perception by young men of
the *Il-Manjeshi* age, that the Seuri were accumulating land at the
expense of the younger men, led in several regions to outright
conflict between groups among which solidary relations of spon-
sorship and authority theoretically should obtain. Today, the new
set of initiates bears even less respect for this senior group because their sponsors, the *Il-Kitoip*, are from the opposite stream.
Thus the attack on the Chief's herders by *Il-murran* of Mosiro
carried weight as a statement of age-set antagonism: he, a Seuri,
was being attacked not only by younger men, but by members of
a group sponsored by the *Il-Kitoip*, the age-set immediately junior to his, who were thus from the opposing stream. The clash

219

was thus underpinned by two distinct dimensions of age-set antagonism, which divided the Chief from the young men both by seniority and by structural alternation.[9]

At a time in anthropology when "violence" is attributed to the implicit constraints exercised by nouns, pronouns, and verbs, to attributions and predicates, the exercise of real force, when one group of young men cracks the heads of another with clubs and threatens them with spears, seems palpable (though of course greatly restrained, both by the closeness of the groups and the absence of firearms in local hands). When "resistance" is elicited from the symbolism of poetry, moods, and evangelism, it is almost a relief when local folk actually take direct action to defend lives or land. And when the post-colonial characterizes sense and sensibility in the cultural contrasts and differences between the globally North and South, there is a satisfying concreteness to episodes of struggle that are in fact artifacts of *real* colonial borders and *actual* postcolonial interventions (which the World Bank's structural adjustment policies, no matter how benign, represent) in national and local policy and practice.

The crack of clubs and the wielding of spears, though limited assertions, are overtly violent acts of resistance, not only to local land grabbers wielding micro-ethnic justification, but, in a more global framework, to the consolidation of a landed class and to the realization of global liberalism in a postcolonial world. These concrete practices, whether representing moves on a larger chess board of political and ethnic struggle or mere responses to local provocation, are not more real simply because they embody force; for, being pragmatic acts, they rely on the illocutionary force they bear, as both assertions of resistance and as claims to land. To understand the locally real today calls for unraveling the strands of an increasingly pervasive system of world relations and of the cultural premises by which motives and interests are defined and action constrained. Then in our own narratives the strands must be rewoven to produce convincing accounts of the complex grounds for the sorts of claims and conflicts that make up what is important to local lives today.

ACNOWLEDGEMENTS

The original version of this paper was presented in the panel on "Fictions of Law, Enactments of Power: Rethinking the Relations Between States and Subjects" at the Annual Meeting of the Canadian Anthropology Society (CASCA), held in Montréal, 27 May 1995. Research reported was supported by the Social Sciences and Humanities Research Council of Canada (SSHRC) and the Québec Fonds pour la Formation de Chercheurs et l'Aide à la Recherche (FCAR). Work was carried out in cooperation with the Arid Lands and Resource Management Network in Eastern Africa (ALARM), which is supported by the International Development Research Center of Canada. For development of the case studies, I am grateful for the assistance of Jeremiah Ole Tumanka from Ewuaso Kedong and Joseph Ole Simel from Lodariak.

NOTES

1. Ironically, "wet" season pasture is usually dry, but after the rains it bursts forth with sweet annual grasses which, if not quickly consumed by livestock or wildlife dies, dries and shrivels, the land reverting to parched aridity throughout the dry season, when the joint community of people and their animals retreat to perennial pastures and permanent water.
2. For elaboration of the Mosiro and Lodariak cases, see Galaty (1994a, 1996) and Simel (1995).
3. Like their neighbors on Ewuaso and Lodariak group ranches, in the early 1970s, adult Maasai males in Mosiro locality were constituted as a legal "group" and granted a single, undifferentiated freehold title. By the late 1980s, encouraged by global liberalization and pressured by the government, group ranches were moving inexorably towards subdivision. Land committees, often the same committees that oversaw the original registration of group members, were charged in the event of subdivision with allocat-

221

ing land among the group members and given the authority to receive and act on requests.

4. However, outside claimants did not passively accept his nullification but argued in court that their holding of "first title" should lead to the nullification being set aside. The court found in their favor. Shifting strategy, those opposing the unjust allocation of land to outsiders, and with the moral and financial assistance of Survival International in London, have sought to have a bill brought before the Kenyan Parliament, which would create a legislative solution to both the Lodariak and Mosiro cases. But in the current pre-election period, it is unclear that the bill will in fact be brought forward. At the same time, prominent figures from Mosiro, a region with a high rate of non-literacy, who might have been expected to lead the community in opposing the allocation, have been bribed and threatened not to pursue the case; one was reportedly given a land rover, while another was said called to the Vice-President's office, where he was accused of being an "anti-government tribalist," before being offered money and a position as a district councilor. So despite both national and international attention given to the case, and the rapid (though provisional) nullification of the illegal allocations, it is far from clear that in the end justice will be done.

5. For discussion of the disastrous land sales that followed the allocation of individual ranches during the 1970s, see Galaty (1992).

6. Discussion of factors leading to the dissolution of group ranches can be found in Galaty (1994b).

7. I have elsewhere described some underlying causes and structure of clashes between Loodokilani and Purko Maasai (Galaty 1980).

8. The *Seuri*, a mature age-set composed of one right and one left-hand division, is sponsor to the right-hand *Il-Kipali* and the left-hand *Il-Manjeshi* groups, which in time will be consolidated into a single, named age-set. Immediately succeeding *I-Seuri* (and preceding the age-set the *Seuri* sponsor) are *Il-Kitoip*, a set which includes the right-hand *I-Rampau* and the left-hand *Irrang'irrang'* groups. *Il-Kitoip* in turn are sponsors for the new right-hand set now in the process of formation and first-recruitment (in some

Maasai sections provisionally called *Il-Memiri*). Thus one full set, encompassing both a right and a left-hand group active as Il-*murran* over a 14 to 15 year period, separates a sponsoring and a sponsored group. The age-set "ladder," senior to junior, runs from the *Seuri*, to *Kitoip*, to *Kipali-Manjeshi*, to *Memiri*; linked in the opposed alternations are, (a) *Seuri* and *Kipali-Manjeshi*, and (b) *Kitoip* and *Memiri*.

9. Among Spencer's scholarly accomplishments are the analysis, over a 20 year period, of the structural implications of these two "models" of East African age organization, which he has called the "gerontocratic ladder" and the "opposing streams," both of which are structurally combined in the Maasai system (Spencer 1976, 1988, 1993a).

Chapter 8

SOME EFFECTS ON A DISTRICT BOUNDARY IN KENYA

❖

Günther Schlee

Paul Spencer (1973: 191-5) has, in his discussion of interethnic alliances between the Samburu and Rendille and the emergence of the Ariaal, an intermediate category of people with clan links to both sides, paid great attention to the attempts of the colonial administration to implement clear distinctions between the "tribes" they perceived and to the boundary which was drawn between their respective districts. His work has recently been taken up by an historian, Simpson, who elaborates on some of the same conflicts (Simpson 1994, chap. 9, cf. Falkenstein [in prep.], chap. 2; Spencer 1973: 193) and adopts a perspective similar to Spencer's

on policies connected to boundaries. But such matters are not
only of historical interest. In some ways Kenya has not changed
much, as the following newspaper cutting illustrates:

BIG SHOTS BEHIND ILLEGAL CATTLE DEALS
by Wangui Gachie

The Minister for Livestock Development ... said yesterday the ministry was concerned about certain influential
people flouting livestock movement regulations in the
country. People had been moving livestock from one district to another without necessary clearing, vaccination
or testing.

Noting that the practice could lead to the spread of
deadly diseases to residents and cattle, the minister decided that the practice cease immediately.

[The Minister said] the Ministry was aware of the
illegal movement within the country adding the practice
had been exacerbated by the closure of the Kenya Meat
Commission.

"The closure of the KMC led to illegal movement of
cattle within the country as pastoralists set out to sell
them to get money for their needs," he said, adding that
now that the KMC had resumed operations, the practice
must be curbed ... some unscrupulous stock traders ...
obtained permits to move cattle from the north and north
eastern districts under the pretext that such cattle were
destined for KMC.

He noted that many of these cattle ended up in Thika,
Murang'a and Nyeri where unsuspecting farmers bought
and mixed herds causing disease outbreaks ...

He addded that the country had attained a high standard of livestock and the government would not allow
anybody to contaminate them (*The Standard*, Saturday
12 August 1989, pp. 1, 9).

The quoted article stems from a Nairobi daily newspaper where
it was the first item containing the main headline. It is written in

straight and plain journalese, but the reader who is not familiar with Kenya may require some explanations nevertheless. The Kenya Meat Commission is a parastatal organization which used to cooperate with the Livestock Marketing Division (LMD). The KMC has held "a legal monopoly of slaughtering for export and for the urban areas" (Raikes 1981:191). The LMD did the buying of stock while KMC owned slaughter houses at Athi River near Nairobi and at Mombasa. In reality,

> the LMD succeeded the African Livestock Marketing Organization soon after Independence. It owns and operates all primary markets for slaughter stock, stock-routes and holding grounds (through which it can control the movement of stock) and operates quarantines and vaccination of slaughter stock. While private traders can use these facilities too, subject to acceptance of the regulations, the LMD carries out most of the direct trade in stock from the northern pastoral areas for canning. (Raikes 1981:192)

The colonial forerunner of the LMD, the African Livestock Marketing Organization, by its very name betrayed its function of keeping the stock from areas inhabited by African pastoralists in separate marketing channels from the cattle of the ranchers in the "White Highlands," the European settler colony. The stock owned by whites were accorded higher grades while the African stock were kept at low price levels. Where these prices were unattractive to the seller, in the 1930s the prices offered to pastoralists were only one quarter of those prevailing elsewhere (Raikes 1981:119); de-stocking campaigns were carried out by force.

But even at times when their stock were not seized by force, the African producers had poor prospects of getting a price comparable to that in the free market of the settler sector, since the two production areas were separated by a quarantine belt and movement of stock was closely controlled, not only between the European and the African sector but even within the latter, where the range was divided into tribal grazing areas (Schlee 1984, 1991).

Already in 1932 a colonial officer writes that the pastoral areas were closed off from all major markets "as if shut up in a tin box made of quarantine regulations."[1] The existence of some infectious diseases appears to have come in quite handy as an excuse for keeping African stock off the European-dominated market.

After a period of closure following mismanagement, the KMC, with a new financing plan, was put back into operation in 1989. During the closure private traders had taken over, but then stock routes were closed again to reestablish the KMC monopoly. I am not in a position to assess the actual veterinary situation and whether the fears of "contamination" of the stock south of the quarantine belt expressed by the Minister are justified. In this chapter I merely want to contrast different official and unofficial views of those regulations and boundaries.

Nomadic livestock producers and private traders have always viewed the present practice as a direct continuation of colonial policies that still work to the benefit of the remaining white ranchers and African elites which have taken over the ranches of those Europeans who have left. Circumventing quarantine regulations for them is both a necessity and a type of sport.

The area to which the minister refers as "the north and northeastern districts" is the arid lowland part of Kenya beyond the quarantine belt. These lowlands are inhabited by nomads speaking Nilotic and Cushitic languages (Samburu, Rendille, Gabbra, Boran, Somali). The localities referred to in the next paragraph, Thika, Murang'a and Nyeri—are situated in the Central Province, a comparatively developed, agricultural area inhabited by the Bantu-speaking Kikuyu.

Apart from this newspaper cutting, I base my argument on a case history about a lorry driver who was intercepted when trying to smuggle livestock along a closed route. I shall further adduce some linguistic and historical considerations with the aim of finding out whether in the Rendille perception of space there is anything corresponding to our concept of a boundary. As colonial and postcolonial policies have heavily relied on cris-crossing Kenya with internal boundaries, the question of perception of space and its subdivisions and the different evaluations of policies attached to these perceptions seem to me a central issue at the cross-section of cognitive anthropology, economics, and politics.

The result is that people inhabiting the same country have quite different views of the legitimacy and usefulness or even the existence of boundaries. The presence or absence of boundaries and the access to resources regulated by them shapes many aspects of social life, among them ethnic affiliations, in one way or another. First the case history.

Not long before the article quoted above appeared in *The Standard*, a Somali lorry driver, a young man of 23, whom I shall call Nasruddin, drove in the middle of the night towards the boundary between Marsabit and Samburu Districts. Nasruddin carried a load of smallstock which comprised animals belonging to seven Gabbra men whose language (Boran) Nasruddin spoke just as fluently as four other languages, namely his mother tongue (Somali), the language of his home area (Rendille), Swahili, and English (which he had learned at school and on the road). Multilingualism is widespread in northern Kenya, especially among Somali traders residing in small rural towns, for whom, together with the contacts established through it, it is an important part of their social capital.

The lorry belonged to Nasruddin's father, a wealthy and influential trader and politician, somebody who, at least in a local framework, comes close to the category sometimes referred to in the press as "Big Shots." Nasruddin had a perfectly valid permit for transporting livestock to Nairobi; only the starting point of the journey given in the paper was still ahead of him; he was allowed to take a load of smallstock from the Samburu District, not from Marsabit District which he was about to leave. It would have been impossible to get a permit to move smallstock out of Marsabit District because of a quarantine. Nasruddin regarded such quarantines as a constant annoyance. For him they meant that other people wanted to sell their stock before him. Thus, he did not follow the idea put to him regarding a particular disease present in a particular area at a particular time. Luckily, such regulations were easy enough to circumvent. Very soon he would reach the district boundary and, after crossing it, everything would be perfectly legal, his papers in order, and he would have nothing else to worry about on the 500-km drive down to Nairobi.

Behind Nasruddin, Mustafa was also driving. He was from a different "tribe" and a different town, but he was of a similar social background and through his mother he was related to Nasruddin. Mustafa was ten years older and already had a lorry of his own, however he was also carrying a load of smallstock like Nasruddin's.

At the district boundary there were some huts, tea kiosks, and a police line. The road passed between the kiosks and the police line. Electricity had never penetrated the area and most kerosene lamps had been extinguished. The small locality was asleep. Nobody would stop them.

But at that moment, the engine of Nasruddin's lorry started to misfire and with a few bangs, louder than gun-shots, the lorry came to a stand right in front of the police line and no matter how desperately Nasruddin turned the ignition key, the engine would not start again. Mustafa overtook Nasruddin's lorry and disappeared into the night. There was no way to stop just then and help his cousin. He would have to abandon him to his fate.

Other helpers came soon. The policemen, woken up by the bangs, had noticed that there was a lorry in trouble in front of their camp and they approached it with their flashlights. They found the lorry full of bleating goats and sheep and the situation was at once clear to their investigative minds. The only thing left was to find out to whom these smallstock belonged and then to apprehend the culprits.

"*Mbuzi ya nani*?"—"Whose goats are these?" they asked. Nasruddin had to think quickly. There were seven owners plus him, the driver, eight culprits in total. Eight culprits would have to pay eight fines. If there was only one culprit, the matter might turn out cheaper, he thought. "They are all mine!", he told them before anybody else could say something different. However, he thought, it would still be better not to be taken to court at all but to bribe the policemen as usual. Normally some hundred shillings would do. But one of the policemen had had a quarrel with Nasruddin's brother and refused to be mollified. In the end Nasruddin offered Ksh 1,000 (ca. $60.00) to each of the four policemen and they rejected the bribe! This event was to be discussed in the whole district for weeks, because nobody ever had met before policemen who do not take Ksh 1,000 when given the chance.

Engines sometimes misfire and sometimes they don't. Very soon and without any repairs the engine could be started again and this time it ran as smoothly as ever. But the journey now proceeded north, and not south. Nasruddin with his lorry and all humans and ungulates in it was taken back under armed escort to the district capital, Marsabit.

Eleven days later the judge passed a verdict which was more lenient than expected. Nasruddin was fined Ksh 5,000. But to mollify the judge, Nasruddin's family had spent Ksh 10,000 pacifying him, a sum which did not appear on any records.

We may now sum up the various transfers caused by this incident and the other effects it has had on the local scene. Ksh 10,000 were paid by a trader to a judge. In economic terms such transfers can be seen as revenue which stems from the private sector and is privately appropriated by members of the state class, thus subsidizing their salaries. However, as through this practice nearly all policy implementation becomes impossible, they are officially not desired and we can hardly classify such payments as having a positive effect on a closed stock route, although the judge might perceive them as just that. Ksh 5,000 were paid as a fine to the State, which can use such money to implement its policies, such as closing stock routes.

As quarantines are officially there for stopping the spread of diseases, we may also ask whether Nasruddin's arrest had any such effect. It probably had not. First of all, it is doubtful that the disease situation south of the closed boundary differed in any way from the one north of it; probably there were the same diseases on both sides anyhow. Therefore, Mustafa's lorry and many other lorries had succeeded in circumventing the quarantine, not to speak of the uncounted herdsmen who just drive their animals afoot through the bush and put them on a lorry only after crossing such boundary. Even if the quarantine had been justified in veterinary terms, it would not have had any veterinary effect because of its lack of proper implementation.

Nasruddin's social capital, though, had greatly increased. He was the hero of the day. He had taken all the guilt on his shoulders. The seven owners of the livestock gladly paid his fine and promised that in future they would hire only Nasruddin's lorry and nobody else's. He had made a profit from all the above described misfortune, and had revived historical perceptions of boundaries and their difficult implementation.

The boundary at which Nasruddin's lorry was intercepted dates back to colonial times, when it was delineated by the British, in order to separate the grazing ground of one "tribe" from that of another. Thus, it originally had an "ethnic" justification. However, those boundaries were drawn along the distinctions made by those who drew them. They were based on British notions concerning African ethnicities, African forms of land use, and African concepts of territoriality. Those colonial constructs did not recognize double affiliations, interethnic clan brotherhoods (i.e., the fact that somebody can be of a different ethnic group yet be of the same clan as yourself), collective adoptions, etc. Even if the pastoralists of northern Kenya had had similar notions of territoriality as the British did, i.e., that of a bounded surface area belonging to a finite set of people, established by rules about membership, that notion did not necessarily mean that an individual, a household, or a lineage would have been greatly restricted in their movements by such a form of territoriality. After all, migrants who can claim membership in more than one group can also claim rights of use of more than one area. However, was there such a notion of territoriality and was the perception of space broken down into two-dimensional units circumscribed by boundaries? A word frequently used by speakers of Cushitic languages to denote the concept of boundary is *mpaka*, not a Cushitic but a Bantu word, probably incorporated in this area quite recently through the administrative use of Swahili. Another word which Cushites use for this concept is *seer*. This term, however, is polysemous, it oscillates between different meanings. In addition to "boundary" it can also mean "day of the week."

> *Maanta a seer oh?* [Rendille] (Which *seer* is today?)
> *Alasmin* (Monday.)

It is likely that the original reference of *seer* refers neither to time, nor to space. In most languages spatial metaphors are applied to time, no time metaphors are applied to space. However, we are not sure what exactly the original spatial reference of *seer* was. The words which we find in use for "boundary" may therefore in this sense be quite recent introductions, dating to colonial times, as we do not find an established term for "boundary" of which we can be reasonably sure that it was also part of the precolonial language use. The etymology of *seer* (*sera* in Boran), goes back to a Semitic word for law (*sar'at* in Geez; Haberland 1963:226), *shari'a* in Arabic, a concept only vaguely related to "boundary," although one can "transgress" both. This Semitic word for "law" may in its turn go back to a concept similar to "path," the metaphorical "right path."

However, some thinkers claim that there are "unnamed categories," while others object to this saying that it is just a device to impose your names and categories on the representation of a world view which purportedly belongs to somebody else. Therefore, if there are such unnamed categories, we should extend our quest. Instead of just looking for a word for "boundary" we should also look for the potentially unnamed idea of "boundary."

In a rather lengthy interview with a very knowledgeable informant, the original text of which is reproduced and analyzed elsewhere (Schlee 1990a), I have tried in numerous ways, some of them even suggestive, to elicit a description of circumscribed surface areas like "the Rendille land" or areas separated by ritual gates (*ulukh*). As a result, "Rendilleland" was represented as a temporary spatial constellation (wherever the Rendille were at a given time), and could overlap with "Samburuland" or with anybody else's whereabouts. The "gates" were very propitious if the right rituals were carried out when passing them but they did not lead from one defined area to another. My attempts to analyze spatial representations of northern Kenyan pastoral nomads (Schlee 1990b, 1992) have revealed, instead of bounded areas, on the one hand, the importance of holy sites, which are zero-dimensional, and on the other hand the importance of routes and paths, which are one-dimensional. Such analysis has suggested a rather peculiar lack of two-dimensional representations. Thus, surface areas seem very marginal to the way nomads describe spatial relations, and together with the concept of bounded surface areas the nomads often seem to lack the possessive feelings about "land," so common among other peoples. This may be one of the factors which explains the weakness of nomad resistance against national parks, the establishment of private ranching, or other forms of land grabbing.

Crossing the Boundary:
An Age-Set Chronology of Ethnic Reaffiliation

In the transitional zone between the Rendille and Samburu we find the Ariaal, a bilingual group with double clan affiliations. Most Ariaal are of Rendille origin; but some, particularly the segments after which the clan settlements are named, stem from the Samburu. The history of the Ariaal shows that there is a constant flow of migrants from the Rendille to the Ariaal and Samburu, but hardly any migration in the reverse direction (Spencer 1973). This can be compared to the ethnic dynamics between the Rendille and their northern neighbours, the Gabbra. The Gabbra throughout their history have accepted Rendille migrants, so that today many Gabbra segments claim Rendille origin although they are fully integrated into their host society, while the only Rendille subclan which stems from the Gabbra, a 17th-Century war spoil, is still slightly discriminated against because of its alien origin. While that subclan did, in fact, partly re-joined the Gabbra in 1990 (Schlee 1994b), the Rendille themselves use the following words, *Rendille inenyet asahta*, meaning "the Rendille sort people out," that is they discriminate, segregate and differentiate.

The formal criterion of distinction between the Rendille and the Ariaal is provided by the age-set rites (Spencer 1973:130). The Ariaal hold *ilmugit* sacrifices of the Samburu type while the Rendille have a different cycle of rituals with the *gaalgulamme* and *naabo* ceremonies.

The Ariaal have a mixed economy with camels and cattle as their large stock, while Rendille neglect cattle in favor of camels. Somebody who favors cattle should therefore join the Ariaal because they adjust their management and movements to the needs of cattle and there he can also acquire Ariaal and Samburu stockfriends. But Ariaal settlements which live in the immediate vicinity of the Rendille and consist mostly of Rendille speakers seem to find no impediments to cattle breeding despite of the ecological hazards involved.[2]

Is it really necessary to formally break with Rendille society by non-participation in the age-set rituals and to declare oneself Ariaal in order to become a cattle herder? In fact, in recent times this pattern seems to have changed. Falkenstein (1995:222) claims that, nowadays, more and more Rendille diversify their herds and take up cattle husbandry without the need to become Ariaal or Samburu. But as recently as 1979, when people had to decide where to have their sons circumcised, I witnessed the continued attractivity of being Ariaal. Thus, there may be other reasons for claiming Ariaal identity than cattle.

In *Identities on the Move* (1994a [1989]: 49-51) I have pointed to cultural attitudes as elements of an explanation which are partly independent of economic and ecological factors. Ariaal have a reputation of good neighborliness, the Rendille a history of internal friction (cf. Schlee 1979 on the *Ilkichili* age-set).

When the time of marriage of the subsequent age-set, *Ilkororo*, was approaching, in September 1988, a whole Rendille clan, *Rengumo*, refused participation in the Rendille preparatory rituals which involve curses or "mixed blessings" that amount to sacrifices of the human integrity and soundness of forcefully recruited individuals. These rituals were said to have turned bad and to be prone to lead to more bloodshed. Rengumo has performed the Ariaal and Samburu type *ilmugit* ceremony instead, thus formally leaving the Rendille fold and joining the Ariaal, although they continue to live among the Rendille, and few of them speak more than a few words of Samburu.

If more Rendille clans follow this pattern, there will be no formal criterion left for distinguishing between Rendille, Ariaal and Samburu apart from the language, a feature which, given the high incidence of biligualism, hardly lends itself easily to administrative measures in case it should ever be decided to divide pastures along tribal lines again.

Statistics like those of Falkenstein (1995:220-3 [in prep.]: chapter 2) will then become impossible. Falkenstein calculated the number of lineages which joined the Ariaal clan *Lokumai* and the number of lineages which left it per age-set period, i.e., the intervals of time to which the numbers of lineages refer are the periods when given age-sets were warriors. They run from 1881–1895–1910–1923–1951–1965, i.e. from circumcision year to circumcision year. Falkenstein's diagram clearly shows an increase of emigration from this Ariaal clan to the Samburu during the colonial period.

Lokumay migration

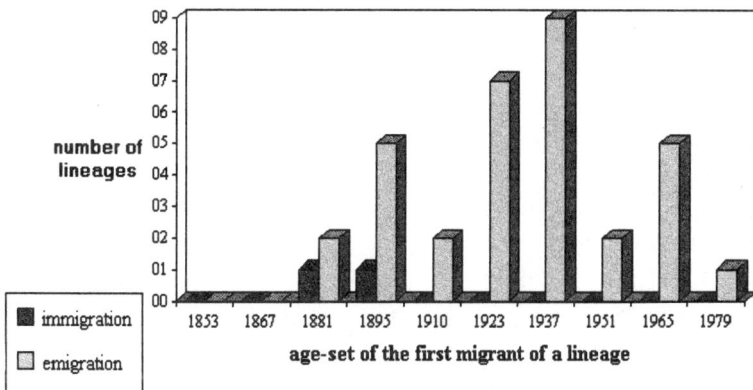

Diagram From Falkenstein (in prep.), chap. 21

Falkenstein attributes this increase to the monopoly of violence established by the colonial state which reduced the risk of raiding, and furthered an interethnic system of exchange between the Rendille, Ariaal, and Samburu. Falkenstein suggests that, "these pacification efforts contributed to the increasing diversification of the pastoral economies of these groups in the colonial period" (1995:222).

There may be another way in which the colonial policy of separating the "tribes" unintentionally furthered that type of interethnic migration, and that takes the form of ethnic re-affiliation. Before colonial control, at least in peaceful periods, it might not have been necessary for Samburu to claim to be Ariaal or Rendille when grazing in predominantly Rendille areas. They could go there as Samburu. Also Rendille or Ariaal in the Maralal area did not have to claim to be Samburu. Colonial policy made just these claims necessary. To that effect, it might not have affected spatial mobility to the same extent as ethnic identification. Nomads always had to use resources on both sides of the (future) Marsabit/Samburu boundary, but crossing the boundary became more difficult without a proper change of ethnic label.

Between the Rendille and Samburu there was a continuum of transition, rather than an ethnic boundary as suggested by the colo-

237

nial administration. During colonial times, negative experiments were made, I think, on all sides, such as the attempts to close the district boundary between Marsabit and Samburu to stock movements. Rendille herdsmen were given access to pastures in Samburu District only in exceptionally dry years. Ecological conditions, however, forced the Rendille to move to higher ground west of the Ndoto chain very frequently. The Lbarta plain around Baragoi, for example, is a quite usual dry-season grazing ground for Rendille. The herdsmen were therefore forced to take their animals to those pastures in spite of the colonial interdictions, and they risked frequent confiscations of parts of their herds; they also risked even occasional arrests.

Age-Set Ceremonies and Mobility: Communal Circumcisions and the *Gaalgulamme* of the Rendille

For the communal circumcisions, held once every fourteen years, the Rendille gather in large clan settlements. A survey of such movements can be found in the *Kenya Range Management Handbook* (Schlee 1991:133ff), from which the data for the subsequent sections of this paper have been taken. The circumcisions are carried out outside those settlements, ideally by members of certain lineages of the *Tubcha* clan, although the above-mentioned conflict in some cases has also interfered with this division of ritual labor. At this point, Rendille who for practical or social reasons have lived in Ariaal settlements, have to decide whether they want to join their Rendille clans of origin again and have their sons circumcised, or stay where they are and thereby add a strong symbolic element to their identification as Ariaal.

In the Saturday year which follows the Friday year of the circumcisions, the Rendille hold the *gaalgulamme* ceremony. This ceremony has alreay been discussed in the anthropological literature (Spencer 1973:46f; Schlee 1979:161f, 224ff, 245; Sclee 1989). I have also elaborated on the settlement order of the clans that gather on the *gaalgulamme* site (Schlee 1979). However, in the following description, the focus is placed on the effect this ceremony has on the movements of people and stock.

Traditionally, the Rendille held the *gaalgulamme* on the eastern shores of Lake Turkana. Unlike the circumcision settlements, where more proximity is the reason for gathering and several rings of houses form a cluster, at the *gaalgulamme* site (ideally) all Rendille form one giant ring of houses in clockwise order of seniority starting from the west. Such settlements may have had a diameter of 2 kilometers. On the occasion described here, Chorr (as the Rendille call the area north of Mt. Kulal and east of Lake Turkana) was chosen as the site because one of the rituals constituting this ceremony was a bath in the lake. All camels were to be present, for two reasons: first, because no Rendille age-set rituals are carried out without the camels being fenced in close to the site or all around the site of the ritual (in contrast to the Samburu-and Ariaal-style *ilmugit* sacrifices), and second, because some of the *gaalgulamme* rituals involve driving camels, as the name of the occasion implies (*gaalgulamme* meaning "camel stampede").

One particular rule concerning the *gaalgulamme* is that no iron weapons, neither spears nor swords, should be taken to the site. Even warriors take only their ritual sticks (*gumo*). During 1980, the Chorr area was considered unsafe because of the Turkana threat, that was aggravated by the rule not to take weapons along. The requirement that a bath should be taken in Lake Turkana was therefore reconsidered and it was decided that the important aspect of the rite was that the warriors should wash themselves with water from a source that never dries up (*tehim ti iiguin*). The Sokorte wells on Mt. Marsabit were thus accepted as a replacement. The Rendille gathered at Bur Gaalgarawah west of Hogisho on the western slopes of the Marsabit highlands, and the warriors went from there to Sokorte to wash themselves.

Thus, from the beginning, the 1980 ceremonies had the stigma of imperfection and one elder concluded afterwards that the ceremonies could be considered *gaalgulamme* in name only. Moreover, only parts of the settlement groups from each clan turned up and from the clan Nahagan none at all. Of the segments which did

239

not move there with their houses, only the warriors went to the ceremonial site. Because of the low ratio of houses (where the water containers are kept) to people, the Rendille ran into problems of adequate supplies of drinking water and a government lorry with a tank had to be sent to the side of the Marsabit-Kargi road relatively close to the site of the gathering.

A ritualized herding task (namely, one in which a camel bull, four she-camels, and their four calves have to be herded for a day, without allowing the calves to suck their dams) has to be carried out by warriors of one clan on the camels of another clan. In the case of the Gaaldeilan warriors, it is Odoola camels on which they have to perform this task. As no Odoola had turned up, they herded some camels of Saale instead.

All this left the Rendille with a feeling of dissatisfaction. The function often ascribed by sociological theory to such rituals, namely the creation of a sense of solidarity and the strengthening of social cohesion, was definitely not achieved by this ritual.

Ecological Constraints

Since 1974 I have observed again and again that among the Rendille a common lament of the elders and women left together with the children in the settlements was that "our livestock has moved far away from us!". This lament could be heard more often as the dry season advanced. Then the camels are all in satellite camps, where they are herded by boys and warriors, and also the smallstock can be driven 100 or 200 km away and be herded by a labor force that, in addition to some elders, boys, and warriors, consists largely of girls. When asked where the livestock was, the respondents often gave very far locations. For example, once substantial herds of cattle (by Rendille standards) were taken all through Samburu District into West Pokot. At other times Rendille herds intermingled with those of the Dasanech who live in the Ethiopian borderland at the northern end of Lake Turkana.

In describing such movements, one is tempted to select the most conspicuous and longest migrations. Some systematic sampling is therefore required. The movements that are described below have all taken place between September 1987 and August 1988. I have taken care to record all movements of major contingents of camels and smallstock, including the longer ones and the shorter ones. I have also recorded those cases whereby stock was kept in the settlement all the time rather than being taken to satellite camps, due to the fact that the settlement itself had moved to good pastures.

The question arises whether that particular year can be taken as representative or not. As far as the distances involved are concerned, it can be said that the period in question was not particularly harsh as far as rainfall is concerned and therefore no conspicuous increase in long-distance movements to avoid drought conditions occurred. My experience, dating from 1974, and the experience of others (H.J. Schwartz, pers. comm.) does not indicate that 1987/88 was an unusual year. Does this mean that the movements recorded for that year represent patterns that can be generalized for other years?.

One caution is necessary. Nomadism in northern Kenya is not of a transhuman or otherwise patterned type but can be termed opportunistic, one goes wherever conditions are best, due to the scattered rainfall. There are general tendencies to move to higher ground in the dry season, and to move closer to roads and markets when one wants to sell animals. Moreover, those are tendencies and not strict patterns. The following examples, therefore, describe options that need to be kept open by pastoralists, and reasons for particular movements rather than fixed routes of migration.

As the camels have to join the settlements for the *sooriyoo* celebrations, this period can, as far as camels are concerned, be subdivided into the span between the *sooriyoo* in the month of Daga (in this case August 18/19, 1987),[3] and the *sooriyoo* in the month of Sondeer I (in this case, February 12/13, 1988), thus (neglecting the one month between the *sooriyoo* festivals of Sondeer I and Sondeer II) the span between the *sooriyoo* in Sondeer (March 13/14, 1988) and the *sooriyoo* in Daga (August 9/10, 1988).

To illustrate my point concerning interethnic contacts and boundaries, it suffices to present some data from the survey, namely, concerning the first of these periods, the period from August 1987 to February 1988.

The migrating units (mostly clusters of satellite camps from different clans) are numbered and the numbers in this ethnographic example correspond to those in Map 1.

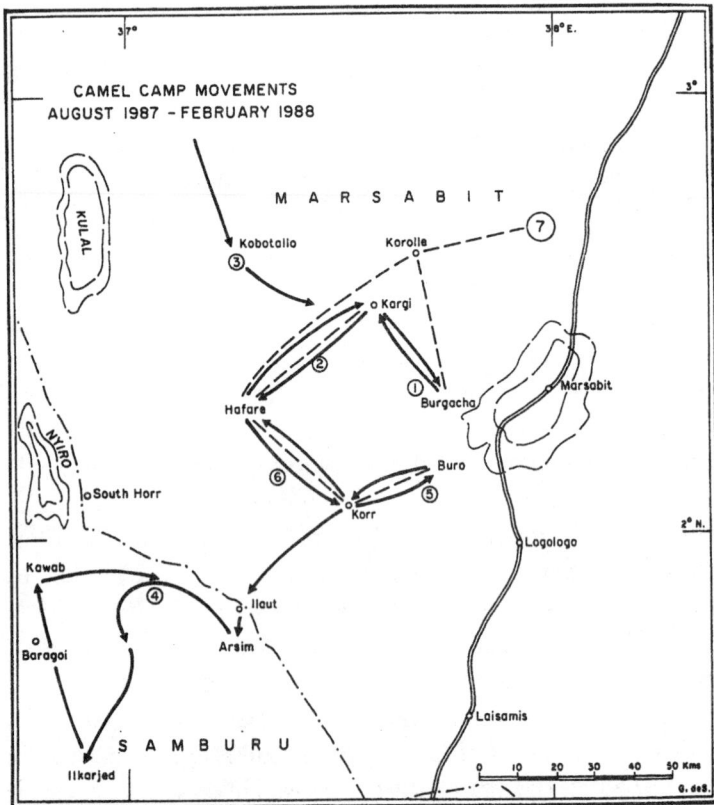

CAMEL CAMP MOVEMENTS
AUGUST 1987 – FEBRUARY 1988

Map 1

→ Movement of camel camps
--→ Regular movements to and from water
⑥ Routes (for description see text)
—·— District boundaries

Of the seven clusters of satellite camps discussed in the survey, three made a migration which went beyond what is administratively handled as the Rendille area, two (clusters 3 and 7) into Gabbra areas, one (cluster 4) crossing the boundary of Samburu District.

Camels from settlements around Kargi and the lava fields east of Kargi: [cluster 3] camels from the clans Tubcha Gaabanayó and Gaaldeilan passed south of the Kobotallo hill and went to the area north of Mt. Kulal. Their farthest point was Alwano east of the Gas waterholes. On the way back they crossed Hasé (Asie on the maps) hill and then passed Kobotallo.

Camels from the Korr area [cluster 4]: the camels belonging to the clan Gooborre went via Illaut and the Arsim waterholes into central Samburu District. They crossed the Siginte pass north of the Ndoto Mountains where there is a ritual gate. Passing through such gate brings a blessing to all camels which move from central Rendilleland to the western pastures and back. They were moved to the Ilkarjed area where there are waterholes in the Malgis valley and from there they crossed the Lbarta plain around Barogoi to Kawab, a hill to the south-west of Mt. Nyiro. On the way back they passed through Siginte again.

In the case of clusters 1, 2, 5, and 6 one finds relatively stable satellite camps from which camels are taken to distant wells and waterholes at regular intervals. To calculate the total distance walked by those camels one would have to add all of their movements to and from the water, and the migration from the settlement to the satellite camp and back. Clusters 3 and 4 were more peripatetic; they moved from waterhole to waterhole building new enclosures at every site rather than oscillating to and from the old enclosures.

However, in other situations one finds no satellite camps at all, for example [cluster 7], the northernmost Rendille settlements (Saale goob Kimogol, Gaaldeilan goob Tarwen, Saale goob Chorrodo, Odoola goob Ballo) stayed around Bubisa in a Gabbra neighborhood. There, conditions were so favorable that the camels did not need to separate from the settlements. Pastures were abundant but dry, and as a result the camels were watered at Korolle. Later the Gabbra and Boran resumed raiding against the Rendille and some of the longstanding neighbors of the Gabbra suffered casualties and lost all their camels (Schlee 1994b).

Ecological aspects of different dry season camel camp movements and the energy balances of different forms of mobility have been discussed elsewhere (Schlee 1988:149ff). Camel nomads face the option of oscillating with their camels between sweet pastures and the water points, or staying close to the water points where only salty pasture is available. The first option has the disadvantage of necessitating longer and longer journeys as the pasture recedes from the water; the second option does not support the entire camel population and has other disadvantages not relevant to our discussion.

One way to break up this dilemma is to move into a different climatic zone. However, as long as south-north migrations like those undertaken by Sudanese camel nomads are precluded in Kenya, such change of climatic zone can only be achieved by moving into different altitude zones. This explains the frequent migrations of Rendille stock into the higher parts of Samburu district, where the rains last longer and the vegetation is still moist when it has already dried up in Marsabit District.

Another solution to the above mentioned dilemma would be to restrict grazing around the water points in the wet season and the months following it, by moving away the herds and the settlements to the remoter pastures (the ones used by the Rendille now at the peak of the dry season). Those pastures would then still be green so that the animals would not need to be taken to the wells. After the rainy season, ponds in depressions and pockets of water in the rocks are also frequent in the remoter parts, so that the settlements and even (if the need arises) the smallstock could find enough water there. Areas around the permanent wells could then be reserved for the dry season.

In such a system of management it would not to be expected that the animals would lose weight in the dry season, because even in the present situation it is not the quality of the vegetation but rather the energy expenses needed to cover the long distances to the water, that are responsible for losses of weight and life. If the recuperation of full mobility of the settlements could not be achieved, another (not optimal but still recommendable) solution would be to restrict the grazing around the wells after the rains to the milk herds needed for domestic use, and to confine all satellite herds to remote pastures.

The communal actions required for such measures, however, are beyond the organizational capabilities of the Rendille. Because of the sectionalist and largely acephalous character of Rendille society, authorities trying to enforce such measures would not be acknowledged. In fact, one of the chiefs at Korr has already made such proposals and has not got far with them, although few Rendille would disagree that in principle what he says is correct. In practice, it would be feared that some segments would ignore the restrictions with impunity, and thus they would reap the benefits procured by the abstinence of others.

One should, however, not blame the Rendille for their stubbornness and individualism, because this attitude is generated by their harsh environment and might be adaptive in other circumstances. If the Rendille were a docile people and had obeyed the misconceived colonial grazing policies and thus followed all suggestions made to them by foreign experts since Independence, they might have died out by now.

It needs to be stressed that such measures, if the Rendille would agree to them and would help to enforce them, would not reduce the range of pastures needed by them but only invert the order in which these pastures are used. With the requisite coordination and communal action, the outlying pastures could be used first and those close to the wells later.

Movements of Smallstock

While a satellite herd of camels can opt either (a) for the far range commuter strategy between dry pasture and water point, or (b) for moving out of the area into higher altitudes with moister pasture and/or areas with a denser distribution of water points, the smallstock satellite camps have only the second option. They cannot opt for the long distance commuter strategy because, sheep and goats unlike camels, are not able to walk 60 km to the wells and back every fortnight.

This is illustrated by the smallstock movements in the period September 1987 to May 1988. The camps moved either to higher pastures or to water points in distant river beds which descend from higher areas. Those movements were varied and far reaching, stretching from the Ethiopian borderland to Isiolo (see maps below). The period covered by the following descriptions differs from that used for the documentation of camel camp movements (above), because unlike the camels the smallstock did not join the settlements for the sorios in February, March and August. They stayed in the satellite camps until May, when the rains had fallen in central Rendilleland, and later moved out again.

This latter cycle of migrations had not been concluded by the time of writing, so that the migrations I describe here (following numbering in Map 2 are those between August 1987 and May 1988.)

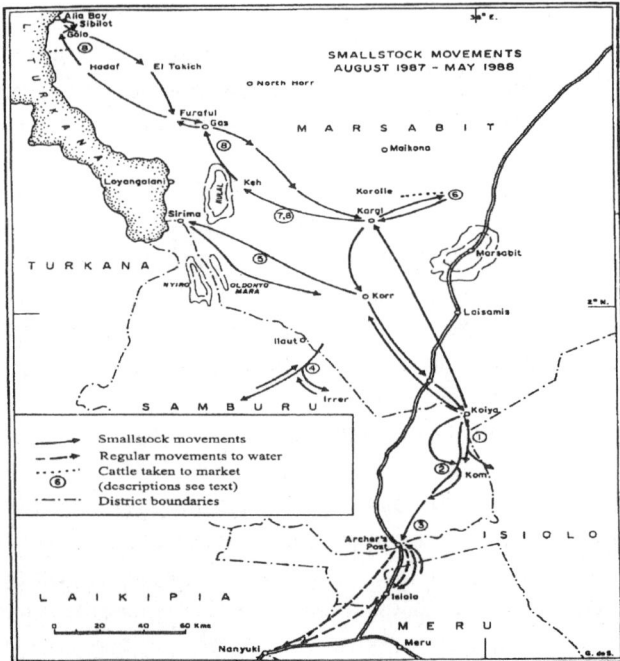

1. Smallstock camps from Kargi and Korr gathered at the Koiya waterholes south-east of Laisamis. [When I last saw Koiya in 1984 there were only waterholes, but now there is said to be a small township that even has a chief. The grazing there might therefore no longer be what it used to be.] Then they moved on to Kom, where they used the waterholes on both sides of the Samburu/Isiolo district boundary but grazed their animals mainly to the west, because east of Kom there were Somali.

2. A second cluster moved south from Koiya by a different route. They followed the chain of waterholes in the Sera riverbed, of which Worr Odoola (the well of the Odoola clan) is the one mentioned most preferentially. After an interval at Kom those camps moved further south-west to the area east of the mountain Ol Kanjo.

3. Cattle herds which had followed those smallstock movements were driven on to Archer's Post where they crossed the Ewaso Ng'iro River to look for pastures in Isiolo and Meru Districts. Herds to be sold were driven on to Isiolo and Nanyuki [interrupted line].

4. Smallstock of Gooborre, Ong'eli, Masula, and Lokumai went via Nkoronit up the Malgis riverbed. A segment turned south to the Irrer waterholes.

5. Smallstock of *Nahagan* and *Saale* from Korr went to the Sirima waterholes between Mt. Nyiro and Loyangalani. On their way back they kept close to Oldonyo Mara (Halicharreh in Rendille).

6. Smallstock from Karai went to Bul (Rable), whence they were taken to the Korolla waterholes in a six-day rhythm (the normal interval being four days), as these waterholes were beyond easy walking distance for smallstock.

7. Some herds were grazed around the Keh waterholes on the eastern flank of Mt. Kulal.

8. A part of cluster 7 was taken on to Alia Bay, making use of the waterholes of Gas, Furaful, Hadaf, and El Takich, drinking also from Lake Turkana while in its vicinity. Security was provided by ten Rendille of the Police Reserve ("homeguards" in local usage) with guns, plus twenty Samburu homeguards alotted to Samburu cattle herds in the vicinity. On the way back those herds crossed the Hasé elevation (Asie).

247

Cluster 6, with its change from a 4-day to a 6-day watering cycle clearly shows the difficulties involved in taking smallstock to dry pastures that are far away from waterholes. However, all other clusters moved out of the central plain of Rendilleland to areas where altitude and relief provided a better distribution of wells and surface water.

The Distribution of the Semi-Permanent Settlements or Main Camps (*goob*)

In the discussion on satellite camp movements it has been mentioned that the settlements (houses, women, children, elders) from which these satellite camp movements radiate outwards comprise a much smaller area than the total grazing grounds used by the Rendille, an area which we have called the plains of central Rendilleland. Yet, it is frequently claimed by visitors and short-term experts that practically all Rendille gather in two clusters around Korr and Kargi.

To find out which claim is true, I carried out a quick, rough settlement-and-house census during September 1988. This census was carried out with the help of one key informant, Mr. Barowa Adicharreh. Morover, the data was subsequently checked by observations made on visits by car or camel to a number of settlements. Those visits showed that Mr. Adicharreh's estimates confirmed my own hypothesis.

The results show that some of the more pessimistic assumptions about the Rendilles' loss of mobility are exaggerated. Statistics show that, in a total of 2,902 Rendille and Ariaal houses surveyed, 2,072 are located more than 5 km from Korr and Kargi, while 830 are within that radius around the two centers. All of those households are of "white" Rendille, as opposed to the Ariaal, with the exception of Ariaal who might have joined settlements named after Rendille lineages. For the "white" Rendille alone this proportion is 1,004:830. As the settlements within the 5-km radius are smaller than those which stay away from the "towns," this proportion becomes inverted if we count the number of settlements.

"White" Rendille comprises 36 settlements with an average of 28 houses outside a 5 km radius around Korr and Kargi, and 41 settlements with an average of 20 houses inside those two circles.

The largest settlement can be found among the Ariaal, whose 1,068 houses are divided into 27 settlements, comprising an average of 39.5 houses each. This reflects two realities, firstly, the remoteness from the "towns," that, as in the case of the "white" Rendilee, favors larger settlements, and secondly, the real possibility of an outside threat. For example, one particularly large settlement (I-4 on the map, east of the Merile-Laisamis road) moved together after two warriors had been shot by Somali.

These statistics do not comprise those Rendille and Ariaal households who had already left their traditional settlement patterns and had moved into towns. Also, the twenty-two houses of the "California" settlement at Korr, mainly consisting of widows and abandoned women, are not included in this count. With the same understanding, the town dwellers of Korr, Kargi, Logologo, and Laisamis—which do not form separate settlements, recognized by their tribesmen as such—were also left out of such census.

On the following map, circles with a radius of 5 km have been delineated around Korr and Kargi.

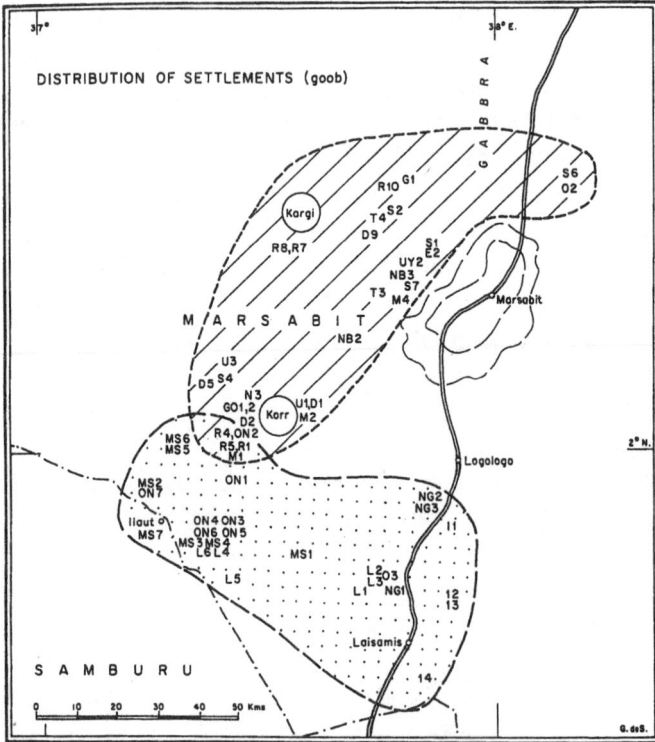

Map 3

Settlements (for descriptions see text)
Rendille settlements 1988
Ariaal settlements 1988

No settlement positions could be marked within any radius, because the density of settlements is remarkably high. The motive for settling within this radius can be assumed to be the proximity to the towns, because grazing and browsing are practically absent there,

250

with the exception of a few weeks in a good year. Thus, 1988 was such a year in which the apparently completely overgrazed vicinity of the waterholes started to flower. Outside this radius, at least, the lactating stock can be kept for longer periods in the settlements, and a combination of availability of pasture and the relative proximity of water and urban facilities can be regarded as motivating such a choice of location. The further a settlement stays away from the towns, the more the search for adequate pasture and a desire to keep the lactating stock as long as possible in the settlements develops.

It must be pointed out that around Logologo and Laisamis there are no such clusters of settlements, although there are (ex-)nomads staying in the towns themselves. There are also hundreds of Rendille and Ariaal living in permanent settlements on Marsabit Mountain engaging in agriculture, cattle keeping, wage labor etc. These are not included in the census or on the map itself.

The first impression derived from plotting these settlement positions in the map is that the Rendille live well to the north of the Ariaal, and that there is a very small area of overlap.[4] This is true of the present situation, but it cannot be assumed to be a stable or regular pattern. Many Rendille settlements which stayed in the area between Ilaut and Logologo in the late seventies moved northwards for the 1979 circumcisions and the 1980 *gaalgulamme* (see above). Some relatively good rains on the northern parts of the range also contributed to maintain this situation until 1990. Before 1979 Rendille and Ariaal settlements were interspersed among each other in the south, and the northern part of Rendilleland belonged exclusively to the "white" Rendille.

On the other hand, there was no interlocking of settlement areas between the Rendille and Gabbra in the late 1970s, as the memory of the massacres of preceding years was still too fresh on both sides. At the time of the survey (1988), there were Rendille settlements in the Bubisa area, which is predominantly Gabbra, and there were Gabbra settlements close to Kargi.[5] Later, in 1990, the relationship between the Rendille and Gabbra deteriorated again, due to the availability of automatic weapons to the Gabbra/Boran after the collapse of the Mengistu regime in Ethiopia.

It has also been claimed that the Ariaal are more nomadic than the Rendille because the proportion of them which has become sedentarized around the mission stations is lower. A glance at the map comfirms that indeed the Ariaal settlements keep away from the towns. Nevertheless the "nomadic" aspect of Ariaal life needs some specifications. If one introduces measurements of mobility (the defining criterion of nomadism) as frequencies of movement and distances covered, one finds that a number of "white" Rendille settlements have made long-distance movements between the Korr, Kargi, and Bubisa areas in recent years, while Ariaal settlements are often found within a radius of a few kilometers for decades.

Ariaal only move their settlements to a new spot if the old one has assembled too much dung. One example is Goob Lengima (MS1), which has stayed on the eastern flank of the mountain Hali Balladan for seven years and shows no inclination to move away from there. The leading elder, Lengima, makes clever use of small water pockets in the rocks of the mountain which can be used for human comsumption and for lambs.

Those categories of stock which can walk longer distances are taken to the wells of Ilaut and Laisamis in the dry season, unless there is still water in the seasonal lake Larabasi on the other side of the mountain. The run-off from the mountain and seasonal rivers coming from the higher areas to the west, in Samburu District, provide occasionally small pockets of green pasture even if there has been little or no rain in the area itself. Because of the long stay in the same area the herdsmen of this settlement always find these spots. Thus, an efficient use of this micro-habitat just supports this one settlement.

Such strategy of making long-term use of highly localized resources by single settlements is not restricted to the Ariaal, but seems to be employed by them more often than by the Rendille. A perhaps untypical Rendille example of a settlement which uses a similar strategy is S7, Goob Haile, which uses some water holes far away from any major settlement cluster or town. These water holes provide just enough drinking water for this one settlement for most of the dry season, so that Goob Haile is only forced to fetch water on camel back from Hula Hula on top of Mt. Marsabit for relatively short periods.

Movements of Slaughter Stock: The Outlets of the District

There is no time in history in which movements of slaughter stock across the boundaries of Marsabit District followed a free market model. The colonial administration often kept Somali traders out of the district because of the policy of tribal segregation mentioned above. Demand was thus curbed. If anybody, nomad or trader, wanted to drive his stock outside the district, he met with the usual difficulties of crossing into other restricted areas. Thus, if he managed to get the required permission or circumvented the restrictions and approached the densely settled Kenyan Highlands with their higher demand, he finally had to overcome a wide belt of no-man's land (now belonging to the Livestock Marketing Division). Moreover, that kind of territory served to enforce quarantine regulations on all stock coming from the nomadic areas.

The reasons given for such territory were of a veterinary type, its effects of an economic nature. It created a dual livestock economy: one with a relatively high price level in the settlers' areas, and another one with a low price level in the nomadic areas (Raikes 1981:118-28). The latter may have been the covert purpose of the quarantine, because as early as 1937 a Government husbandry expert gives the following evaluation of the possibilities of exterminating the diseases of the nomadic stock and the reasons for not exterminating them:

> For many years the pastoral native reserves have been in perpetual quarantine. This has been caused partly by the presence of disease, but largely by economic considerations. The expenditure at any time of comparatively small sums on veterinary services for these areas

would have enabled them rapidly to be liberated from quarantine *with disastrous effect upon the price of stock and stock products within the Colony.* (Emphasis, Original; Raikes 1981:118)[6]

While effectively blocking the market outlets of the nomadic areas, the colonial administration gave quite different explanations for the low level of sales. According to them, the nomads did not want to sell their animals. It is in this period that the myth of the conservative nomad with his irrational emotional attachment to his animals evolved. The nomads were forced to sell a given proportion of their stock to prevent "overstocking" and "overgrazing" and they were forced to sell at prices for which their purportedly more rational and market-oriented competitors, the white ranchers, would never have sold. Such prices sometimes amounted only to about one quarter of those achieved in the protected areas (e.g., Raikes 1981:119). Whether the nomads would have sold if access to the market had been given to them and prices had not been discriminatory, has never been investigated. Instead, the stereotype of the irrational nomad was used in order to justify "destocking measures" which amounted to expropriation because of the pitiable compensations paid. Just an example from the archives:

> There is little doubt that the District is carrying more camels than it should. Whenever the question of selling off camels to the Meat Marketing Board is raised the Rendille look wooden and say they haven't got any, the Gabbra make a long story about the camel being man's best friend, the motor car of the desert and the Bank of England rolled into one. Until a rough census is made it will not be easy to enforce a destocking policy as regards camels. (Kenya National Archieves, DC Marsabit, 1948)

In other words, a vague opinion by a layman about the carrying capacity of an area, plus a humorous description of what some nomads are claimed to have said, are enough to demand a "rough census" followed by a suspension of the property rights of the nomads.

In the current Kenyan situation though, apart from fines for border transgressions, de-stocking campaigns and quarantines, another form of interference with the nomadic livestock economy are the "auctions," as the purchasing fairs of the parastatal marketing organization are called locally. Just like quarantines, they tend to be manipulated. Such manipulations usually favor the large suppliers and town dwelling traders, at the expense of the nomads. If, for example, shortly before or during the auction it is announced that only oxen in a given weight bracket are to be bought, no smaller or larger ones and no cows, then the local supplier can select animals of the required category, while a nomad who has come from far with two or three animals which happen to be of the wrong category has to drive them back. If, they are no longer in a condition to be driven back, the nomad will have to sell them at dumping prices to the local traders.[7]

Another disadvantage for suppliers who have come from as far is that the prices are often not paid in cash but in certificates which can be cashed only weeks later. Whatever a nomad may have gained by selling animals is thus partly or entirely spent on his maintenance in town during this waiting period.

Conclusion

The outlets of Marsabit District are still characterized by artificial bottlenecks, barriers, handicaps, traps, and stumbling stones. Much remains to be done in the fields of marketing and grazing management. The types of policies implemented have in principle remained those to which Spencer has drawn our attention, a fact that casts doubt upon the learning ability of evolving political systems. Thus, the ingenuity of herders and traders in circumventing these policies is a factor which has remained constant since colonial times an ingenuity that allows them to deal with borders—their perception and their construction.

NOTES

1. F.O.B. Wilson in a letter, cited by Zwanenberg (n.d.) and Raikes (1981:118).

2. Fratkin (1986: 278) presents a somewhat idealized situation in suggesting that Rendille have camels but no cattle, the Samburu cattle but no camels, and the Ariaal as owners of both types of large livestock.

    Incidentally, Fratkin (1986:276-7) misquotes Schlee (1979) on saying that I attribute a fixed genealogical depth to Rendille lineages and typical sizes to subclans and clans, while in fact there is an enormous variation. Also, there is no such thing as a collective circumcision rite by the Rendille on Mt. Kulal.

    Nevertheless, apart from those details, his hypothesis concerning "stability and resilience" provides interesting reading.

3. Most of the following lunar dates are reconstructed, not ob served. Rendille might see the new moon one or two days later than it is marked in this calendar.

4. 03 is the only "white" Rendille settlement in the core area of the Ariaal (north of Laisamis on the map).

5. The turning point of the Rendille/Gabbra relationship were the 1979 circumcisions, when a new Rendille warrior age set was initiated, one that was free from the stains of earlier bloodshed.

6. Raikes (1981:118), after van Zwanenberg (n.d:14), who cites an official report from 1937.

7. For more examples of how auctions can be manipulated, see Walz 1992.

Chapter 9

REINVENTING *GADA*: GENERATIONAL KNOWLEDGE IN BOORANA

❖

Mario I. Aguilar

In a recent study on culture and anthropology, Michael Carrithers has argued that "there are some landmarks, some aesthetic standards and recalled traditions, which people use to guide their relationships and their institutions," and he further suggests that "people have the creativity and social intelligence to make use of these resources to remake their cultures" (1992:199). From that perspective, ideas related to culture, or what Barth has called "culture-bearing units" when referring to ethnic groups (1969:11-13), tend to reproduce themselves throughout generations, so that modes of thought are resilient, while symbols used or localized practices implemented can change.

That, I would argue, has been the case of the Oromo in East Africa. Through intense processes of historical and political change, elements of a resilient Oromo philosophy and cosmology have become central to the self-perception of Oromo as a distinct group, a nationality, and a cultural unit.[1] While already in the 16th century the monk Bahrey spoke of the organizational and cultural parameters of the Oromo of that time (Bahrey 1954),[2] the last thirty years of scholarship by Oromo and non-Oromo scholars have suggested that while there are many diverse ways of being Oromo, there are also unifying elements that suggest a creative culture, rather than a collection of isolated and localized segments of Oromo speakers (e.g., Hassen 1990; Hultin 1975). To that effect, it has also been suggested that while change has certainly affected all Oromo, they have not lost their traditional institutions, their traditions, and their cultural ways of understanding the world (Baxter 1994).[3]

In this chapter I want to outline three important elements that have made the Boorana, viewed as the central and ancestral Oromo group, a resilient and creative recipient of Oromo culture, not only in southern Ethiopia, but also in Kenya. Those three elements are generational knowledge, religious traditions (cosmology), and a unified philosophy, namely the Peace of the Boorana (*nagaa Boorana*). Those three elements are re-enforced and re-called when the *gada* festivals are celebrated, and therefore they are contained in the social ideology recreated through the *gada* system.

It is my argument that those elements have made the re-invention of the system in Kenya possible, through contested perceptions of age and new social creations of gerontocracy by members of an age-conscious society. The problem of understanding the *gada* system as a system of age is not, then, to understand how it works, but how it does not work. From that point of view, I would argue, the problem of the coming-of-age in *gada* stems from the fact that some Oromo pass through the system, while

258

others, including significant numbers of Boorana, fail to pass through it.

The Boorana in Kenya

I focus on the Boorana of Kenya, rather than on those Boorana that live in the so-called Oromoland (Oromia) in Southern Ethiopia. From that emic and Oromo perspective, the Boorana of Kenya constitute part of an Oromo diaspora, of Oromo peoples living inside the political boundaries of a modern nation state known as Kenya, but outside Oromoland. From an etic perspective, that of myself as anthropologist, the Boorana of Kenya and Ethiopia are symbolically linked by habitual ritual activities that in themselves make them look towards places of origin such as Dirre and Liban in southern Ethiopia (Aguilar 1993d, 1994a, 1995e, 1996e). From that perspective, peoples are connected though language and culture, regardless of the imposition of political and economic boundaries.

Thus, perceptions of nations and states such as Ethiopia and Kenya carry emic (from within) and etic (from without) discourses that make ideas of knowledge ever more complex. This is not the place to deal with those methodological and epistemological issues; let it suffice to say that for our purposes here, knowledge and tradition are not perceived as static sources to be learned and quoted from. Knowledge is to be understood as a process of present and future re-invention of the past, that allows the social and cultural creation of invented traditions.[4] Those creative social and cultural processes, in turn, allow people to cope with historical, social, and political changes over extended periods of time, whereby cultural knowledge resides not only on individuals who "know," but also on teachers of culture, such as women, fathers, and kin.

That has been the case of the Boorana in Kenya, whereby it is possible to suggest that the Boorana tradition (*ada*) is perceived by them as a unified body of knowledge, its implementation, however, depends on a public and open discussion of practice and law by communal assemblies (Bassi 1996a), or the reaching of consensus expressed in a sense of communal well being and societal peace (Aguilar and Birch de Aguilar 1993).

The Boorana of Kenya live in the Eastern and North-Eastern provinces, in territories that constituted during the British colonial period the Northern Frontier District. Large concentrations of Boorana live in Marsabit and Moyale, while other smaller numbers reside around the Waso Nyiro river and Isiolo. Other peoples close to the Boorana in Kenya are the Orma who live around the Tana River in Eastern Kenya,[5] and the Gabra, who move with their camels around northern Kenya.[6]

Colonial histories and historical ruptures created boundaries that divided the Boorana of Kenya from those that live in southern Ethiopia. Their respective histories however, have been somewhat similar, as both segments of this Boorana totality had to face a colonial challenge to their political and economic structures and a constant undermining of their cultural, cosmological, and epistemological constructions of the world. Thus, the Boorana in Kenya had to suffer a somehow similar and at the same time more intense cultural isolation than those experienced in the territories controlled by Menelik II at the end of the 19th century (Aguilar 1996d). On the one hand, the colonial line that divided Ethiopia and Kenya made them an isolated group, that also lost their actual spatial mobility; on the other hand, the colonial boundaries established in 1934 and the institutionalization of the *pax Britannica* meant that groups of Boorana in Kenya—such as the Orma, the Waso Boorana, and the Marsabit and Moyale Boorana—did not any longer have the fluidity of communication with other Boorana and Oromo across colonial borders.

During pre-colonial times, and certainly at the beginning of the colonial administration, conflict between different ethnic groups was common, especially during rites of initiation into warriorhood or adulthood. Therefore, one of the major tasks of colonial officers was to keep groups from fighting each other, a process of colonial creation of order, that, in reality, meant the drawing of administrative lines on maps in order to prevent violence and raiding.[7] Thus, while nomadic peoples can and will always move across imagined political borders, the lack of authorized movements did affect their participation in political assemblies, public ritual moments, and large festivals of initiation. Fewer Boorana, for example, could at any given time travel together to take part in public movements such as pilgrimages, either to sacred places or to the *Aba Muda* (Knutsson 1967).[8]

To order such movements, the colonial enterprise engaged in "processes of neutralization, re-creation, and rearrangement" of particular places and their geography (Mudimbe 1994:134-40), that in the case of the Kenya Colony meant isolating the White Highland, and other tribal territories from those occupied by nomadic and semi-nomadic pastoralists (see Chap. 8, infra). In the words of Charles Chenevix Trench, "the north was another world," and it was perceived as "the silent north" by Glanday, both administrators during the British colonial period in northern Kenya (Chenevix Trench 1993:48, 122).

The white settlers themselves pushed for those colonial demarcations to be enforced, as diseases could be passed on to their own animals as a result of an indiscriminate transportation of cattle from the northern territories to the markets in the central parts of Kenya. Thus, with the creation of the Northern Frontier District by the British colonial power, pilgrimages became more and more difficult, and the Boorana in Kenya became more preoccupied with their daily dealings with the colonial administration and with the Somali threat over their resources, rather than with any fluid communication with the Boorana in Ethiopia.

The territories around the Waso Nyiro river suffered the same colonial imposition of boundaries mentioned above, so that by 1934 the 1,500 Boorana who had been settled into the area after having been brought from Wajir in 1932 were separated by the movement of Samburu and Rendille into what became the administrative district of Samburu. Areas of grazing were demarcated in order to prevent ethnic clashes, and towns and markets were developed as centers of trade, taxation, and ordering.[9] In those colonial parameters, the Boorana of the Waso Nyiro river area increased their daily contact with Somali and, through a process of 'somalization', became, like the Somali, Muslims (Baxter 1966). While their actual process of religious change or conversion can be traced to their settlement into the area in 1932, from the colonial reports of 1952 (Aguilar 1995b), it is possible to say that the cultural assimilation of Somali traits included not only the adoption of Somali Islam but also their way of dressing.

However, ritual and symbolic links with other Boorana remained strong despite their daily participation in an ethically perceived Muslim community and a so-called "Muslim world." Places of origin, such as Dirre and Liban in Ethiopia continued to be considered their homelands and places to be visited in the future. Thus, geographical isolation and spatial immobility did not prevent them from perceiving issues of time as creative and flexible. During daily prayers, for example, those sacred niches in Ethiopia and the original division of Boorana into two segments, two moieties (Ghona and Sabo), are constantly mentioned (Aguilar 1993a).

In those current parameters of perception rather than identity, to be a Waso Boorana is to be a Muslim, according to the opinions of outsiders and insiders, especially older men in Waso Boorana society (Aguilar 1997a). However, in the opinion of younger men, women, and some outsiders such as Paul Baxter and myself, a Waso Boorana identity is also constructed and reconstructed periodically, around the same principles of the Peace of the Boorana (*Nagaa Boorana*) and the societal consciousness of being part of a larger number of people, who have at different moments in the past shared the same system of religious and political organization known as *gada* (Aguilar 1993b; Baxter 1990).

The general perception of *gada*, then, reflects its centrality in the formation and recreation of Boorana (Oromo) culture, however, it cannot be essentialized as a static mode or a process of Oromo incorporation for everyone. It is a very strong symbol of Oromo ethnic identity, but "it may have multiple meanings" (Bassi 1996b:150). Thus, those different perceptions and meanings are constructed by different generations, especially in places such as the Waso area where the actual social and cultural continuity of the *gada* system has not been ritually or politically implemented (Aguilar 1996a).

Gada as a Cultural System

Discussions on *gada* became central to the understanding of Oromo and Boorana after the publication of Legesse's book on *Gada* (1973). The system—understood by some as a political and ritual system, by others solely as a religious system—represented the centrality of a configuration of Boorana segments that, due to historical and political developments became a symbolically unified system of classification and identification. Those discussions have perceived *gada* in different ways, due to the fact that researchers have been, in contact with different peoples in different areas and at different times.

It is a historical fact though, that by the 16th century *gada* as a political system had enabled a nation to function in a state of cultural and political diversity. The system, as such, suffered serious disruptions due to external and internal colonial policies over the past centuries and became more and more suppressed by the expansionist and centralized cultural policy of the Abyssinian rulers of Ethiopia. In that context of change and suppression, it is possible to argue that the role of the *Kallu* (Knutsson 1967), as the recognized ritual figure and authority of such system in the case of Boorana, became more and more understood as a ritual one. Nevertheless, assemblies as models of social consensus assumed an important role in the discussions that preceded steps towards a constant cooperation between localities and districts. In other words, assemblies maintained the running of a ritual and political system on a day-to-day basis, and in the midst of difficult social and political circumstances.

It is my suggestion that systems that require elaborate celebration and processes of learning by participants and members of a society as such do not disappear, however they are transformed over time. In the short term, elements of such systems are kept through the structural changes of ritual and political systems. On the long term, public elements disappear only to be re-incorporated during periods of strong ethnic and nationalistic sentiment. That has been the case with the Oromo diaspora that has tried to understand better and to re-invent their traditions and their views of the world that after all make them different from other peoples. Those re-inventions of tradition have also been part of the processes lived by the Boorana in Kenya during the last twenty years.

People of *Gada* in Kenya

As already suggested, the operation of the gada system was disrupted by the beginning of the colonial expansion and government in Kenya as well as Ethiopia. With the disruption of the system, peoples such as the Boorana of the Isiolo area and the Orma of the Tana River developed particular cultural traditions while accepting changes in their political and religious social structures (Aguilar 1994d, 1995a, 1997b, 1997c). Thus, they were portrayed by anthropologists as people who had lost their traditions (Dahl 1979a; Ensminger 1992) and had become very different from those Boorana portrayed in the writings of Haberland (1963), Knutsson (1967), or Legesse (1973). The fact that the *gada* festivals had never been celebrated in areas such as the Waso area of Eastern Kenya spoke to researchers of the disappearance of a system, and the fact that people converted to other religious systems and became part of other nation/states substantiated that claim.

From the Waso Boorana point of view, that "loss of their traditions" had been understood as the causal explanation of many disasters, and had justified their claims to have become impoverished, while their grandfathers were rich and expected to overlook thousands of herds of cattle after retiring from an active social life. However, events taking place during the 1970s and recently during 1995 gave other signals, suggesting the resilience of systems of age and the actual symbolic connections between Boorana in Kenya and those in Ethiopia.

Already during the 1970s a delegation of Boorana, mainly Sakuye from the Isiolo District of Kenya, visited Ethiopia and spoke to the Boorana *Kallu* there. The visit responded to letters exchanged between Boorana of Kenya and Ethiopia whereby concern was expressed by Boorana in Ethiopia, over the fact that those resident in the Isiolo District of Kenya had lost their traditions. A further visit took place by the late 1970s, when a delegate of the *Kallu* tried to collect contributions in a period of famine and unrest in Ethiopia (Hogg 1981). A similar famine had taken place in Kenya in a very hard period for the Waso Boorana, following the tragedies of the *shifta* war (1963–1967), and the efforts to provide food and animals to the Waso Boorana by churches and international agencies.

Even when those particular visits and exchanges between Kenya and Ethiopia did not change matters of practice, either religious or political, there arose a certain cultural consciousness as to the fact that there were historical and symbolic connections between the Oromo of Kenya and Ethiopia. During the internment in camps in the mid-1960s, the Waso Boorana began questioning the actual wisdom of a further alliance with the Somali. In such context, and through the elaboration of memories, expressed during my fieldwork in the area in the late 1980s, Waso Boorana women suggested that there was a conscious process of distancing themselves from Islam, and from the Somali. Children who were with their parents in those camps, or were born in those years, are now part of an age bracket of 30 to 35 years old, who have in practice followed other practices, or have become part of a world of mixed temporalities, where Boorana ethnicity and tradition has become more important than an imported Somali Islam.

Research that followed those events, labelled the Waso Boorana as Muslims (Dahl 1979a; 1979b; 1996:164; Hogg 1981). Civil servants sent to the area talked and still talk about "those Muslims."[10] It is true that research in the area during the 1970s accounted for the localized political influence of a generation of older men whose fathers and themselves had converted to Islam.

By the late 1980s and 1990s religious practices in the area had been influenced by the appearance of men who had been part of sufi brotherhoods in Mombasa, as well as other traditional practitioners who had been in touch with traditional ways from the north. A further diversification of religious practices had taken place after the 1970s, as practices related to Sufi brotherhoods and the actual localized responses to illness in the community became perceived as Boorana rather than Muslim phenomena. However, those perceptions are not only fragmented but are also constructed in relation to the actual potency of knowledge that different healers and ritual men (*abayen*) exercise in the different Boorana communities living in the Waso area.

Together with the fact that younger men had taken positions of leadership in the Boorana *manyatta*, those religious revivals created a decentralization of the central mosques' spheres of influence in the area. Younger men who were more in tune with national developments were also employed by non-governmental organizations, and development plans supported by the Christian churches were based on the premise of local traditions, communal consensus, and traditional knowledge. Thus, while assuming that most Boorana in the Waso area perceive themselves as Muslims, there has been a considerable shift in the power of the elders as given by outside forces, and as perceived by communities who respected older men and their connections with the mosque and the Islamic leaders or foreign Muslim missionaries resident in towns such as Garba Tulla, Kinna, or Merti (Aguilar 1995d, 1996g).

From that perspective, it is possible to argue that by the 1990s there had been a resurgence of cultural traits and a new awareness on the part of the Boorana of Kenya, especially in the case of the Waso Boorana, in terms of their common identity with other Boorana and their close cultural association with other Oromo. One could ask whether that communal cultural perspective was present before. In a sense it was, but it was suppressed by (a) the massive conversion of Boorana men to Islam, and (b) the actual disastrous results of the Boorana movement for secession from Kenya during the *shifta* war (1963-1967) which on the one hand

hand, impoverished them and on the other allowed them to rethink their past allegiance to Islam, and to the Somali movement in East Africa (Aguilar 1995b).

The changes in social and political perception that took place among Boorana, and indeed in the whole of Kenya after independence is also significant as to understand processes of identity and ethnicity formation. Western education became the norm, and the vehicle for accessing resources and opportunities in the post-colonial nation state. Before independence, the Northern Frontier District had been cut off from the rest of Kenya and movements in and out of the district were restricted for both those living within and those living without that area. The education system enforced the political ideology of nationalism, where the term "Kenyan" was used as to embody the creation of new and educated citizens of such nation, who would forget their ethnic backgrounds and work for the development and progress of the whole nation.

Children of the Boorana managed, through the involvement in education by the Christian churches and the Muslim foundations, to get into the educational system. However, they found it difficult to compete for further carriers in political and economic centers dominated by Kikuyu and Luo and all those groups that already at the time of Kenya's independence had voices and interests in the Kenyan nationalist movement. Perceptions of Boorana by other Kenyans have been colored by the Boorana conversion to Islam and the fact that they still maintain pastoralism as their way of life, even in times of natural or political disasters. Thus, they are considered a backward people who live outside the progress and unity achieved by the modern nation of Kenya.

It can be argued, though, that throughout many historical changes, the Boorana in Kenya, have remained people of *gada,* ever conscious of age models, and their importance in their lives. In other words, the Boorana can be considered an age-conscious people, because the whole social system functions on the basis of perceptions related to age and generational patterns. From that Kenyan Boorana perspective—or rather from the perspective of the Boorana in Kenya—it is possible to argue that *gada* needs to be understood as a mode of thought and knowledge that informs the way of life of any Oromo, rather than solely as a structural and functional system that can be mathematically explained and interpreted. The question "What is *gada*?" is somehow different from "how did/does *gada* function as a system?."

From that premise of social practice, the system only comes into existence if the actual *gada* festivals are regularly celebrated. If it is not celebrated at all, it is still possible to suggest that people who have been part of the system have also assumed cultural traits from such cultural modes of classification and organization. The system itself can be used as a political or a religious or a military system. However, its importance resides in the fact that, as a philosophy, it embraces cultural ways of being Boorana and Oromo, and therefore helps the creation and recreation of identity and community.

The people of *gada*, from that point of view, are constituted not only by those who still re-enact the rituals of the system, but also by all those who at one point or another have been under the social, economic, cultural, and political influence of such a system. To that effect, the strength of the system lies in the fact that as a structural, organizational, and ideological model of society based on age, it can embrace all kinds of people, who maybe in their daily practices continue practicing their own ways of organizational patterns. The reified, essentialized system, becomes, with such kind of understanding in mind, an ever changing umbrella under which people can be integrated at any time into the system, and that requires an ideological parameter of age rather than the actual "real" existence of the system in place.

Boorana Generations

With that reshifting of relational cultural parameters, it was clear from our analysis, that what actually had changed in Waso Boorana society by the end of the British colonial period in Kenya was the actual importance of particular generations. That cultural change took place in the religious and political spheres of influence in places such as Isiolo, Garba Tulla, or even Marsabit and Moyale. In an age-conscious society, as suggested above, perceptions of age and their relation to leadership had changed, due to sustained historical changes. Thus, conversion to Islam was a process that effected cultural changes—particularly those that were somehow understood as leadership patterns–in a different manner than through the traditional *gada* system.

Legesse has suggested that there were two parallel systems that ran in Boorana. On the one hand, the age-set that took over the political leadership did so for a particular and limited period of time; on the other, it allowed for a democratic and somehow egalitarian (i.e., communal) way of exercising authority (1973:50-2). Bassi in his recent work has confirmed the qualities of communal interaction present in Boorana assemblies, whereby decisions arise out of consensus through the composition of assemblies that can be attended by any social member of localized communities (Bassi 1996a).

On the other hand, the system was given authority by a ritual system based on principles of kinship and patrilineal descent, whereby the descendants of the first *kallu* gave final sanction to those generational roles effective for a period of eight years. The two systems came together in the pilgrimage to the *Abba Muda*, whereby the ritual and the political gave actual recognition to each other. Those two models operating within the same system became effective according to the needs and contextual possibilities of a particular group of Boorana, those under the cultural influence of the system's localized cultural and political organization.

Since the 16th century, and with the expansion of the Oromo, there was a tremendous diversification of the system and of those religious traditions celebrated among the diverse Oromo peoples. Christianity and Islam became part of various Oromo and Boorana communities, creating a diversification of the ritualized pilgrimage to the *Abba Muda*, mainly due to the external factors of colonial domination and the political fragmentation of Oromo leadership units.

Thus, the *gada* system remained in place; however, it was also shaped in a creative, complex, and diversified manner, difficult for the outside researcher to assess without further comparative research in different areas of Boorana. To a certain extent, the Boorana have always remained Boorana, even when converting to other systems of beliefs and practices such as Islam or Christianity. However, their own participation in Islam and Christianity has certainly influenced their particular perceptions of age and the role of generations in the private and public spheres of Boorana life.

Ideas related to biological generations cross the boundary between old and young in Boorana. However, in a diversified context of age interaction, I use the term "generation" following Karl Mannheim, who suggested that generations are perceived and therefore constituted by particular groups that share an ethos, rather than a certain biological age (Mannheim 1952). From that point of view, older men are those who perceive the world in a particular way, in most cases rather differently than a younger generation after them. That younger generation not only suggests a new view of the world, but also has the need and the impulse to make an impact, in order to break from tradition and the established norm. In the case of the Oromo of Wallaga (Ethiopia), for example, Jan Hultin has suggested that "in accordance with the Oromo conception of time and history, each new *gada* class had, as a group, to match in deeds the reputation of its historical antecedents and to set an example for future classes" (Hultin 1979:285).

The rituals of rebellion are not only important because they unify society as a whole, but because they allow the young to recreate the past in a particular social context whereby the agency of continuity or change is perceived by them as belonging to themselves. Once that past reality and tradition have been challenged, those younger generations readily comply with an ideologically recreated world of their own, imposed on others through the same use of authority and tradition.

In the contextual case of Boorana Islam, generational perceptions of proper behavior are slightly different than in the *gada* system, especially concerning the role of older men in the running of public affairs and with respect to the ever more fragmented realms of politics and religion in the diversified context of Ethiopia and Kenya. While in *gada* a responsible age-grade took over the political leadership at prescribed intervals and for a fixed period of time, the understanding of most World Religions is somehow rather different. Those who are older are perceived as having more power of decision, due to the fact that they are assumed to be more knowledgeable and more experienced in life.[11]

It is only in an idealized Boorana world that democratic principles of succession to office are present: in the contemporary world of Northern Kenya, for example older men represent their communities, in the daily mediation between particular communities and the Kenya administration. During my fieldwork, older men were always invited to meetings with the district officer or to the communal meetings with development agencies trying to provide water or veterinary assistance to that particular area of Kenya.

Such a model of social action is closer to the gerontocratic model of Spencer than to the generational and democratic model of *gada,* as described by Legesse. Older men are described by the administration and by the missionaries resident in the area as elders and therefore as people to be listened to, because their own communities will listen to them as well. In that context, there is still the feeling that if older men agree with proposals from the administration, everybody eventually will do the same.

The colonial interpretation of "authority" was responsible for such creation of elderhood in Boorana as colonial administrators assumed models of knowledge related to biological age, rather than to local perceptions of tradition, cosmology, and the passing of age. The "elders," as portrayed by colonial officers, were a unified group of older men who knew everything and controlled everything. Those assumptions could have been taken from models of Maasaihood, and the power of the elders to curse and to bless, or to withhold cattle (so as to postpone possible marriages). However—and as Spencer has suggested in his writings—younger members in such

271

a society finally obtain their privileges, despite an elder's discontent (1993a:151-2).

To that effect, colonial officers who were themselves expected to submit reports on local culture to their superiors created texts regarding culture, which in turn were read by their successors.[12] From that perspective, those who knew the tradition were perceived as those who should assume the active leadership of Boorana communities.

Elders, Women, and the Ada

The knowledge of tradition has always been important for the running of the *gada* system, so that Gemetchu Megerssa has argued that "it is this expert knowledge which protects and ensures the continuity of the tradition itself. It is the knowledge about the basic laws believed to operate in the workings of the entire system and which make up parts of the system" (1993:59). Knowledge of tradition, of the *ada Boorana* remained the normative body of knowledge that gave authority to older men in Waso Boorana, even when for Islam knowledge of the Q'uran was a more desirable kind of acquired knowledge.

Older men in Waso Boorana became faithful Muslims after their conversion; however, they were not able to read and write and therefore could not embody knowledge as perceived in Islam. Yet they remained the source of knowledge of the *ada* for younger generations of Boorana. They were integrated into councils and assemblies by the colonial authorities because of their power of influencing others among Boorana communities. They were also consulted by district officers appointed by the Kenya government because of their knowledge of past practices and developments in the Waso area.

Knowledge of the tradition, then, secured daily and habitual memories of *gada* and of Boorana knowledge. Thus, even when *gada* communal festivals were never performed in the Waso area, daily activities such as the *Buna Qalla* (sacrifice of coffee-beans) and daily prayers remained a constant source of relational and symbolic connection between Kenya and Ethiopia, between a diversified way of being Boorana and those Boorana proper in Southern Ethiopia (Aguilar 1995c).

The place of women in such a process of continuity cannot be underestimated (Aguilar 1994c). After all, and as I have suggested in my own writings, Boorana men in the Waso area tend to live in the public sphere of the town, the mosque, the market, and the government administration. Children go to school, however, and from their birth they spend more time with their mothers than with their fathers. Due to the fact that women have a less prominent role in the practices of Islam, Boorana women in Garba Tulla, for example, perceive their traditions as more important, and many of them leave Islam if they are divorced by their husbands or if their husbands die.

The cosmology of Boorana in all its richness then, is recreated on a daily basis through those domestic ceremonies whereby women direct and perform ritual roles through the use of Boorana symbols such as coffee-beans, milk, and butter (Aguilar 1996b). It is significant that in the case of the Maasai, Spencer has argued that "the perpetuation of the age system depends as much on women as on men" (1988:7).

That is certainly the case in Boorana, where older women instruct younger women on the traditions and prepare them for their roles as wives and mothers, and for childbearing, especially sons. However, older women are also expected to be given children for their care, so that barren women or those whose children have grown up and have left would ask for a loan or a "gift" of a child from relatives (Dahl 1990:133). Certainly older women depend on younger women; however, they make sure that huts and utensils are constructed and designed in the proper manner by those younger women.

Utensils and artifacts, as women's property, do not have only a functional value, because, and as suggested by Gudrun Dahl,

> when the Boorana are surrounded by these familiar things, they are constantly receiving messages relating to the

central values of their culture, and when the Boorana
woman handles her milk pots or her mats she is also in
a way formulating statements about her own identity
(Dahl 1990: 135).

The fertility of women and herds depends on the keeping of peace,
understood not only as the absence of war, but as a harmonious
interaction between human beings, animals, nature, the spirits,
and God. It depends on the actualization of the Peace of the
Boorana (*Nagaa Boorana*), a daily ritual activity performed by
married women and their families.

Nagaa Boorana

If the most valued ideal of all Boorana has always been "Peace"
(*Nagaa Boorana*), actualized through the proper celebrations of
the *gada* festivals and the consensus achieved through the communal assemblies, that state of affairs has also prevailed in the
daily lives of the Boorana of Kenya. Without that peace, there
would exist "a confused and distempered universe" (Baxter
1978:181), where herds would not increase, where there would
be injustice, and where children would not be born (Knutsson
1967).

That keeping of "the Peace of the Boorana" (*Nagaa Boorana*),
therefore, requires a constant flow of ritual and symbolic actions,
and even daily greetings and blessings (Baxter 1990), an ideological internal cohesion that in itself secures societal harmony
(Bassi 1996a:181). This kind of ethno-philosophy, therefore, permeates all social life in Boorana and constitutes, in the case of the
Waso area, a striking contrast to a situation of constant insecurity,
violence, and conflict (Aguilar 1993c, 1996f).

All ritual moments help to restore peace, as all violent and con-
flictive moments also do so. As a cultured center principle of social
understanding, the *Nagaa Boorana* reflects the possibility of the
existence of an ideal Boorana world, and does not account for the
possibility of unpeaceful moments in other societies affected by

Boorana interests. Thus, processes of globalization and national centralization have not affected the Waso area, geographically remote on the one hand, culturally ethnocentric on the other. Such remoteness stems primarily from the re-invention of a system of age (*gada*) that allows every Boorana to feel an important constituent of a society that treasures peace and harmony through changes in particular generations.

Conclusion

As argued in this chapter, generational knowledge, religious traditions (cosmology), and a unified philosophy have been the prominent elements in preserving Boorana as a "culture-bearing unit" (Barth 1969:11-3). In the midst of conflict with the Somali and through a cultural displacement of Boorana within a Westernized, modern state such as Kenya, cultural traits of the *gada* system have prevailed. Those symbols and traditions have not only been maintained, but they have been re-affirmed as central to Boorana life during the 1990s. They have been used as to recreate Boorana identity, as a different identity from that of the Somali, the Samburu, or the Rendille of Northern Kenya.

It is not an accident then, that it was in that cultural and generational climate that the *gadamoji* ceremonies took place, between June and July 1995, at the sacred site of Wayye Diida, eight kilometers from the township of Sololo Ramaata in Northern Kenya. The new *gadamoji* (elders), empowered by the celebration of such a ritual, acquired a new status in Boorana society, and their role changed from public to somehow domestic. In the domestic realm, they acquired a central role in the passing on of *gada* values, as well as the Boorana (Oromo) cultural values.

As rightly suggested by Anncsa Kassam, reflecting on those events,

> the *gadamojjii* elders who were of the right biological
> age would be treated as women: they would no longer be

allowed to carry a spear or engage in any offensive or defensive action; they would be addressed using a female pronoun ... they had now entered the spiritual realm of things and for the rest of their lives they would serenely follow the path of prayer. Their sole responsibility would now be to maintain *nagaya*, the peace of the Boorana, in society. (1995:34)

That maintenance of peace, I would argue, will maintain a society proud of *gada*, and proud to be part of a larger Oromo nation, after all an age-conscious society, based on a sustaining principle of peace, applicable to life, through the many changes still to come in a contemporary and future Kenyan society.

ACKNOWLEDGMENTS

Ideas from this chapter, in a much shorter version, were initially presented at the Annual Meeting of the African Studies Association, San Francisco (USA), 23-26 November 1996, and later published in *The Oromo Commentary* (Aguilar 1997e). I am grateful to its editor Dr. Melkuria Bulcha, for allowing the elaboration of those ideas in this volume, and to the Oromo scholars who attended that meeting and helped to enrich this paper.

NOTES

1. One of the landmarks of such presupposition in academia was the publication of Baxter, Hultin, and Triulzi 1996.
2. Mohammed Hassen has argued that already before the 16th century there was an Oromo presence within the Christian Abyssinian kingdom. Further, he has suggested that those sedentary pastoralist Oromo who were under Abyssinian rule were living in different social and cultural circumstances than the pastoralist Oromo who underwent a systematic expansion (Hassen 1994:61).

3. It is clear to me that while some Oromo nationalists limit the Oromo areas to those associated with an independent state, namely Oromia, my parameters for research on Oromo include those Boorana, Gabbra, and Orma in Kenya, including Nairobi, and the Oromo diasporas in the US, Canada, Australia, and Europe. In other words, I include all those who speak the Oromo language as their mother tongue, as well as those who live outside Ethiopia due to political or economic circumstances (cf. Aguilar 1997d).

4. Eric Hobsbawm has defined an "invented tradition" as "a set of practices, normally governed by overtly or tacitly accepted rules and of a ritual and symbolic nature, which seek to inculcate certain values and norms of behavior by repetition, which automatically implies continuity with the past" (1983: 1).

5. While in a progressive expansion early this century, the Boorana reached the Tana river, they did not associate themselves with the Orma, who in the past had also kept institutions such as chiefs and councilors and aspects of the *gada* system (Ensminger 1992: 45).

6. The Gabra speak the same language as the Boorana, and in the past they have shared the same political system, to the extent of keeping a ritual system of exchange (Schlee 1994b:136). Though they have been considered "vassals" of the Boorana, Gabra and Rendille also have age-set systems of the *Gada* type (Schlee 1989:82-92, cf. 1994b:132).

7. The Boorana were known for raiding enemies at initiation, whereby those who were being assumed as adults had to kill an enemy and come back with the dead person's genitals (Baxter 1979:72, Hultin 1990). However, lines of separation were also effective in order to help the sharing of economic resources such as grazing and water. For example, the so-called Stigand line was created by the colonial administration in 1938, so as to separate Rendille and Gabra. Moreover, in times of drought, the Gabra grant permission to the Rendille in order to graze in their assigned territories, recognizing that in the past Rendille occupied those lands (O'Leary 1994:101).

8. Thus, pilgrimages to sacred places cannot be understood only as acts of piety, but they also constitute major exercises in pastoral mobility. In the case of the Gabra Galbo, that pilgrimage as witnessed by Schlee in 1986, involved 140 households, thousands of camels, and large flocks of smallstock (Schlee 1990a: 45-6).

9. The Northern Frontier District as an administrative region was declared a "closed district" in 1926, and a "special district" in 1934. Special permits were required to visit the region and courts of justice and economic systems of trade were different from the rest of Kenya. This created a region totally different than the rest of the Kenya colony, and people who never had to mix or live with the "other" Africans of Kenya (Aguilar 1996c:363).

10. District Officers in the Garba Tulla Division were quite often changed, during my years of fieldwork. To be appointed to the area was to be sent to a hardship post, and an area where security was one of the key issues. So, for example, a District Officer originally from Siaya in Western Kenya was appointed during 1992. He was changed after a couple of weeks, as he could not cope as he said "with these Muslims." During 1988, District Officer Njoroge, a Kikuyu, was appointed to the area due to the fact, that otherwise retired from the civil service, he had as a younger man been posted to the area after the unrest of the 1960s. He commanded people around, and certainly he worked through a colonial model of reliance on the "elders" (older men) rather than consulting younger professional and educated Boorana.

11. This Boorana perception of authority can only be upheld as long as one perceives Waso Boorana society as illiterate, with a daily emphasis on orality, memory, and tradition. As in the case of the followers of any of the so-called religions of the Book, that perspective tends to change, when some people around can read and interpret with some authority the so called sacred texts (in the case of Islam, the Q'uran).

12. Colonial records contain, in the case of the Boorana of the Waso area, descriptions of age-sets, age-grades, and material on the

gada system that must have been obtained from informants who themselves tried to reconstruct from oral narratives those institutional practices that had not been present in the area for some years already.

BIBLIOGRAPHY A

❖

Selected Works by
Paul Spencer

The Samburu: A Study of Gerontocracy in a Nomadic Tribe. London:
Routledge and Kegan Paul and University of California Press,
1965.

"The Function of Ritual in the Socialisation of the Samburu Moran," In:
Socialisation: The Approach from Social Anthropology, (ed.)
P. Mayer. London: Tavistock, 1970.

"Party Politics and the Processes of Local Democracy in an
English Town," In: *Councils in Action: Comparative Studies*,
(eds.) A.I. Richards and A. Kuper. Cambridge: University
Press, 1971.

*Nomads in Alliance: Symbiosis and Growth Among the Rendille
and Samburu of Kenya.* London: Oxford University Press,
1973.

"Drought and the Commitment to Growth," *African Affairs* 73
(1974): 419-27.

"Scarcity and Growth in Two African societies," In: *The Population Factor in African Studies*, (eds.) R.P. Moss and R.J.A.R. Rathbone. London: Athlone Press, 1975.

"Opposing streams and the gerontocratic ladder: Two Models of Age Organisation in East Africa," *Man* (n.s.) 11 (1976):153-75.

"The Jie Generation Paradox," In: *Age, Generation and Time: Some Features of East African Age Organisations*. (eds.) P.T.W. Baxter and U. Almagor. London: Hurst, 1978.

"Three Types of Ethnic Interaction Among the Maasai-Speaking People in East Africa," In: *Space, Hierarchy and Society*, (eds.) B.C. Burnham and J. Kingsbury. B.A.R. International Series 59. Oxford: The Clarendon Press, 1979.

"Polygyny as a Measure of Social Differentiation in Africa," In: *Numerical Techniques in Social Anthropology*, (ed.) J.C. Mitchell. Philadelphia: I.S.H.I., 1980.

"Pastoralists and the Ghost of Capitalism," *Production Pastorale et Societe* 15(1984):61-76.

Society and the Dance: The Social Anthropology of Process and Performance, (ed.) New York and London: Cambridge University Press, 1985a.

"Introduction: Interpretations of the Dance in Anthropology," In: *Society and the Dance:The Social Anthropology of Process and Performance*, (ed.) P. Spencer. New York and London: Cambridge University Press, 1985b.

"Dance as Antithesis in the Samburu Discourse," In: *Society and the Dance: the Social Anthropology of Process and Performance*, (ed.) P. Spencer. New York and London: Cambridge University Press, 1985c.

"Homo Ascendens et Homo Hierarchicus," In: *Age, Pouvoir et Societe en Afrique Noire*, (eds.) M. Abeles and C. Collard Paris: Karthala, 1985d.

The Maasai of Matapato: A Study of Rituals of Rebellion. Manchester: University Press for the International African Institute, 1988.

"The Maasai Double Helix and The Theory of Dilemmas," In: *The Attraction of Opposites*, (eds.) D. Maybury-Lewis and U. Almagor. Michigan: University Press, 1989a.

"The Diffusion of Form and the Infusion of Meaning in Dance," In: *Folk Dance Today*. Paris: I.O.F.A. UNESCO, 1989b.

Anthropology and the Riddle of the Sphinx: Paradoxes of Change in the Life Course, ed. P. Spencer. ASA Monograph 28. London: Routledge, 1990a.

"The Riddled Course: Theories of Age and Its Transformations (Introduction)," In: *Anthropology and the Riddle of the Sphinx: Paradoxes of Change in the Life Course*, (ed.) P. Spencer. ASA Monograph 28. London: Routledge, 1990b.

"Time and the boundaries of the economy in Maasai," In: *Property, Poverty and People: Changing Rights in Property and Problems of Pastoral Development*, (eds.) P.T.W. Baxter and R. Hogg. Manchester: Department of Social Anthropology and International Development Centre, University of Manchester, 1990c.

"The Loonkidongi Prophets and the Maasai: Protection Racket or Incipient State," *Africa* 61,3(1991):334-42.

"The Pacification of the Maasai and the Transformation of the Prophet"s Tribute," *Anthropozoologica* 16: 65-72.

"Becoming Maasai: Being in Time," In: *Being Maasai: Ethnicity & Identity in East Africa*, (eds.)T. Spear and R. Waller. London: James Currey, 1993a.

With Telelia Chieni. "The World of Telelia: Reflections of a Maasai Woman in Matapato," In: *Being Maasai: Ethnicity & Identity in East Africa*, (eds.) T. Spear and R. Waller London: James Currey, 1993b.

"Dance and the Cosmology of Confidence," In: *The Politics of Cultural Performance*, (eds.) D. Parkin, L. Caplan and H. Fisher. Oxford: Berghahn, 1996.

The Pastoral Continuum: The Marginalization of Tradition in East Africa. Oxford: Clarendon Press, 1998.

Maasai: Society in Time, Space and Cosmos. (In preparation)

BIBLIOGRAPHY B

❖

Works Cited

Adorno, T.W. *Aesthetic Theory*. London: Routledge and Kegan
 Paul, 1984.

Aguilar, M.I. "The Role of the Sarki Dance in Waso Boorana/Somali
 Symbiosis and Conflict," *Anthropos* 88 (1993a):184-90.

_____. "The Peace of the Boorana," *New People* 27(1993b): 10-1.

_____. "*Nagaa*: the forgotten quest for peace in modern Kenya," *The
 Month* 26,5 (1993c):183-7.

_____. "Dialogue with Waso Boorana Traditional Religious
 Practices," *African Ecclesial Review* 35,2 (1993d): 101-14.

_____. "The Eagle Talks to a *Kallu*": Waso Boorana Ritual Percep-
 tions of Ethiopia," In: *New Trends in Ethiopian Studies* II:
 Social Sciences. ed. H.G. Marcus. Lawrenceville, NJ: The Red
 Sea Press, 1994a.

_____. "Anthropology and Anomalies in Kinship Patterns,"*Anthro-
 pology in Action* 1, 1 (1994b):25-6.

_____. "Portraying Society Through Children: Play Among the
 Waso Boorana of Kenya," *Anthropos* 89(1994c):29-38.

_____. "The Social Experience of Two Gods in Africa," *African Ecclesial Review* 36,1 (1994d): 32-44.

_____. *Ministry to Social & Religious Outcasts in Africa.* Eldoret, Kenya: AMECEA Gaba Publications, 1995a.

_____. "African Conversion From a World Religion: Religious Diversification by the Waso Boorana in Kenya," *Africa* 65,4 (1995b):525-44.

_____."Recreating a Religious Past in a Muslim Setting: "Sacrificing" Coffee-beans Among the Waso Boorana of Garba Tulla, Kenya," *Ethnos* 60, 1-2 (1995c):41-58.

_____. "Walking the Waso Boorana Path to the Peak," *The Month* 28,1 (1995d):37-41.

_____. "Expanding the Concept of Oromia: The Waso Boorana Case," *The Oromo Commentary* 5,1 (1995e): 17-20.

_____. 1996a. "Keeping the "Peace of the Waso Boorana": Becoming Oromo Through Religious Diversification," In: *Being and Becoming Oromo: Historical and Anthropological Enquiries.* P.T. W. Baxter, (eds.) J. Hultin and A. Triulzi Uppsala: Nordiska Afrikainstitutet.

_____. "The Eagle as Messenger, Pilgrim and Voice: Divinatory Processes Among the Waso Boorana of Kenya," *Journal of Religion in Africa* 26,1 (1996b): 56-72.

_____. "Writing Biographies of Boorana: Social Histories at the Time of Kenya's Independence," *History in Africa* 23(1996c):351-67.

_____. "Historical and Cultural Interaction, Symbiosis and Clientage: Waso Boorana and Somali in Eastern Kenya (1932-1992)," *Journal of Oromo Studies* 3(1996c): 1-17.

_____. "Symbolic Integration to Oromia: Boorana Traditional Practice, Language and God in Eastern Kenya," *Journal of Oromo Studies* 3(1996e): 62-8.

_____."Peace and Consensus in the Midst of War: Conflict Resolution in Boorana," *The Oromo Commentary* 6,1 (1996f): 28-30.

_____."Dialogue with Islam: an African perspective," *African Ecclesial Review* 38,6 (1996g): 322-40.

_____. "Reinventing *Gada*: Generational Knowledge in Boorana," *The Oromo Commentary* 7 (1): 10-4, 1997a.

_____. *Dios en Africa: Elementos Para una Antropologia de la Religion*. Estella, Navarra, Spain: Verbo Divino, 1997b.

_____. "Historical Anthropology and Anthropological History: Rethinking the Social Production of an African Past," In: *Rethinking African History*. Edinburgh: Centre of African Studies. 1997d.

_____. "Local and Global, Political and Scholarly Knowledge: Diversifying Oromo Studies." In *African Affairs* 96,2 (1997d): 277-80.

_____. *Being Oromo in Kenya*. Lawrenceville, N.J.: Africa World Press, 1998.

_____.and Birch de Aguilar, L. *Women's Organizing Abilities: Two Case Studies in Kenya and Malawi*. Washington, D.C.:ODII, 1993.

Ahr, C. *Fruchtbarkeit und "Respekt": Filmethnologische Untersuchung eines Geschlecterkonflikts um ein Ritual bei den Maasai*. Gottingen: Re, 1988.

Amoss, P.T. and S. Herrell eds. *Other Ways of Growing Old*. Stanford: University Press, 1981.

Arens, W. "Introduction," In: *A Century of Change in Eastern Africa*. ed. W. Arens. The Hague, Paris: Mouton, 1976.

_____.and I. Karp. "Introduction," In:, *Creativity of Power*. (eds.) W. Arens and I. Karp. Washington, D.C. and London: Smithsonian International Press, 1989.

Aretxaga, B. "Striking with Hunger: Cultural Meanings of Political Violence in Northern Ireland," In: *The Violence Within: Cultural and Political Opposition in Divided Nations*. Boulder: Westview, 1993.

Arhem, K. "The Symbolic World of the Maasai Homestead," In: *Body and Space: Symbolic Models of Unity and Division in African Cosmology and Experience*. (ed.) A. Jacobson-Widding Uppsala Studies in Cultural Anthropology 16. Stockholm: Almqvist and Wiksell International, 1991.

Atieno-Odhiambo, E.S. "The Song of the Vultures: A Case Study of
    Misconceptions about Nationalism in Kenya," *Journal of East-
    ern Africa Research* 1(1971) 111-22.
Bahrey. 1954. "The History of the Galla," In: *Some Records of Ethiopia,
    1593-1646.* (eds. And trans.),C.F. Beckingham and G.W.B.
    Huntingford London: Hakluyt Society, 1954.
Barth, F. *Ethnic Groups and Boundaries: The Social Organization of
    Culture Difference.* London: George Allen and Unwin, 1969.
Bassi, M. I. *Borana: Una Societa Assembleare del'Etiopia.* Milan: Franco
    Angeli, 1996a.
_____. "Power's Ambiguity or the Political Significance of Gada,"
    In: *Being and Becoming Oromo: Historical and Anthropologi-
    cal Enquiries.* (eds.) P.T.W. Baxter, J. Hultin and A. Triulzi
    Uppsala: Nordiska Afrikainstitutet, 1996b.
Baxter, P.T.W. The Social Organization of the Galla of Northern Kenya.
    Unpublished D.Phil. Dissertation, Lincoln College, Univer-
    sity of Oxford, 1954.
_____. "Acceptance and rejection of Islam among the Boran of the
    Northern Frontier District of Kenya," In: *Islam in Tropical
    Africa*, ed. I.M. Lewis. London: Oxford University Press for
    the International African Institute, 1966.
_____. "Boran Age-sets and Generation-sets: Gada, A Puzzle or a
    Maze?," In: *Age, Generation and Time: Some Features of East
    African Age Organizations.* eds. P.T.W. Baxter and U. Almagor
    London: C. Hurst, 1978.
_____. "Boran Age-sets and Warfare," In: *Warfare Among East Afri-
    can Herders*, eds. K. Fukui and D. Turton. Osaka: National
    Museum of Ethnology, 1979.
_____. "Oromo blessings and greetings," In: *The Creative Commun-
    ion: African Folk Models of Fertility and the Regeneration of
    Life*, eds. A. Jacobson-Widding and W. van Beek Uppsala: Acta
    Universitatis Upsaliensis, 1990
_____. "The Creation & Constitution of Oromo Nationality," In:
    Ethnicity & Conflict in the Horn of Africa, ed. K. Fukui & J.
    Markakis, London: James Currey, 1994.
_____. and U. Almagor. *Age, Generation and Time: Some Features*

of East African Age Organizations. London: C. Hurst, 1978.
_____. J. Hultin and A. Triulzi, (eds.) *Being and Becoming Oromo: Historical and Anthropological Enquiries*. Uppsala: Nordiska Afrikainstitutet, 1996.

Beall, C.M. "Theoretical Dimensions of a Focus on Age in Physical Anthropology," In: *Age and Anthropological Theory*, (eds.) D.I. Kertzer and J. Keith Ithaca and London: Cornell University Press, 1984.

Beattie, J.H.M. and R.G. Lienhardt. *Studies in Social Anthropology: Essays in Memory of E.E. Evans-Pritchard by his Former Colleagues*. Oxford: Clarendon Press, 1975.

Beidelman, T.O. "Women and Men in Two East African Societies," In: *Explorations in African Systems of Thought*, (eds). I. Karp and C.S. Bird. Washington, D.C. and London: Smithsonian Institution Press, 1987[1980].

Bell, D. "Introduction: the Context," In: *Gendered Fields: Women, Men and Ethnography*, eds. D. Bell, P. Caplan, and W.J. Karim. London and New York: Routledge, 1993.

Bernardi, B. *Age Class Systems: Social Institutions and Polities Based on Age*. Cambridge: University Press, 1985.

Birch de Aguilar, L. 1995. "Masks, Society, and Hierarchy Among the Chewa of Central Malawi," *Anthropos* 90(1995):407-21.
_____. *Inscribing the Mask: Interpretation of Nyau Masks and Ritual Performance Among the Chewa of Central Malawi*. Fribourg, Switzerland: University Press, 1996.

Bourdieu, P. "The Berber House," In: *Rules and Meanings: The Anthropology of Everyday Knowledge*, (ed.) M. Douglas. Harmondsworth: Penguin Books, 1977 [1973].

Bundy, C. "Street Sociology and Pavement Politics: Aspects of Youth and Student Resistance in Cape Town, 1985," *Journal of Southern African Studies* 13,3 (1987):303-30.

Burton, J.W. "Representations of the Feminine in Nilotic Cosmologies," In: *Body and Space: Symbolic Models of Unity and Division in African Cosmology and Experience*. Stockholm: Almqvist and Wiksell International, 1991.

Caplan, A.P. 1976. "Boys" Circumcision and Girls" Puberty Rites

Among the Swahili of Mafia Island Tanzania," *Africa* 46,1 (1976):21-33.

_____."Gender, Ideology and Modes of Production on the East African Coast," In: *From Zinj to Zanzibar: History, Trade and Society on the Coast of East Africa*, ed. J. de Vere Allen Wien: Franz Steiner Verlag, 1982.

_____."Women's Property, Islamic Law and Cognatic Descent," in R. Hirschon (ed.), *Women and Property, Women as Property*, ed. London: Croom Helm, 1983.

_____. "Children are our Wealth and We Want Them": A Difficult Pregnancy on Mafia Island, Tanzania," in D. Bryceson ed., *Women Wielding the Hoe: Lessons From Rural Africa for Feminist Theory and Development Practice*. Oxford and Providence, RI: Berg, 1995a.

_____."Law and Custom: Marital Disputes on Mafia Island, Tanzania," In: *Understanding Disputes: The Politics of Law*, (ed.) P. Caplan, Oxford, U.K. and Providence, RI: Berg, 1995b.

_____. *African Voices, African Lives: Personal Narratives From a Swahili Village*. London and New York: Routledge, 1997.

_____. "Where Have all the Young Girls Gone?: Gender and Sex Ratios on Mafia Island, Tanzania," In: *Agrarian Economy, State and Society in Contemporary Tanzania*, (eds.) P. Forster and S. Maghimbi Aldershot: Avebury Press, (in press).

Carrithers, M. *Why Humans Have Cultures?: Explaining Anthropology and Social Diversity*. Oxford: University Press, 1993.

Carsten, J. and S. Hugh-Jones. 1995. "Introduction," in J. Carsten and S. Hugh-Jones, *About the House: Levi-Strauss and Beyond*. Cambridge: University Press.

Carter, C. "We are the Progressives": Alexandra Youth Congress activists and the Freedom Charter, 1983-85," *Journal of Southern African Studies* 17,2 (1991):197-220.

Carter, G. and T. Karis. *From Protest to Challenge* IV. Stanford: Hoover, 1977.

Carton, B. Forthcoming. *"Blood From Your Children": African Generational Conflict in South Africa*. Charlottesville: The University Press of Virginia.

Chenevix Trench, C. *Men Who Ruled Kenya: The Kenya Administration 1892-1963*. London: The Radcliffe Press, 1993.

Chieni, T. and P. Spencer. "The World of Telelia: Reflections of a Maasai Woman in Matapato," In: *Being Maasai: Ethnicity and Identity in East Africa*, eds. T. Spear and R. Waller London: James Currey, 1993.

Chikane, F. "Children in Turmoil: The Effects of Unrest on Township Children," In: *Growing Up in a Divided Society: the Contexts of Childhood in South Africa*, eds. S. Burman and P. Reynolds Johannesburg: Ravan Press, 1986.

Clark, M. "Contributions of Cultural Anthropology to the Study of the Aged," in L. Nader and T. Maretzki eds, *Cultural Illness and Health: Essays on Human Adaptation*. Washington, D.C.: American Anthropological Association, 1973.

_____.and B.G. Anderson. *Culture and Aging: An Anthropological Study of Older Americans*. Springfield: Charles C. Thomas, 1967.

Clough, M.S. *Fighting Two Sides*. Niwot. Colorado: University Press of Colorado, 1990.

Cohen, D.W. *The Combing of History*. Chicago and London: University of Chicago Press, 1994.

Cohen, D.W. and E.S. Atieno Odhiambo. *Burying SM: The Politics of Knowledge and the Sociology of Power in Africa*. Portsmouth, N.H.: Heinemann, London: James Currey, 1992.

Cohen, L. "Old Age: Cultural and Critical Perspectives," *Annual Review of Anthropology* 23(1994): 137-58.

Colson, E. 1962. *The Plateau Tonga on Northern Rhodesia: Social and Religious Studies*. Manchester: University Press for the Rhodes-Livingstone Institute, 1962.

Curtis, A. *Memories of Kenya*. London: Evans, 1986.

Dahl, G. 1979a. *Suffering Grass: Subsistence and Society of Waso Borana*. Stockholm: Department of Social Anthropology, University of Stockholm, 1979a.

_____. "Ecology and Equality: The Boran Case," in L"equipe Ecologie et Anthropologie des Societes Pastorales (eds.), *Pastoral Production and Society*. Cambridge: University Press, 1979b.

_____. "Mats and Milk Pots: The Domain of Borana Women," in
A. Jacobson-Widding and W. van Beek (eds.), *The Creative
Communion: African Folk Models of Fertility and the Regen-
eration of Life*. Uppsala: Acta Universitatis Upsaliensis, 1990.
_____. "Sources of life and identity," in P.T. W. Baxter, J. Hultin and
A. Triulzi (eds.), *Being and Becoming Oromo: Historical and
Anthropological Enquiries*. Uppsala: Nordiska Afrikainstitutet,
1996.

Diseko, N. 1992. "The Origins and Development of the South African
Student's Movement (SASM): 1968-1976," *Journal of Southern African Studies* 18,1 (1992): 40-62.

Duder, C.J. and G.L. Simpson. "Land and Murder in Colonial Kenya:
the Leroghi Land Dispute and the Powys "Murder" Case," *Journal of Imperial and Commonwealth History* 25, 1997.

Englund, H. "Between God and Kamuzu: The Transition to Multiparty
Politics in Central Malawi," In: *Postcolonial Identities in
Africa*, eds. R. Werbner and T. Ranger. London and New
Jersey: Zed Books, 1996.

Ensminger, J. *Making a Market: The Institutional Transformation of
an African Society*. Cambridge: University Press, 1992.

Evans-Pritchard, E.E. *The Nuer: A Description of the Modes of Livelihood and Political Institutions of a Nilotic People*. New York
and Oxford: Oxford University Press, 1940.

Falkenstein, M.K.S. 1995. "Concepts of Ethnicity and Inter-Ethnic
Migration Among the Ariaal of Kenya," *Zeitschrift fur
Ethnologie* 120 (2): 201-25.

_____. Ethnicity, Market Integration and Urbanization among the
Ariaal. Doctoral Thesis, University of Bielefeld, Sociology of
Development Research Center, In Preparation.

_____. G. Schlee, and S. Tonah. 1995. "Ernahrungssicherung in
Nomadengebieten Nordkenias," *Zeitschrift fur Ethnologie* 120,1
(1995): 89-146.

Fortes, M. "Age, Generation, and Social Structure," In: D.I. Kertzer and
J. Keith (eds.), *Age and Anthropological Theory*. Ithaca and
London: Cornell University Press.

Fosbrooke, H.A. 1948. "An Administrative Survey of the Masai Social System," *Tanganyika Notes and Records* 26: 1-50.

Fratkin, E. 1986. "Stability and Resilience in East African Pastoralism: the Rendille and Ariaal of Northern Kenya," *Human Ecology* 14: 269-86.

_____. E.A. Roth and K. Galvin. 1994. "Introduction," In: *African Pastoralist Systems: An Integrated Approach*, (eds.) E. Fratkin, K.A. Galvin and E.A. Roth. Boulder and London: Lynne Rienner, 1994.

Fry, C.L. "Toward an Anthropology of Aging," In: *Aging in Culture and Society: Comparative Viewpoints and Strategies*, ed. C.L. Fry. New York: J.F. Bergin, 1980.

_____. "Introduction: Anthropology and Dimensions of Aging," In: *Dimensions: Aging, Culture, and Health*, ed. C.L. Fry et al New York: Praeger, 1981.

Fukui, K. and D. Turton, eds. *Warfare Among East African Herders*. Osaka: National Museum of Ethnology, 1979.

Galaty, J.G. "Models and Metaphors: On the Semiotics of Maasai Segmentary Systems," In: *The Structure of Folk Models* (ASA Monograph 20), eds. L. Holy and M. Stuchlik London and New York: Academic Press, 1980.

_____. "The Land is Yours": Social and Economic Factors in the Privatization, Sub-division and Sale of Maasai Ranches," *Nomadic Peoples* 29(1992):26-40.

_____."Rangeland Tenure and Pastoralism in Africa," In: *African Pastoralist Systems: An Integrated Approach*, eds. E. Fratkin, K. Galvin and E. Roth Boulder and London: Lynne Rienner, 1994a.

_____.1994b. "Ha(l)ving Land in Common: The Subdivision of Maasai Group Ranches in Kenya," In: (eds.), *The Pastoral Land Crisis: Tenure and Dispossession in Eastern Africa*. Special Issue of *Nomadic Peoples* 34/35, eds. J. Galaty, A. Hjort, C. Lane and D. Ngala. Munster: LIT Verlag, 1994b.

_____. 'Property' in the Strict Sense of the Term: the Theory and Practical Rhetoric of Land Tenure in East Africa." Unpublished paper presented to the invited session, "Development as Ideology and Practice: Africanist (retro)spectives," American Anthropological Association Annual Meeting, San Francisco, November, 1996.

Gann, L.H. and P. Duignan. *The Rulers of British Africa, 1870 - 1914*. Stanford: Stanford University Press, 1978.

Goody, J. *The Expansive Moment: Anthropology in Britain and Africa 1918-1970*. Cambridge: University Press, 1995.

Graham, D. "Indirect rule: the Establishment of "Chiefs" and "Tribes" in Cameroon's Tanganyika", *Tanzania Notes and Records* 77/78: 1-9, 1976.

Grillo, R.D. 1974. "Ethnic Identity and Social Stratification on a Kampala Housing State," In: *Urban Ethnicity*, (ed.) A. Cohen. London: Tavistock Publications.

Haberland, E. 1963. *Galla Sud-Athiopiens*. Stuttgart: W. Kohlhammer.

Hassen, M. 1990. *The Oromo of Ethiopia: A History 1570-1860*. Cambridge: University Press.

_____. "The Pre-sixteenth-Century Oromo Presence Within the Medieval Christian kingdom of Ethiopia." In: D. Brokensha (ed.), *A River of Blessings: Essays in Honor of Paul Baxter*. New York: Maxwell School of Citizenship and Public Affairs, Syracuse University.

Heatherwick, A. ed. *Dictionary of Nyanja Language*. Updated and edited reprint of Scott (1929). London: Religious Tract Society, 1951.

Herdt, G. "Sexual Repression, Social Control, and Gender Hierarchy in Sambia Culture," in B.D. Miller (ed.), *Sex and Gender Hierarchies*. Cambridge: University Press, 1993.

Hillman, E. "Maasai Religion and Inculturation," *Louvaine Studies* 17: 351-76, 1992.

Hirson, B. 1979. *Year of Fire, Year of Ash. The Soweto Revolt: Roots of a Revolution?*. London: Zed, 1979.

Hobsbawm, E. 1983. "Introduction," In: *The Invention of Tradition*, (eds.) E. Hobsbawm and T. Ranger Cambridge: University Press.

Hodgson, D.L. "Patriarchal Authority and the Case of the Disobedient Daughter: Marriage, Maasai and the Tanzanian State." Unpublished Manuscript, 1994.

_____. The Politics of Gender, Ethnicity and "Development" Images, Interventions and the Recognition of Maasai Identities in Tanzania, 1916-1993." Unpublished PhD Dissertation, University of Michigan, 1995.

Hogg, R. "The Social and Economic Organization of the Boran of Isiolo District Kenya," Unpublished Ph.D. thesis, University of Manchester, 1981.

Hollis, Sir A.C. 1905. *The Maasai: Their Language and Folklore.* Oxford: Clarendon Press, 1905.

Holmes, L.D. 1976. "Trends in Anthropological Gerontology: From Simmons to the Seventies," *International Journal of Aging and Human Development* 7,3 (1976):211-20.

Holy, L. "Strategies for Old Age Among the Berti of the Sudan," In: *Anthropology & The Riddle of the Sphinx: Paradoxes of Change in the Life Course,* (ed.) P. Spencer. London and New York: Routledge, 1990.

Hultin, J. "Social Structure, Ideology and Expansion: The Case of the Oromo of Ethiopia," *Ethnos* 40, 1-4(1975): 273-84.

_____. "Political Structure and the Development of Inequality Among the Macha Oromo", In: (ed.) L"equipe Ecologie et Anthropologie des Societes Pastorales, *Pastoral Production and Society.* Cambridge: University Press, 1979.

_____. "The Conquest of Land and the Conquest of Fertility: a Theme in Oromo Culture," In: *The Creative Communion: African Folk Models of Fertility and the Regeneration of Life.* Uppsala: Uppsala Studies in Cultural Anthropology 15, 1990.

Jacobs, A. "The Traditional Political Organization of the Pastoral Masai." Unpublished D.Phil. dissertation, Nuffield College, University of Oxford, 1965.

Jochelson, K. "Reform, repression and resistance in South Africa: A Case Study of Alexandra Township, 1979-1989," *Journal of Southern African Studies* 16,1 (1/March 1990): 1-32.

Kane-Berman, J. *Soweto: Black Revolt, White Reaction.* Johannesburg: Ravan, 1978.

Karp, I. *Fields of Change Among the Iteso of Kenya.* London, Henley and Boston: Routledge & Kegan Paul, 1978.

Kasfir, S. (ed.) *West African Masks and Culture Systems*. Tervuren: Musee" Royal de l"Afrique Central, 1988.

Kassam, A. "Notes on the Booran Oromo *Gadamojjii* Ceremony held at Sololo (Kenya) June-July 1995," *The Oromo Commentary* 5,2(1995): 23-34.

Keith, J. 1980. "The Best is Yet to Be: Toward an Anthropology of Age," *Annual Review of Anthropology* 9: 339-64.

Kertzer, D.I. and O.B.B. Madison. "Women's Age-set Systems in Africa: The Latuka of Southern Sudan," In: *Dimensions: Aging, Culture, and Health*. C.L. Fry et al New York: Praeger, 1981.

_____. and J. Keith, eds. *Age and Anthropological Theory*. Ithaca and London: Cornell University Press, 1984.

Kipury, N. *Oral Literature of the Maasai*. London and Nairobi: Heineman, 1983.

Kituyi, M. *The State and the Pastoralists*. Bergen: Christian Michelsen Institute, 1985.

Knutsson, K.E. *Authority and Change: A Study of the Kallu Institution Among the Macha Galla of Ethiopia*. Gothenburg: Etnografiska Museet, 1967.

Kuper, A. *Anthropology and Anthropologists: The Modern British School*. London and New York: Routledge, 1983.

Legesse, A. *Gada: Three Approaches to the Study of African Society*. New York: The Free Press, 1973.

Lewis, I.M. *A Pastoral Democracy: A Study of Pastoralism and Politics Among the Northern Somali of the Horn of Africa*. London and New York: Oxford University Press for the International African Institute, 1961.

Liebenow, J.G. *Colonial Rule and Political Development in Tanzania*. Evanston, Illinois: Northwestern University Press, 1971.

Llewelyn-Davis, M. "Women, Warriors and Patriarchs," In: *Sexual Meanings: The Cultural Construction of Gender and Sexuality*, eds. S.B. Ortner and H. Whitehead. Cambridge: University Press, 1981.

Lloyd, P.C. 1974. "Ethnicity and the Structure of Inequality in a Nigerian Town in the Mid-1950s," in A. Cohen (ed.), *Urban Ethnicity*. London: Tavistock publications.

Lodge, T. *Black Politics in South Africa since 1945.* London: Longman, 1983.

_____.and B. Nasson. *All Here, and Now: Black Politics in South Africa in the 1980s.* New York: Ford Foundation and the Foreign Policy Association, 1991.

Lonsdale, J. "The conquest state, 1895-1904," In: *A Modern History of Kenya 1895-1980,*ed. W.R. Ochieng London: Evans Brothers, 1989.

Low, D.A. and R.C. Pratt. *Buganda and British Overrule 1900-1955.* London: Oxford University Press, 1960.

Mannheim, K. "The Problem of Generations," In: *Essays on the Sociology of Knowledge*, (ed.) P. Kecskemeti. London: Routledge and Kegan Paul, 1952.

Mayer, P. and I. Mayer. *Townsmen or Tribesmen.* Cape Town:Oxford University Press, 1970

Megerssa Ruda, G. Knowledge, Identity and the Colonizing Structure: the case of the Oromo in East and Northeast Africa. Unpublished Ph.D. Thesis, School of Oriental and African Studies, University of London, 1993.

Mudimbe, V.Y. *The Idea of Africa.* Bloomington and Indianapolis: Indiana University Press, London: James Currey, 1994.

Mufson, S. *Fighting Years:Black Resistance and the Struggle For a New South Africa.* Boston: Beacon Press, 1990.

Munro, J.F. *Colonial Rule and the Kamba.* Oxford: Clarendon Press, 1975.

Myerhoff, B. *Number Our Days: Culture and Community Among Elderly Jews in an American Ghetto.* New York and London: Meridian (Penguin), 1994 [1979].

Myrick, B. "Colonial Initiatives and Kamba Reaction in Machakos District: The Destocking Issue, 1930-1938," In: *Three Aspects of Crisis in Colonial Kenya,* ed. B. Myrick, D.L. Easterbrook, and J.R. Roelker Syracuse, N.Y.: Maxwell School of Citizenship and Public Affairs, Syracuse University, 1975.

Ogot, B. A. ed. *Kenya Before 1900: Eight Regional Studies*. Nairobi: East African Publishing House, 1976.

O'Leary, M. "Patterns of Range Use, Nomadism, and Sedentarization: The Case of the Rendille and Gabra of Northern Kenya," In: *A River of Blessings: Essays in Honor of Paul Baxter*, (ed.) D. Brokensha. New York: Maxwell School of Citizenship and Public Affairs, Syracuse University, 1994.

Owusu, M. 1976. "Colonial and Postcolonial Anthropology of Africa: Scholarship or Sentiment," In: *A Century of Change in Eastern Africa*, ed. W. Arens The Hague, Paris: Mouton.

Parkin, D. *Neighbors and Nationals in an African City Ward*. London: Routledge and Kegan Paul, 1969.

_____. "Eastern Africa: The View From the Office and the Voice From the Field," in R. Fardon (ed.), *Localizing Strategies: Regional Traditions of Ethnographic Writing*. Edinburgh: Scottish Academic Press, and Washington D.C.: Smithsonian Institution Press, 1990.

Pinnock, D. "Breaking the Web: Gangs and Family Structure in Cape Town," In: *Crime and Power in South Africa: Criminal Studies in Criminology*, eds. D. Davis and M. Slabbert Cape Town: D. Philip, 1985.

Radcliffe-Brown, A.R. 1952 [1940]. "On Joking Relationships," In: *Structure and Function in Primitive Society*. London: Cohen and West, 1952 [1940]

Raikes, P.L. *Livestock Development and Policy in East Africa*. Uppsala: Scandinavian Institute of African Studies, 1981.

Rangeley, W.H.J. "*Nyau* in Kotakota District," *The Nyasaland Journal* 2,2 (1949): 35-49.

Ranger, T.O. "African Reactions to the Imposition of Colonial Rule in East and Central Africa," In: (eds.), *Colonialism in Africa 1870-1960*, vol. I., eds. L.H. Gann and P. Duignan. Cambridge: University Press, 1969.

Riley, M.W. "Foreword," In: *Age and Anthropological Theory*, eds. D.I. Kertzer and J. Keith Ithaca and London: Cornell University Press, 1984.

Robertson, A.F. "The Development of Meaning: Ontogeny and Culture," *Journal of the Royal Anthropological Institute* (n.s.) 2(1996): 591-610.

Roth, E.A. "Demographic Systems: Two East African Examples," In: *African Pastoralist Systems: An Integrated Approach*, eds. E. Fratkin, K.A. Galvin, E.A. Roth. Boulder and London: Lynne Rienner, 1994.

Saitoti, T. ole. *Maasai*. (Photographs by Carol Beckwith.) London: Elm Tree Books, 1980.

Schapera, I. *Some Problems of Anthropological Research in the Kenya Colony*. International African Institute Memorandum 23. London: International African Institute, 1949.

Scharf, W. and B. Ngcokoto. "Images of Punishment in the People's Courts of Cape Town, 1985-7: From Prefigurative Justice to Populist Violence," In: *Political Violence and the Struggle in South Africa*, (eds.) N. Chabani Manganyi and A. du Toit London: Macmillan, 1990.

Schildkrout, E. "Ethnicity and Generational Differences Among Urban Immigrants in Ghana," In: *Urban Ethnicity*, (ed.) A. Cohen. London: Tavistock Publications, 1974.

Schlee, G. *Das Glaubens—und Sozialsystem der Rendille: Kamelnomaden Nordkenias*. Berlin: Dietrich Reimer Verlag, 1979.

_____. "Nomaden und Staat: das Beispiel Nordkenia," *Sociologus* 349,2 (1984): 140-61.

_____. "Camel Management Strategies and Attitudes Towards Camels in the Horn," In: *The Exploitation of Animals in Africa*, (ed.) J.C. Stone. Aberdeen: African Studies Group, University of Aberdeen, 1988.

_____. *Identities on the Move: Clanship and Pastoralism in Northern Kenya*. Manchester: University Press for the International African Institute, 1989.

_____. "Holy Grounds," In: (eds.), *Property, Poverty and People: Changing Rights in Property and Problems of Pastoral Development*, (eds.) P.T.W. Baxter and R. Hogg Manchester: Department of Sociology and International Development Center, University of Manchester, 1990a.

_____. "Policies and Boundaries: Perceptions of Space and Control of Markets in a Mobile Livestock Economy." Working Paper 133. Sociology of Development Research Center, University of Bielefeld, 1990b.

_____. "Erfahrungen nordkenianischer Wanderhirten mit dem Kolonialen Und Postkolonialen Staat," In: *Nomaden: mobile Tierhaltung*, (ed.) F. Scholz Berlin: Das Arabische Buch, 1990c.

_____. "Traditionalist Pastoralists: Land Use Strategies," In: Republic of Kenya, Ministry of Livestock Development, *Kenya Range Management Handbook* II, 1991.

_____. "Ritual Topography and Ecological Use," In: *Bush Base: Forest Farm: Culture, Environment and Development*, (eds.) E. Croll and D. Parkin London: Routledge, 1992.

_____. *Identities on the Move: Clanship and Pastoralism in Northern Kenya*. Nairobi: Gideon S. Were Press, 1994a.

_____. "Ethnicity Emblems, Diacritical Features, Identity Markers: Some East African Examples," In: *A River of Blessings: Essays in Honor of Paul Baxter*, (ed.) D. Brokensha. New York: Maxwell School of Citizenship and Public Affairs, Syracuse University, 1994b.

_____. "Cross-cutting Ties, Grenzen, Raub und Krieg." Working Paper 203. Sociology of Development Research Centre, University of Bielefeld, 1994c.

Scott, D.C. *Dictionary of Nyanja Language*. London: Religious Tract Society, 1929.

Simel, J.O. "Premature Land Subdivision, Encroachment of Rights and Manipulation in Maasai Land: KeekonyokieSection." Working Paper, Prepared for the Kenya Team of the Arid Lands and Resource Management (ALARM), Nairobi, 1995.

Simmons, L. *The Role of the Aged in Primitive Society*. New Haven, CT: Yale University Press, 1945.

Simpson, G.L. On the Frontiers of Empire: British Administration in Kenya's Northern Frontier District, 1905-1935. Unpublished Ph.D. Thesis, West Virginia University, 1994.

Sitas, A. "The making of the "Comrades" Movement in Natal, 1985-1991," *Journal of Southern African Studies* 18,3 (Sept. 1992): 629-41.

Sorrenson, M.P.K. *Origins of European Settlement in Kenya.* London: Oxford University Press, 1968.

Spear, T. "Being "Maasai," but not "People of Cattle": Arusha Agricultural Maasai in the Nineteenth Century," In: *Being Maasai: Ethnicity & Identity in East Africa, eds.* T. Spear and R. Waller. London: James Currey, 1993.

_____. and R. Waller. "Introduction," In: *Being Maasai: Ethnicity & Identity in East Africa.* London: James Currey, 1993.

Stewart, F.H. *Fundamentals of Age-Group Systems.* New York: Academic Press, 1977.

Surplus People's Project. *Forced Removals in South Africa.* Cape Town: Surplus People's Project, 1983.

Talle, A. "Women as Head of Houses: The Organization of Production and the Role of Women Among Pastoral Maasai in Kenya," *Ethnos* 52,2 (1987): 196-218.

_____. *Women at a Loss: Changes in Maasai Gender Relations and Their Effects on Gender Relations.* Stockholm Studies in Social Anthropology 19. Stockholm: University of Stockholm, 1988.

Tate, H.R. "Journey to the Rendile Country, British East Africa," *Geographical Journal* 23(1904a.): 220-8, 280.

_____. "Nairobi to Samburu & Rendile," *East African Quarterly* 90-101, 1904b.

Teleki, S. 1889. "Count Teleki's Discoveries in Eastern Africa," *Scottish Geographical Magazine* 5: 96-100.

Tetelman, M. "We Can": Black Politics in Cradock, South Africa, 1928-85. Unpublished Ph.D. Thesis, Northwestern University, 1997.

Thompson, S. "Metaphors the Chinese Age," In: *Anthropology and the Riddle of the Sphinx: Paradoxes of Change in the Life Course.* ASA Monographs 28, (ed.) P. Spencer London and New York: Routledge, 1990.

Tignor, R. *The Colonial Transformation of Kenya.* Princeton, N.J.: Princeton University Press, 1976.

Tonkin, E. *Narrating Our Pasts: The Social Construction of Oral History*. Cambridge: University Press, 1992.

Trimingham, J. *Islam in East Africa*. London: Oxford University Press, 1964.

Turner, V. *The Forest of Symbols: Aspects of Ndembu Ritual*. Ithaca and London: Cornell University Press, 1967.

Van Zwanenberg, R. n.d. "Nomadic Pastoralism and the Process of Impoverishment: A Historical Comparison of Kenya and Uganda." Unpublished Paper Presented to the History Research Seminar, University of Dar es Salaam, n.d.

Vogel, S. *Aesthetic of African Art: The Carlo Monzini Collection*. New York: Museum of African Art, 1986.

Von Hohnel, L. *Discovery of Lakes Rudolf and Stefanie*, Vol. II. London: Frank Cass, 1968.

Wagner-Glenn, D. *Searching for a Baby's Calabash: A Study of Arusha Maasai Fertility Songs as Crystallized Expression of Central Cultural Values*. Ludwigsburg: Philipp Verlag, 1992.

Wallman, S. *Kampala Women Getting By: WellBeing in the Time of AIDS*. London: James Currey, 1996.

Walshe, P. *The Rise of African Nationalism in South Africa*. London: Hurst, 1970.

Walz, Gabriele. *Nomaden im Nationalstaat: Zur Integration der Nomaden in Kenya*. Berlin: Dietrich Reimer Verlag, 1992.

Wilson, M. *Good Company: A Study of Nyakyusa Age-villages*. London: Oxford University Press for the International African Institute, 1951.

CONTRIBUTORS

❖

Mario I. Aguilar is chairman and head of the department of Social Anthropology at the University of St. Andrews, Scotland. His recent publications include *Being Oromo in Kenya* (1998), and *Dios en África: Elementos para una antropología de la religión* (1997).

Laurel Birch de Aguilar lectures at the department of Social Anthropology, University of St. Andrews, Scotland. She is the author of *Inscribing the Mask: Interpretation of Nyau Masks and Ritual Performance Among the Chewa of Central Malawi* (1996).

Pat Caplan is professor of Social Anthropology at Goldsmiths College, University of London. She has carried out research in Tanzania, South India, Nepal and Britain, and is the author of numerous books. The most recent of which are *Understanding Disputes* (1995), *African Voices, African Lives* (1997), and *Food, Health and Fertility* (1997).

Benedict Carton is assistant professor of African History at George Mason University and the author of a forthcoming volume,

Blood from your Children: African Generational Conflict in South Africa (University Press of Virginia).

John G. Galaty is professor of anthropology at McGill University, and recently served as President of the Canadian Association of African Studies. Specializing in the study of East African pastoralists, he has conducted fieldwork among the Maasai of Kenya and Tanzania. His most recent edited works include *Herders, Warriors and Traders: Pastoralism in Africa* (1991) and *The Pastoral Land Crisis: Tenure and Dispossession in Eastern Africa* (1994).

Guenther Schlee is professor of Social Anthropology at the University of Bielefeld. His recent publications include *Identities on the Move* (1989, reprinted Nairobi 1994), and *Inklusion und Exklusion* (1996).

George L. Simpson is assistant professor of History at High Point University, North Carolina. He received his Ph.D. in 1994 from West Virginia University, with the thesis "On the Frontiers of Empire: British Administration in Kenya's Frontier District 1905-1935."

Paul Spencer professor of African Anthropology, retired from the department of Anthropology and Sociology of the School of Oriental and African Studies, University of London, in 1997. His most recent book is *The Pastoral Continuum: The Marginalization of Tradition in East Africa* (1998).

Aud Talle is professor of Anthropology at the department and Museum of Anthropology, University of Oslo. She has carried out fieldwork among pastoralists in Kenya, Somalia and Tanzania, having published *Women at a Loss: Changes in Maasai Pastoralism and Their Effects on Gender Relations* (1988).

Michael S. Tetelman is visiting assistant professor at the History Department, Northwestern University.

INDEX